HORSESHOES
AND
HOLY WATER

HORSESHOES
AND
HOLY WATER

MEFO PHILLIPS

Published in Great Britain in 2005 by
Virgin Books
Thames Wharf Studios
Rainville Road
London W6 9HA

A catalogue record for this book is available from the British Library.

ISBN 07535 1038 3

Typeset by Phoenix Photosetting, Chatham, Kent
Printed and bound by
Mackays of Chatham, Kent

To Peter
My non-horsy, golf-loving husband
and lorry driver extraordinaire

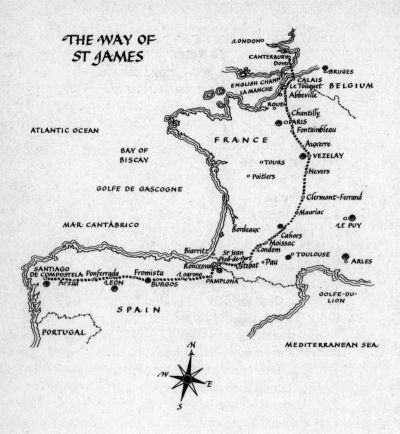

THE WAY OF
ST JAMES

LONDON
CANTERBURY
Dover
BRUGES
ENGLISH CHANNEL
LA MANCHE
CALAIS
Le Touquet
BELGIUM
Abbeville
ROUEN
Chantilly
PARIS
Fontainebleau
FRANCE
Auxerre
VEZELAY
ATLANTIC OCEAN
TOURS
Nevers
Poitiers
BAY OF
BISCAY
Clermont-Ferrand
Mauriac
GOLFE DE GASCOGNE
LE PUY
MAR CANTÁBRICO
Bordeaux
Cahors
Moissac
Biarritz
Condom
St Jean
Pied-de-Port
TOULOUSE
Pau
ARLES
Roncesvalles
Ostebat
SANTIAGO
DE COMPOSTELA
Ponferrada
Fromista
Logrono
PAMPLONA
Arzua
LEON
BURGOS
GOLFE-DU-
LION
SPAIN
PORTUGAL
MEDITERRANEAN SEA

N
W
E
S

CONTENTS

ACKNOWLEDGEMENTS

Enormous thanks are due to all the companies and individuals who sponsored us to ride to Santiago de Compostela in aid of the East Kent Pilgrims' Hospices: to the countless people who helped us with the preparation and along the way in France and Spain, particularly the Confraternity of St James, Dr Bompy and Dr Fernando; to our abandoned families and to Francis Elton (Fred) who accepted my absence from work for several months with remarkable patience; to Clara and Eve for encouraging me through every chapter of this book as I wrote it, complete with wayward use of language; to my editor Kerri Sharp for not flinching when an entire unsolicited manuscript landed on her desk, and to Susie, Peter, Bessie the Bedford, and most of all Leo and Apollo, our humorous hairy companions who willingly carried Susie and me for 1700 miles.

FOREWORD BY CLIVE ANDERSON

I got to know the author of this engaging account of an extraordinary journey through France and Spain about twenty years ago, when I was a London barrister and Mefo worked for Girlings, a firm of solicitors in Canterbury.

From time to time Girlings briefed me to represent some of the wide range of their criminal clients in Canterbury or Maidstone Crown Court. There's quite a lot of crime in East Kent: it has its poor districts as well as rich, agricultural areas and industrial zones, bored teenagers and retired pensioners, army barracks and closed down mines. And in addition there is the enormous traffic through Dover and the other channel ports and the illegal trade that inevitably comes with it: baccy for the parson, crates of wine for personal use, opiates for the streets.

No doubt Girlings prefer to make their money these days in more sedate areas of the law – conveyancing, wills, matrimonial and civil litigation and the like – but in those days if you were in Kent and thinking of murdering your wife, burgling your neighbour's house, hitting someone in a pub, nicking a car, smuggling illicit substances into the country – or were unaccountably accused of doing some, or all, of the above – you were well advised to turn to Girlings for legal representation.

But it might also have meant you got me. And I often got Mefo at court with me. I hope we had an unbroken run of forensic triumph on behalf of innocent clients unjustly accused of breaking the law. Obviously I can no longer recall any cases we lost. But I can certainly remember chatting to Mefo over endless cups of coffee, the occasional lunch and tea.

In criminal litigation there is a lot of hanging around. Waiting for your case to be reached in the list, waiting for your client to arrive at court, waiting for the judge to make up his mind, waiting for the jury to reach a verdict. Waiting. So gradually I got to know quite a lot about Mefo's life in and away from the law courts – her family and friends, lifestyle and horses.

I knew she was interested in writing something more creative than instructions to counsel, but I had no idea that she was going to produce such an entertaining account of such an epic journey. I don't know which is more impressive, the book or undertaking the journey in the first place. It is both well written and well ridden. But mad – two middle-aged sisters on two scarcely suitable horses travelling 1700 miles along the ancient pilgrim route to Santiago de Compostela. Mefo is not a religious person, so why is she devoting several months to a pilgrimage? Her sister suffers from vertigo on all the bridges, hills and mountains of France, Spain and the Pyrenees in between. Their back-up lorry is if anything less suited to the rigours of the journey than the rest of them and they manage to take along a bicycle, which is almost always out of commission.

A hard ride, but an easy read, in which you get to know something of Mefo along the way. Her second husband is portrayed heroically at the wheel of the lorry between playing endless games of golf waiting for the horses to catch up. Her parents and her children left behind in England put in appearances, the Girlings office also waiting for her return is an offstage character in itself, an earlier brush with cancer is touched but not dwelt upon. There is a lot to be learned here about the towns, churches, villages and people of France and Spain, and the other pilgrims met en route. And plenty more about horses – including the French for horse droppings.

All in all, a classic piece of travel writing, requiring no plea in mitigation from me.

Clive Anderson

PROLOGUE

This isn't a history book.

The Way of St James is very well known, and fat volumes have already been written about the cultural legacy of this pilgrim road to Santiago de Compostela in north-west Spain by others far more knowledgeable than me. So I'm not going to describe its evolution from a Roman trade route – nicknamed the Milky Way because it tracked the stars westwards – to a path full of religious significance in any great detail here.

This is an alternative view, from the broad back of a spotted horse: a tale of life on the sometimes unconventional pilgrim trails through France and then Spain in the company of a sister with vertigo, our own two horses, a non-horsy husband with golf clubs, a raucous lorry and a useless bicycle.

Only briefly, therefore, here is the background: the story of St James the Great.

After the death of Christ, James obeyed His command to start spreading His message all over the world and took himself off to

Spain to make converts. Apparently he was there for two years before returning to Palestine, where he was beheaded on the orders of Herod Agrippa in AD 44, becoming the first of the Apostles to be martyred. His faithful followers loaded his body into a stone boat, and paddled off to the Bay of Padrón in northwest Spain at such an astonishing speed that they completed the voyage of four thousand miles in a week.

There the sceptical Queen Lupa ordered James's body to be unceremoniously buried on a hillside ruled by a potentially disciple-eating snake (or dragon, depending on which account you prefer), but the snake rolled over and expired when it saw the sign of the Cross. Astonished, Queen Lupa was instantly converted to Christianity, with the result that James was properly buried in a large stone coffin.

Time passed, and the burial site was forgotten. It was not until some 800 years later that its whereabouts were revealed to a hermit in a vision featuring a star and celestial music, and the spot became known as the Field of the Star, or Campus Stellae. The more prosaic say the name comes from Compostum, or burial ground, but either way it was amended to Compostella and a church was built over the site.

By now the final enclave of Christians in northern Spain was ready for rebellion against the Moorish domination of the rest of the country, but the Christians had no hero, no charismatic leader. The news that St James's tomb had been found in miraculous circumstances was amazingly timely, and St James himself on a white horse, his sword flashing, led the Christians to victory at the battle of Clavijo in Rioja. His reputation was established as Santiago Matamoros, St James the Moor-Slayer, and he became the patron saint of Spain, appearing in battle all over the country during the next several centuries – even at the side of El Cid.

In 1078, building began on the cathedral of Santiago to replace the church. It wasn't long before thousands of pilgrims began flocking to the shrine of St James there, and it quickly became so popular that it rivalled the pilgrimages to Rome and Jerusalem, helped and encouraged by successive Spanish kings, the Church and local enterprise. Four major routes from France evolved, their starting points at Paris, Vézelay in Burgundy, Le Puy at the foot of the Auvergne, and Arles above the Camargue. English pilgrims made their own way across the Channel to join these four roads, or sailed down the Bay of Biscay to ports nearer Ostabat, close to the Pyrenees where the Paris, Vézelay and Le Puy roads fused, or further still to the northern Spanish coast.

Pilgrims travelled light, carrying a staff, scrip or wallet for food and a leather bottle for water, and some wore cloaks and broad hats with the scallop shell attached that became the emblem of the St James pilgrimage. Canons of the cathedral began issuing certificates, or Compostellas, to pilgrims who successfully completed the whole journey – or who said they had, because there was no proof except that they'd arrived in Santiago.

I discovered, through the once powerful Benedictine monastery at Cluny in France, that there's a link between my home town of Faversham on the north Kent coast and Santiago de Compostela. The monastery was a major sponsor of the pilgrimage and built churches and abbeys along the final road in Spain, known as the Camino Francés, which stretched the five hundred miles from the Pyrenees to Santiago, while monks from Cluny, travelling in the opposite direction, colonised monasteries and abbeys in England – and among them was Faversham Abbey, founded by King Stephen.

Flattened on the orders of Henry VIII, most of the ruins of Faversham Abbey now lie underneath the local grammar school playing fields, and some are under my horse's paddock next to those fields, fringed by the still-surviving abbey barns. The monastery at Cluny was dedicated to St Mary of Charity and so is Faversham Church, with its elegant see-through crown spire, the last of a link created when the popularity of the pilgrimage to Santiago was at its height.

During the months it took my sister Susie, my husband Peter

and me to travel to Santiago, we had animated discussions about St James and how he ended up in that city, if indeed he did. Susie's deeply interested in religion, involved with God, and Peter and I are sceptics. My God gets called upon occasionally in sticky situations but Peter doesn't dwell much on the subject at all, and while Susie believes the bones of St James lie in a silver sarcophagus in Santiago cathedral, Peter and I suspect that it's all just a politically inspired legend.

What does it matter? Everyone we met on the Way of St James was making the pilgrimage for a reason, from the man dragging the life-sized cross to the Lycra bicyclists whispering up behind our startled horses on silent wheels. One depressed American woman had been advised by her psychiatrist to throw away her pills and walk the Camino instead, and she was still striding cheerfully along when we bumped into her hundreds of miles beyond the Pyrenees.

I imagine nothing's changed much since the earliest pilgrims set out: a mixture of zealots, adventurers, thanksgivers, seekers of a short cut to heaven, those escaping fierce spouses, and a few rogues hoping to fleece the true pilgrims. Then, as now, the Way was maintained because the army of visitors was good for the Spanish economy.

Susie and I had our own definite, separate reasons for going, and Peter was persuaded by me to come along and drive the horse lorry (after I'd tempted him with a map showing every golf course in France) – and so one day in early spring we set off to ride the Milky Way, the road beneath the stars.

PART ONE: FRANCE

1. YOURS WITH SEVERAL BITS BETWEEN HIS TEETH

What's happened to the football match? No-one's playing. The grammar school pupils are pressed against the fence, gawking at my horse. What's he doing? Oh, no … it's that mare we bought for Susie. She's seducing him! Geldings aren't supposed to be able to …

Mine can.

Leo! Get *off*!

This could be an unusual pilgrimage.

Tall books lined the stairwell, the best place in the house, a gateway to magic from the time I learned to read: Edward Lear's *Book of Nonsense*, *Astrology for Children*, Maeterlinck's *The Bluebird*. I used to sit for hours on the stairs poring over them in the fragmented light from the landing window, its leaded panes distorted by the blast from an off-course doodlebug that exploded in 1942 in the woods next door.

Among the books was *A Tale of Two Horses*, the children's version of *Tschiffeley's Ride*, the extraordinary true story of a man's trip from Patagonia to Washington with two mustangs.

Aged eight, my imagination was so fired by this book that I pictured myself setting off on my Shetland, Twink, to ride the length of America, undeterred by the fact that we would have to swim the Atlantic first. I never forgot it, but it took a bad dose of cancer almost 40 years later to spur me into realising the dream of a long, long ride of my own.

My sisters Penny, Susie, Tessa and I were the pony-mad daughters of a farmer father and a writer mother, brought up in the house on a hill overlooking the Channel that kept its kinky window panes unchanged for thirty years. Our father loved animals in general but not necessarily horses in particular, and his bedtime stories of the brave black mare he rode throughout the war were a total fabrication, as he cheerfully admitted when we'd grown up. He also told us that our mother unscrewed her arms and legs at night and hung them off the end of the bed, and we believed that as well. Our mother, with arms and legs intact at least during the day, had been horsy all her life.

Our childhood was crammed with show-jumping rabbits, guinea pigs raced on the lawn wearing harnesses made from our mother's stockings, a succession of small ginger huskies and cowardly mouse-phobic cats, and hibernating hedgehogs seized out of the coal shed. But most of all it was dominated by ponies, mud and arguments with each other as to who was going to hold the haynet and who was going to get thistle fingers filling it. We raced around playing cowboys, taught our woolly ponies to buck to order and had the occasional success potato-racing at gymkhanas. Meanwhile, our mother wrote books about horses and royalty, and made TV documentaries about the countryside, which were peopled by the four of us falling off our ponies and, on one occasion, mowing down the cameramen who suggested that we should gallop towards them along the beach bareback, in bikinis.

As we grew up, we didn't grow out of our interest in horses – it was perpetuated by our mother, who rode her old Irish pony until she was 85 and struck down by Alzheimer's. When she was

80 they took part in a dressage-to-music competition, which they won on the basis of their combined ages of 102, and our mother's startling performance wearing a false moustache and our father's regimental dress uniform from the war.

Penny kept horses throughout serial marriages, several children and years of teaching dressage, which she practised periodically on Susie, me and any of our available offspring. Her commands were eccentric – it took ingenuity to work out that '*Crap* on the saddle!' actually meant 'bear down, balance your horse and it'll slow up'. Strange postures were adopted.

Susie settled into a long marriage with her barrister husband John (a practical man who kept saws under their bed to avoid them getting rusty in his workshop) and life in the countryside bringing up their children, whose diminutive ponies she rode occasionally, teaching calligraphy and leading her sheep in small headcollars round the lanes. For twenty years she was warden of St Rumwold's, her ancient village church untroubled by electricity, sometimes pumping the organ into wheezing life for the Communion service or trying to keep the candles lit for Evensong, intrigued by the teachings of the Bible and nicknamed Mrs Parochial Gray by the rest of her sisters.

Tessa, married to artist and cartoonist Bill Papas, had no time in her whirlwind existence to own a horse again, although when she and Bill were living in Greece they adopted a donkey foal that went sailing with them. Unfortunately, the donkey grew into a giant with an indecent passion for my sister, so found himself banished to an island and a donkey's proper working life, far from his previous existence cruising the Mediterranean with a blonde.

As for me, I found some interesting jobs because I could ride. I spent one summer as a trail guide in the Rocky Mountains, and one chaotic spring touring round Europe with an American rodeo being flung out twice a night from a speeding stagecoach, to the delight of the rodeo's chimpanzee if not of the bemused Italian and French audiences. It was at this time that I was introduced to the Appaloosa breed of horse. The name evolved because of the interest taken in them by the Nez Perce Indians from the Palouse River in Idaho when horses arrived in America with the Spanish conquistadors; the Indians admired their distinctive spotted coat patterns so much that they went on to develop the breed. What struck me most about the rodeo Appaloosas was how good natured and adaptable they were; they switched obligingly from saddle horses to broncs with the simple addition of a bucking strap cinched round their middles, and back again to patient plods tied in the horse lines for hours.

Married for the first time and with two young children, I opted for safer though often colourful work in criminal law for a firm of solicitors in Canterbury, and rode and owned horses when I had the opportunity. Divorced years later, a sailing policeman taught me about life on the water, and horses took second place to boats; I bought *Jorrocks*, a beautiful witch of a 1936 sailing sloop built of pitch pine and teak and mahogany, and I moved to Faversham where she sat comfortably in her mud berth on the creek.

The operation that annihilated the cancer left me with the aggravation of a dodgy digestion, and I needed to be fit all the time to feel well. Applying gallons of paint and varnish to *Jorrocks*'s massive hull in the spring and then the effort of sailing her in summer did the trick – there was no lazy self-steering on this boat, no ropes leading conveniently back to the cockpit: she was all heavy teak tiller, and halyards which threatened to fly me up the mast like an undersized bell-ringer into the belfry. But winter sailing in home waters can be a bleak foggy business; I met my future husband Peter who views sailing as 90 per cent boredom and 10 per cent sheer terror, even in summer, and it didn't take much to convince me that *Jorrocks* would be better off cuddled in a tarpaulin from November to April. But by December I was flabby, stodgy and out of sorts.

The solution was obvious: I would buy a horse. So I acquired a jet-black Russian gelding who kept his anarchic temperament under wraps for a month, and parted with him again when his constant efforts to throw himself under approaching lorries rather than pass dangerous looking purple flowers in the hedge reduced me to a quaking wreck. And then I remembered the amiable Appaloosas from the rodeo days.

The advertisement for Leo read 'goes anywhere with anyone', but he was a successful show horse, and I'm sure a trip to Spain wasn't what he had in mind. He was just six years old when I bought him in 1999, well-mannered, cosseted, with chestnut spots on a pale coat and whites to his eyes like a human, giving him a permanent air of surprise.

In some ways he wasn't typical of the breed, many of which have sparse manes and tails; Leo's tail was a huge curly waterfall, and his mane was so thick that it parted in the middle. And he didn't conform to a modern trend for a lightweight Appaloosa – he was a comfortable, solid middleweight, a throwback to his Spanish ancestry, with style, a sense of humour and a penchant for showing off. But what he did have in abundance was the Appaloosa's gentle temperament, a willingness to try whatever I asked of him.

I began to think seriously about a long distance ride.

It was Susie who came up with the idea of the Way of St James. I had never heard of it, but she'd learned of its existence through her own dream of a proper pilgrimage, a natural progression for her because of her thirst for knowledge about religion and history. She thought she'd walk it with the family lurcher, but John put his foot down – he didn't mind Susie walking the Way, but he didn't think it would be safe for their dog. He didn't want to go himself, and Susie didn't particularly like the idea of travelling alone, so I suggested that she and I might go together. With Leo. With Susie on a horse as well, so we could keep pace with each other.

What about our starting point? Susie envisaged the Camino Francés, setting out from the monastery at Roncesvalles on the southern side of the Pyrenees, and then we got more ambitious and thought of leaving from Vézelay in France. But finally, ever the dreamer, I thought, oh well, let's ride the whole way from England. From Canterbury. As far as we knew, no travellers had ridden the entire length of the pilgrim routes on their own horses since 1500-and-something. We got very excited as the plan unfolded, but there were two problems: one was that I was working full time, and the other was that Susie had no horse.

The first problem was quickly solved: I suggested a sabbatical to my employers. They were used to my wild ideas so agreed in the sure knowledge that this was just Plan 286 and nothing would come of it. By the time they realised I was serious, luckily for me a trainee was with the firm who'd be able to look after my work for the three months I expected to be away, so they indulged me anyway, although they thought I was mad.

A horse for Susie proved to be more difficult.

The mare we bought was a disaster, but it wasn't only because she persuaded Leo to roger her all round the field. She may have been breathing lust at him, but she snorted fire at everyone else from the time we got her home, and Susie soon found out that advancing years had done nothing for her nerve. The horse would clop along at a disconcertingly tremendous speed if she felt like it, but if she didn't, she was a mountain of obstinacy travelling in reverse, and there was no knowing whether she'd go forwards to Santiago or backwards to John O'Groats. The blatant seduction of my innocent gelding was the final straw – Leo was thrilled with his emergence into a macho world after his sheltered upbringing, but the prospect of travelling piggyback to Spain wasn't attractive. The mare had to be sold, and we were back to square one.

We went to see Apollo. He was a very loudly marked Irish–Appaloosa cross with enough black spots to give you a migraine, a smart little horse who'd recently arrived in England to be sold on. He was full of rubber-lipped kisses for everyone, and he was sparky enough for me to worry that Susie would find him unnerving, but surprisingly she didn't. We decided to get him, but just as we were finalising the details, the dealer phoned to say the farrier had come to put new shoes on him and Apollo had thrown a wobbler. Somewhere, sometime, a blacksmith in Ireland must have hit him, perhaps with a hammer, because Apollo had such a phobia that the minute the farrier's apron and tools were produced he turned into a kicking maniac.

We changed our minds.

Next came tragedy, when Tessa's husband was killed in a flying accident returning home to Oregon from Canada. Susie and I flew out to spend a week in their house, which was so full of relatives that we had to share Tessa's bed along with a Siberian husky, a half-wolf and assorted cats that slept on our heads. Wriggling about uncomfortably, we talked for hours about the pilgrimage; Tessa needed a project, something to plan for, and it was decided that she would meet up with us somewhere along the way. Flying back to England, immersed in thought, Susie and I each concluded that we liked Apollo far too much to let him go – so he joined us, phobia and all.

Planning began in earnest.

We'd decided to ride for charity, in aid of the East Kent Pilgrims' Hospices. They were appropriately named, in view of our pilgrim route, but the reason for our choice was more than that: I was very aware that had things gone differently for me, I could have ended my days in the Canterbury Hospice; and we'd had friends die there, cradled in the atmosphere of compassion and comfort, humour and strength. The hospices were only partly funded by the local health authority and the rest of the huge running costs came from every imaginable source, from the pockets of schoolchildren to the challenge funds of the largest employers in Kent. Susie and I thought that the unlikely idea of two middle-aged women riding their own horses from Canterbury to Santiago de Compostela might attract sponsorship.

But first there was the question of our exact route so we could suggest, say, a penny a mile to our sponsors. I bought a map that showed all the bridleways in France apparently interlinking the whole way from Calais to St-Jean-Pied-de-Port at the foot of the Pyrenees, from where we would follow the Pas de Roncesvalles across the mountains into Spain. It was perfectly simple, and we plotted a way based on this map that would take us south-east of Paris to Vézelay and the start of one of the four traditional roads to Santiago – but that road looked as though it might become boring around Bordeaux: flat and a bit monotonous.

How about a diversion south through the Auvergne on a lesser-known pilgrim trail? Susie looked doubtfully at an atlas – she'd suffered from vertigo for years, and the words Massif Central plastered across the area didn't look too promising. But I assured her truthfully that I'd been told by a friend we wouldn't have to go anywhere particularly high, and I promised to stay away from gorges. We could cut down to Aurillac, and then pick up the major Le Puy route at Cahors. Susie wasn't convinced but she agreed, if only to shut me up, so I walked *Jorrocks's* navigational dividers laboriously down the snaky tracks on the French equestrian map, added 500 miles for Spain, and came up with a total of 1500 miles. A substantial £15 per sponsor. We went to Stanfords in London and ordered dozens of Série Bleue maps, the equivalent of Ordnance Survey, from a young man with violent hay fever; taking advantage of his lowered resistance, Susie persuaded him that Stanfords should sponsor half their cost.

The next question was the departure date. We decided on April 2002, a comfortably long way ahead; by then our various children would be grown up and in theory independent: only my daughter Clara would still be at university. I knew I'd be in the doghouse with her because her finals were in the summer and so was her twenty-first birthday, but our mother was developing Alzheimer's and our father was doddery on his feet – if we didn't go soon, we wouldn't go at all.

Susie designed a map of our route and a logo of a scallop shell with two spotted horses inside it, and we put together a leaflet describing ourselves, the hospices, the horses and the Way of St James. We pondered over a name for our expedition, but the problem was solved by a friendly forensic expert I was instructing in connection with a court case. Our discussions veered away from work towards imaginative ways of encouraging sponsorship, perhaps short of parading through Canterbury like two wrinkly Lady Godivas which might have the opposite effect. Susie and I adopted his suggestion that we should call ourselves Santiago Tales, and he amused himself for months afterwards by ending his letters to me with 'yours to the sound of galloping hooves', 'yours with several bits between his teeth' and 'yours *not* in the saddle at all hours'.

We distributed leaflets and sponsorship forms to everyone we could pin down: Peter's golf club members; Susie's calligraphy students; clients of my firm; barristers, magistrates and Crown Court judges; a retired Canon; family and friends. Not surprisingly, some of our potential sponsors decided to wait and see if we made it to Santiago before contributing, but many helped towards our expenses and specific items like horseshoes, return tickets across the Channel, all-weather jackets with multitudinous pockets, and reflective strips for the horses' bridles in case we got lost in fog.

We went to London to join the Confraternity of St James, where I lurked behind Susie in their office in case my less than holy profile put them off, but they were unfazed, helpfully providing publicity, guidebooks and pilgrim passports for stamping in the towns and villages on the Way. The ultimate stamp would be in Santiago when we would be awarded our certificates, or compostellas. If we got that far.

Our farrier Jason, for one, didn't believe we'd get there, and with good reason: 'no foot no horse', of course, and here was one who had to be sedated the minute the blacksmith appeared, and here was the other who had flat feet with thin hoof walls, quite unsuitable for long-distance riding. He humoured Susie and me, though, buying us tools and showing us how to remove horseshoes (that is, if we could get near Apollo in the first place), and how to hammer down loose nails. He advised us to paint their hooves with corn oil in hot weather to keep them moist, and he suggested a special hoof-enhancing food supplement for Leo – it cost the earth but it worked, and Leo grew a new set of fortified feet.

In August 2001 an article about us was published in the local newspaper, and suddenly it wasn't armchair travelling any more. We were in print: we would have to go. DEFRA provided the necessary forms for Leo and Apollo, and it was a relief to see that no rabies regulations applied to horses, but they did need clean bills of health and export certificates to be completed just before we left. We also had to supply an address in Santiago. This was tricky as we didn't know anyone there, but a friend of a Spanish friend gave us the address of his flat in the city, and we just hoped the authorities wouldn't bother to check on the likelihood of Leo and Apollo trotting up two flights of stairs to the spare bedroom.

The next question was a back-up vehicle. The phone bills mounted as Susie and I discussed and argued over the problem – it was a romantic idea to travel as light as Dick Whittington, but it simply wasn't practical. Susie was worried we wouldn't be proper pilgrims if we didn't go it alone, but I was worried we'd take so long I'd come back and find myself without a job.

I suggested a horsebox.

It took a long time to talk Susie round to this idea but eventually, when she was finally wavering, I blew my only savings on Bessie the elderly Bedford. At the same time I reminded Peter he'd once told me he'd like to be a lorry driver, and produced the map of French golf courses.

Bessie's roof leaked. There was rot in the lorry's hardwood body, and the first time Leo walked in he split a board in the ramp. The living area was an empty Luton head and a space seven feet square containing two lockers and a home-made dresser, all of which needed rebuilding. Soggy hardboard bellied down from the ceiling, the interior was painted lurid orange, and 39 queen wasps taxied out of gaps in the planks with their wings humming dangerously in the thin November air.

But the engine ran sweetly, the cab was comfortable and Bessie had character. I looked meaningfully at Peter, muttered something about the ground being far too wet to play golf at this time of year, and promised him steak dinners every Saturday night. With an unfathomable expression, he parked Bessie outside the sitting-room window for the winter, fed the extension lead through the letterbox into the nearest power point and, leaving Susie to cope with the bulk of the fundraising for the time being, he and I set to work.

Friends helped with the fitting out, installing a set of horsebox windows I bought through the internet and replacing any rotten sections in the planks. Peter, by now resigned to the fact that he was going to miss his golf club's centenary year, unrolled a huge strip of white fibreglass sheeting I acquired for a song and created a watertight roof over the top of the old one. He made luxuriously padded partitions for the horses so they couldn't knock themselves, installed new lockers, mended the dresser and rewired the lorry so we could run the domestic electricity off a second battery. Jack plugs for Frigo the coolbox and the twelve-volt stereo system from *Jorrocks* went in, and I imagined soothing evenings of Saint-Saëns and Schubert. The paintwork was my job: three shades of cheerful yellow on the walls, and a white ceiling in Peter's and my bedroom in the Luton head. I had to lie on my back to paint it, and with Clara's mattress added, the only one small enough to go in, we'd have headroom of all of twenty inches. How on earth were we going to fit in there for three months?

Furnishing was done on a shoestring: blue carpet offcuts, and a portable gas stove from Lena's Nautibits, the second-hand chandlery in the boatyard; and from *Jorrocks* came the kettle, cutlery, pots and pans, and all her 1950s-vintage feather cushions with fraying yellow covers. The local shipwright mounted scallop shells on pine plaques for Bessie's exterior, the Chamber of Commerce provided signs that announced FAVERSHAM, MARKET TOWN OF KINGS and the Pilgrims' Hospices gave us one that said SANTIAGO TALES, SUPPORTING PILGRIMS' HOSPICES IN EAST KENT. Bessie was beginning to look conspicuous, but palatial enough for me to breeze round the boatyard and persuade a Thames barge skipper and the crane driver, as well as one of our sponsors, that two weeks each spent relief driving so Peter could come home for the odd break would be the holiday of a lifetime.

We were getting there.

At the beginning of February it dawned on Susie and me that we'd better do something about getting ourselves and the horses fit. I took up riding before I went to work, and Leo and I skittered out through the boatyard at dawn to the cacophonous din of loose rigging slapping against metal masts, which he learned to ignore, along with the heavy traffic when I rode through the middle of Faversham. Periodically, Apollo arrived from Susie's home to stay, and once Leo had got over his initial disappointment that Apollo wasn't a mare, the two horses became best friends.

The more we rode, the more uncomfortable on our saddles Susie and I became, but Peter bought me some encasing equestrian knickers called Cumfy Rumps as a precaution against the nightmare scenario of three months without being able to sit down, and there was an additional solution: sheepskins over the tops of our saddles. Mine had the added advantage of gluing me to Leo, necessary after an early mishap when he shot forwards as a dog leaped out of the hedge and, much to his embarrassment, I fell off over his tail.

I meant to finish work at the end of March, but it didn't happen. Departure day was set for Monday, 8 April; on the fifth I was still at work, dictating copious notes so the trainee wouldn't panic and leave. The last weekend passed in a blur of shopping for more camping equipment, an air mattress for Susie, three months' supply of concentrates for the horses and a £2 compass that slid over my wristwatch strap. We decided to take Susie's elderly bicycle just in case it came in useful, and all Peter's golf clubs were crammed into their bag ready for the Channel crossing, which was to include my car packed to the roof with horsy supplies, John and an assortment of our children to help us get under way on the other side.

Susie, on a recce during the previous summer, had managed to book the horses in at an equestrian centre close to Calais for the first night – but on a later recce with me, we could find no sign of the wonderful linked bridlepaths marked on our map. Was this going to be a pilgrimage spent clattering down the autoroutes?

2. GOD(S)PEED

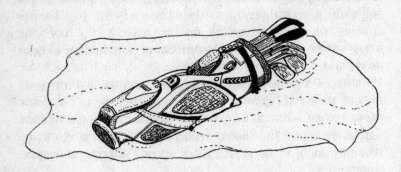

8 April.

Departure day, and the lorry still isn't packed. The plan is to travel in Bessie to Canterbury for a blessing in the cathedral by Patrick the Archdeacon, and then to ride most of the way to Dover where Leo and Apollo are staying the night in the grounds of a stately home. Then we'll return to our respective houses for one last night, ride the rest of the way to Dover tomorrow and load the horses in the lorry to cross the Channel. At 9 a.m. Leo and Apollo are pronounced healthy by the local vet, who tells us how well they look and doesn't comment on the size of Apollo's paunch, which is impressive even after weeks of exercise.

Driving down the road from Faversham to Canterbury I think: well, it's too late now. We're really going to do it. I try to persuade myself to deal with just one day at a time: today's mental note is to give the cat a worm pill this evening. I'm apprehensive about the blessing, but I'm convinced that if I don't take part, the God whose existence I doubt will certainly strike me dead at Calais. Susie looks serene, in a tight-lipped sort of way. Peter's more concerned that Bessie's decided to entertain us with a shrieking noise from one of her brakes, which he says is sticking. It wasn't sticking yesterday.

In St Radigund's car park the horses deposit huge piles of dung all over the horsebox ramp and several designated car spaces, but there's no time to clear up – we're late for the Archdeacon. Leo and Apollo take off at a butcher boy's trot along Palace Street, and here are our children, and all our friends and workmates with banners and flowers as we pass through the towering Christchurch Gate and into the precincts. The press are here as well, and the lady from the *Faversham Times* obligingly holds Leo as Susie and I follow Archdeacon Patrick through the door into the cathedral, our footsteps clacking loudly on the flagstones. As we enter a chapel next to the monument to Thomas à Becket, I realise that probably the last horse riders who came into the cathedral were the ones bursting in to kill him. Someone practising the organ sends the notes soaring into the vaulted ceiling, and a few early tourists peer at the curious sight of two women in breeches and gaiters walking along with a priest.

Patrick suggests we just stand, and then he blesses us with pilgrim prayers. The words flow over me but the sense of occasion is overwhelming as the sunlight slants through the high windows: here we are at last on this glowing spring day, finally leaving after two long years of planning. I hear Patrick asking that we should be peaceful in the evening and weary at night. Not too weary, I hope.

Outside, Meridian TV has arrived. I've kissed my friends goodbye and hugged them all – now it's time to get on the horses and pose self-consciously. The Hospices' fundraiser is here to wave us off and so are some of my firm's partners, among them Fred, impossibly smart in trilby hat and cashmere overcoat with its moth hole carefully concealed. The girls from work laughingly tell me I'm mad. Leo's moulting white hairs all over Patrick's black cassock as he blesses the horses too, pressing down on Apollo's head so he nods respectfully. 'May your burden be light,' Patrick says to him, and I wonder if this is a reference to Susie's weight.

We clatter up the cobbles in the Burgate with posies pinned to our Confraternity sweatshirts. Someone's standing in front of the banner that reads GOD SPEED, irreverently concealing the S, and everyone follows us on foot, my son Oliver running alongside to hand me a hopeful sun hat he's just bought. The traffic on the ring road is held up so that we can cross, and then suddenly we've left them all behind and we're trotting up the main road past the prison, turning off into the lanes and then across country on the North Downs Way.

There's a detour to make so we can visit our mother, now in a home outside Canterbury. It's hard to see her there after a lifetime as a free spirit, dependent in a wheelchair pushed by our father, her swollen scaly feet in slippers. At the moment she thinks she can't walk, but she recognises us at once and her eyes light up when she sees the horses – but for the Alzheimer's she would have been demanding to come with us too. We say goodbye, prickly with guilt, but our mother is quite tranquil and our father still ferociously independent. He merely reminds us to send postcards.

It's relaxingly sunny and warm as we join the North Downs Way again, but just as we're beginning to think it might not all be hard work, I notice thirty cows and twelve loose horses hurtling towards us in the same field. Susie and I scramble off Leo and Apollo, who by now are gyrating in circles while we try to wave off the leering heifers and hunters, and Leo rumbles endearments at likely young fillies as I drag him to the gate at the other end of the field and wait for Susie and Apollo to tango across together. It takes ten minutes to push back the puffing hordes while simultaneously trying to squeeze our horses out through the gate – one shove from an overexcited cow and they'd all be through, hightailing it up the motorway to Dover. We feel exhausted already, and are thankful when we make it to the stately home without any more incidents.

Back at my house everything's in chaos. The place is filthy, still nothing's packed, but I've remembered to worm the cat. The trainee from work arrives, punctuating supper with last-minute requests for instructions, but I'm finding it hard to think about the law any more – DEFRA's order to scrub the horsebox before we cross the Channel seems to be much more important. The trainee and I mull over the question of specific intent relating to indecent assault charges while I'm swilling buckets of pink disinfectant round Bessie.

To bed at 2 a.m., nothing finished.

At dawn we're milling round the house, loading the lorry with plastic containers of clothes, bits of electric fencing, the Marmite and a spare battery along with Susie's awkward bike. Clara's ousted from her bed, her mattress commandeered, and Peter lovingly arranges his golf clubs on top of the duvet in Bessie. Next to the lorry my car's sinking low on its axles, pregnant with horse food.

On the bridlepath to Dover, Susie and I manage a sedate canter with no racing, but the bridlepath becomes a footpath and the Ordnance Survey map hasn't noted the change. My planned route is in tatters when we meet fixed stiles we're both too old to contemplate jumping, and we have to pass under the dual carriageway, noticing at the last moment that there's a lake in the middle of the tunnel which looks ominously deep and black. Lorries thunder overhead. Normally I wouldn't dream of riding a horse this way, but this is no ordinary journey and anyway there's no way round. Leo takes a deep breath and plods through, up to his knees, ignoring the noise – but looking back, I can see the mutinous outline of Apollo saying no at the tunnel entrance. I ride out of sight, and seconds later he and Susie appear at speed to the sound of tidal waves; Apollo has no intention of being left behind by his friend, and he never says no again.

The footpath follows a track so narrow and overgrown that we have to get off and lead the horses, whippy branches cracking on the saddles. We can't see the end until suddenly we're poised at the top of a flight of steps into a car park, and there's no way round this either. Walking down steps when you have four feet to think about takes time, and each horse watches carefully when we show him where to place his hooves. I wonder if the rest of the pilgrimage is going to be as eventful as these first two days.

Leo and Apollo stride up Bessie's ramp in the public gardens just outside Dover and attack their haynets with fervour. No travel nerves there. The noise from the sticking brake is worse than yesterday as we squeal along Dover's streets, collect our travel passes and line up to be booked through on to the ferry. The clerk looks doubtfully at the lorry.

'Where are the securing points?'

'Securing points?'

'It's got to be chained down on the ferry. It can't travel otherwise.' She glances only briefly at the complicated DEFRA forms and our passports, and hands back the paperwork. We sit in stunned silence. I can see us failing to clear the first hurdle – I'm sure Bessie was made long before the days of securing points. They won't let us on. We'll have to go home. The clerk notices our consternation. 'Wait a minute. I'll make a phone call.'

Two minutes later we're bumping on to the ferry, and the car-deck crew attach chains to all Bessie's strategically placed securing points that none of us has noticed before. When I check the horses, shut in darkness now, they're still munching hay. We head for the bar.

At Calais, Bessie screeches through Customs. Several of our children are crammed in the lorry's living space, transfixed by the handlebars of Susie's bike or poised in the capacious muck bucket, but no-one's interested in our documents nor in who's travelling with us. At Hydrequent equestrian centre Madame has prepared two stables with deep straw beds, but Leo doesn't want to know – he likes being outdoors, and the prospect of being shut in puts him into such a hyped-up sweaty state that his spots turn blue. Seven ponies have to be removed from their bare windy paddock so our horses can relax with the turkeys scratching at the thin grass.

The horse section of the lorry is in an unspeakable state. This is going to be Susie's bedroom in a few days' time. We scrub it out again with the pink disinfectant and jam everything out of my car into one side, together with most of the contents of the living space in Bessie, or there'll be no space to live in. Apart from the damp whiffy state of the rubber matting, the slot on the other side of the partition is now habitable, and I remove Peter's golf clubs from our mattress when he's not looking and tie them to the back of the horse partition with all the spare headcollar ropes.

For now, we've decided to break ourselves in gently, and the first two nights are to be spent in pre-booked gîtes. In the neighbouring town of Marquise we have a huge farewell dinner before John takes my car and all the children back across the Channel. It seems very odd to be saying goodbye in tones of such finality – Susie's due to return briefly for a wedding party in May, but I can only promise Clara that Peter and I will fly back for her university graduation ceremony in July if we haven't reached Santiago by then. She reminds me again that I'm going to miss her twenty-first birthday.

I'm a disgraceful mother. I have left home.

So now it's just Peter, Susie and me. We climb silently into Bessie's cab in the darkness, and roar away from the four parking spaces she's occupied in the main square at Marquise. A wrong turning on the way to the gîte means Peter's lorry driving skills are immediately tested when he has to turn round on a narrow cart track, in pitch blackness and a sudden downpour, and already he's being rude about our navigation.

The gîte is freezing cold. I have Peter to keep me warm but Susie, peering apprehensively at the distance from her top bunk to the floor, has only a woolly nightie. I think the hot-water bottle's in the lorry. Somewhere. It's strange to be three in a room and I wonder if good manners will triumph, even in sleep, so that none of us snores or farts.

3. LOOKING FOR A *TOUTE DROITE* DIRECTION

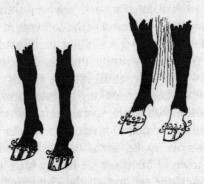

It turns out to be a politely quiet night but I'm awake at six, waiting for the day to begin. Peter's heaved grumbling out of bed at least two hours before his normal wake-up time of ten o'clock, and we leave Hydrequent in cold sunshine, planning to ride just twelve miles south to our final pre-booked stop at Lacres – but something seems to be wrong with our map-reading, and it turns out to be 22 miles. And Leo thinks something's wrong with the road – he ought to be walking on the other side of it. Firmly English, he veers to the left every time I relax, and I discover early on that my posture is terrible, my shoulders round after years of slouching over a desk. Efforts to straighten up leave me with a second backache to add to the one I've already had for several months, since trying to haul my reluctant mother to her feet last year, but all the same there's excitement shimmering in the air: we're on our way.

We look for bridlepaths. There aren't any, and the camber of the road slopes down so steeply that the horses are unbalanced. There's no question of trotting as we ride along main roads, minor lanes and up long hills to see tarmac running endlessly into the distance, all lined with the orderly stumps of pollarded trees. Peter's somewhere ahead of us in Bessie, but as we forgot to switch to French SIM cards in our respective mobile phones we aren't able to contact each other all day.

The Bois de Boulogne is a terrible disappointment. The map does show bridlepaths here, but ours hugs a tiny verge beside the road. Susie and I share a sticky bun for lunch at a woodland table; we've already spent so much money on the gîte and last night's dinner that it's going to be cheese and Marmite sandwiches from now on – we're on a very limited budget, and if our ageing teeth could cope with ship's biscuit, I'd have loaded a supply of that.

From the busy town of Samer the most direct route to Lacres is down the N1, but it's a continuous stream of high-speed cars and lorries, and it's out of the question. We approach a surprised Frenchman washing his car in the middle of the town – Susie and I just want directions, but Apollo insists on kissing him as well while he instructs us to *suivez* La Blanche Jument, a long narrow country road that leads straight back to the N1. More directions are needed but there's no-one on this lonely lane to give them, so we fantasise about tea and a hot bath instead. We seem to have been riding for weeks.

Round the corner there's a farmyard to hover in looking useless, and Madame comes out to investigate – when we explain our predicament, she departs in her car and returns moments later with Peter and Bessie trundling along behind her. At our gîte a short half-mile away our hostess presents us with a bucket of fresh milk straight from the cow, and there's nothing for it but to make two pints of hot chocolate each, hardly a recipe for another quiet night, while she helpfully books us in for tomorrow with a relation who farms near Montreuil. We daren't ask how far it is.

In the cold morning Susie and I are thankful for our sponsored all-singing all-dancing jackets, heavy and snug in the bitterest wind. Their pockets are packed with sandwiches, Mars

Bars, squash, my mobile phone (now with appropriate SIM card) and horsy snacks. We daren't get off the horses – I weigh too much to get on again from the ground without a leg up, and Susie's so small she needs a milestone to stand on anyway.

Already a mental readjustment is needed. We left late yesterday and even later today – Susie and I have different body clocks, and mine ticks faster than hers. She tells me I'm a driven personality, and she's probably right, but a promise to my employers to be back by mid-July has something to do with it, coupled with a fervent intention that we shouldn't find ourselves riding through Spain in the heat of August. However, for the moment we've abandoned the idea of trying to find bridlepaths and we're sticking to a more direct route on minor roads, which should be quicker. I've taken over the navigation – Susie has to find her glasses each time she needs to look at the map, and if I squint I can still read the tiny writing without mine. My marine navigation qualification should stand me in good stead, but finding my way at sea is a doddle compared to rummaging round the contours and forests of France. The £2 wrist compass is coming into its own.

At Neuville-sous-Montreuil our new hostess welcomes us for two nights, but while the horses have a big cowfield to themselves for both, tonight her gîte is full and we must all sleep in Bessie. But it doesn't work out like that. Bessie's brake has been sticking and shrieking all day; it needs to be fixed before we go any further, and fortunately for us there's a lorry garage down the road at Attin, run by shaven-headed Serge with a big gap-toothed smile. He is soothing, he understands the problem: he comes from a showjumping family. He knows about horseboxes, and smoothly he removes Bessie's rear wheel before telling us we must leave her at the garage overnight with the brake and valve soaking in oil. We're not sure about sleeping in the lorry in a miasma of diesel and oil where one false step in the dark would mean an unscheduled descent into the inspection pit, but Serge says there is *pas de problème*: he'll lend us his works van and we can stay at his friend's hotel. Three to a room again, Susie snores in a flat monotone until Peter shouts at her to shut up before tuning up himself – but I don't get the chance to snore because Susie stops breathing altogether in mid-snort, and then I'm awake for the rest of the night checking periodically she's still alive.

We rattle back to Attin just when everyone has gone for lunch, which in France means for at least three hours, and after treating Serge's van to a whistle-stop tour of Montreuil we return to the garage to find Bessie is ready and squeakless, and I'm now £170 poorer. I hope I don't go home to find the house has been repossessed – last night's hotel was an unscheduled expense as well, so tonight's supper is skinny cheese omelettes in the lorry before Susie retires to her gîte with the hot-water bottle.

It's Peter's and my first night in Bessie, and Clara's mattress is superbly comfortable. I lie awake for a while in the murmuring night, listening to the piebald cows chewing in their barn and hoping I don't fall out of bed, as it's a drop of four feet from the Luton head to the lorry floor. Unfortunately, Bessie's wooden body means she has no insulation and, as the temperature dips below freezing, I settle down to a night of stopping up draughts and swearing, while Peter wraps himself up in the duvet like a sausage in a roll.

Breakfast is *en famille* in the farmhouse. Busy Madame with her short chic haircut has four children under twelve but her husband, the handsome man in the photograph in the kitchen, was killed in a tractor accident four years ago. He was the farmer, and Madame's a professor of medical science, but now she's adapted to running the family farm and the gîte, bringing up the children on her own. Every movement she makes is brisk and efficient: she kneels by the kitchen hearth, blows down a deer's hollow antler and the fire explodes into life.

Child number four is a little girl with swimming brown eyes who sits in a high chair and pretends to eat breakfast. Apparently she's refusing to eat in the mornings, and she repeatedly stuffs her mouth so full of bread and hot chocolate, swallowing nothing, that disaster is imminent – but Madame removes her at speed, still in her high chair, skating her expertly across the tiled floor and out of the door. The other children ignore the drama; the eldest is busy struggling with his English grammar and the pronunciation of 'aren't' and, anyway, they want to ride the horses. Leo and Apollo are bounding with energy, ready to go, but they tone it down to a slow and careful walk round the old tennis court with their little riders, and I'm relieved to see that Mademoiselle Brown Eyes hasn't choked to death but is now bouncing round on Peter's shoulders.

The horses shed their restraint the minute we're out on the road. Apollo leaps into a gallop when an invisible St Bernard dog rumbles at him behind its gate, leaving Susie struggling to pull him up at red traffic lights, and when we reach a level railway crossing Leo jumps all the tracks at once. A day's rest on rich pasture has left the horses supercharged, dancing sideways with impatience every time we stop.

Madame's arranged for us to stay with another family at Valloire, but it's only about twelve miles away and at this rate we'll be there in an hour and a half. I'm uneasy that already we're dropping behind schedule; the countryside is flat here and I think I should be pushing on while I can, but the fact is that Susie and I aren't fully fit, and neither are the horses. We don't yet have the nerve to bang on doors and ask unwary householders if they can accommodate two horses, three people and a lorry for the night, so we're reliant on the kindness of people like busy Madame to find us somewhere to stay, wherever it may be. It was never going to be possible to book ahead from England, because we have no idea where we might be on any particular day.

The road's a straight pencil pointing to the river Authie before running alongside drowning marshes on the other side towards Valloire, and at least now we're out of the Pas de Calais and into Picardie, so maybe we're making some progress. We ride past an old abbey, to Susie's pleasure as she sees an opportunity to improve my religious education, and next to it our new hosts have a manicured estate, totally enclosed and with an electric gate that sighs open when we ring the bell. At their smart stables we're clearly expected to groom Leo and Apollo, but we're too tired to do any such thing and try to explain in our best French that when they're turned out in a field they'll roll and do it themselves. To Leo's delight, the field next door contains the family's tall aristocratic horses, including an elegant mare called La Demoiselle. He refuses to roll, secure in his belief that his sweaty body is irresistible, and it's as well there's a fence between them.

Peter's parked Bessie discreetly by the stables, and we have the run of a centrally heated garage where there's a basin, a loo and a clutch of baby mallards under a lamp. Monsieur Immaculate's soft leather riding gaiters are carelessly flung over a rail, and I look speculatively at my own rough Spanish ones, their inside calves already caked with grease from Leo's coat.

Susie carts me off to the abbey. It's guided tours only and the guide isn't here, so we wait in the sunshine on a courtyard bench and are dead asleep by the time she appears. I creak to my feet, too tired to concentrate on her patter in speedy French – Susie's attentive, but I can only vaguely take in the names Cistercian, and Thérèse Papillon who ran the abbey as a TB sanatorium during the war. The accoustics in the chapel are so resonant that in my disinhibited state of tiredness I have an urge to see if my mouse-volume singing voice will expand to operatic dimensions, but luckily for our guide we're distracted by the sight of a piece of string dangling two large statues, which she assures us are made of papier mâché. Susie's looking both impressed and holy, but I'm just dying for a bath.

Back at the estate Monsieur Immaculate's been making phone calls to try to find us accommodation for tomorrow, but he's had no success and he tells us that our route is *bloqué*, our journey doomed. We will find nowhere to stay in France. But he notes

Susie's and my mulish expressions and hastily volunteers to make some more phone calls in the morning.

As soon as night falls the temperature drops like a stone, so we dig out the new portable gas heater and read its perplexing instructions. They emphasise that it shouldn't be lit indoors, but it's hardly man enough to warm up the estate and canopy of night sky as well, so we light it anyway and huddle over it with our supper in the lorry. This is Susie's first night in Bessie and she departs to the horse section with her air mattress, sleeping bag and a torch; taking no chances, she parcels herself up in all the spare horse rugs as well. By morning we're all frozen, and when I scamper to the garage at 7 a.m. the grass is white with frost and vapour writhes eerily from the lake. I hope Monsieur Immaculate is still asleep because I don't have a nightie and he might not be impressed by the sight of someone in an outsized red T-shirt and gumboots sprinting across his perfect lawn.

By the time we're ready to leave, Leo's so hyped up with excitement that he won't line up by the lorry ramp so I can get on him, and Monsieur obviously thinks I have a small common horse with very bad manners. However, he looks amazed when Susie and I tell him politely that we've cleared up all the horse dung in his field, and we learn something new: dung is '*crottes*' in French, a word that rolls satisfyingly off the tongue and anglicises nicely to crots. Monsieur kindly refuses to accept payment for the night and indeed has made another thirty phone calls which have resulted in a billet for tonight at Forest-l'Abbaye, on the other side of the Forest of Crécy. I don't have enough hands to control Leo while I look at the map, but he gives us detailed directions in rapid French which neither Susie nor I can follow. We daren't ask him to repeat them, so we nod knowledgeably and leave with effusive thanks.

Five minutes later we're lost, and there are hooves approaching behind us – Monsieur Immaculate is out hacking with his daughter, and Leo's ecstatic to see La Demoiselle again. She and Monsieur's gelding are clipped, shiny and wearing every kind of tendon boot, exercise boot and overreach boot imaginable, while Apollo and Leo are unclipped, still hairy with the last of their winter coats and totally unbooted, highlighting Apollo's striped hooves fetchingly framed by a frill of woolly curls. Leo's galloping on the spot, sluicing down with sweat as Monsieur moves smoothly alongside in his soft gaiters, his knicker line so invisible that he must be wearing his Cumfy Rumps, to point us in a *toute droite* direction. We thunder uncontrollably up the road and seconds later are lost again, deciding to wait until the even beat of horseshoes has diminished into the distance before venturing back the way we came.

The only way I can get Leo to stand still so I can look at the map is to let him bury his head in the hedge and munch; now that I have a chance to look at it, the route is quite straightforward and we soon reach the Forest of Crécy. According to the map there's a bridle path that runs straight through it from north to south, and Forest-l'Abbaye is right where we emerge. All the same, I'm alarmed that the map shows this public forest is divided into hundreds of tiny rectangular parcels of land all bordered by tracks and neatly numbered from one to 412. One wrong turn and we could be lost for weeks.

Keep an eye on the compass. Just head south.

The forest is glinting with light and sunshine, too well behaved for brambles, the track leading from one airy glade to another through rows of deciduous trees bursting into loud green leaf, and the horses are happy to canter, their hoofbeats muffled in the mulch underfoot. They leap over the occasional fallen branch, Apollo skimming the top with minimum clearance, perhaps to reflect a previous career as a showjumper, and the novice Leo hurling himself over with two feet to spare just in case he catches a twig with his hoof. My back aches like hell.

And then suddenly we plunge into darkness – we've entered

the Kingdom of Mordor, a wood where the French authorities have obviously run out of steam and young saplings. The path is narrow, dense now with fir trees so tightly packed that no light penetrates; every tree rattles with brittle black branches and the ground underneath is as dead as school corridor linoleum. Leo and Apollo are bug-eyed, looking for trouble, and Susie's checking for Orcs. We whisper our way through to avoid disturbing any evil forces that might be about, and equally suddenly we're back in blinding sunlight, out on the road with the forest behind us, to find Bessie and Peter waiting in Madame Becquet's little paddock.

We're all parked together in the tiny field for the night, and Leo and Apollo are delighted to be so close to us, poking their noses through the groom's door into our supply of wine bottles by the doormat. Leo notices a mare in the next paddock, ancient and swaybacked, her coat harsh as a bottlebrush, and he fancies her every bit as much as La Demoiselle. That mare Susie and I bought has a lot to answer for. Peter christens her Mrs Robinson, and she snorts and roars flirtatiously as Leo suavely arches his neck over the fence.

Madame Becquet shouts down the telephone at the proprietor of the Château de Béhen, about fifteen miles away, and informs him we'll be staying with him tomorrow night. She tells him off for speaking far too fast and hangs up on him abruptly in mid-conversation, but when I call him back I find to my surprise that he speaks beautiful English – he sounds bemused, but he's prepared to let us stay.

The night's punctuated by restless hooves pacing round the lorry and subdued harrumphs of excitement from Mrs Robinson. At breakfast the horses make a nuisance of themselves, snuffling into the washing-up bowl and demanding croissants and, when none are forthcoming, Apollo seizes Susie's air mattress off the ramp and trots off with it clenched in his teeth. I'm waiting for the explosion but luckily it taps against his knees and scares him into dropping it before there's a puncture and, meanwhile, Leo's galloping sideways with excitement again, anxious to be on his way. We've been told that trekking horses get bored, but there's certainly no sign of it yet – I'm more concerned that Peter's bored, but he's patiently tackling one book after another. He complains that we wake him up when we're getting ready in the morning, but at least he can go back to sleep again.

The road leads south in the chilly sunshine, crossing the Somme at Petit Laviers west of Abbeville; but it's not really the Somme, it's the Canal Maritime and we rattle across a metal swing bridge no more substantial than the one across Faversham Creek. I'd like to imagine the ill-fated French army of 1346, piled up on the south side of the river waiting for the tide to go out as they pursued the English to the Battle of Crécy with disastrous consequences, but the Canal is slate grey and orderly, totally without atmosphere.

In the late afternoon we ride into the village of Béhen, circumnavigate the church twice by mistake, and find ourselves outside the fairy-tale château with swans waddling in the garden.

4. A MOST EXPENSIVE KISS

A gangly figure with dishevelled hair is bounding out of the château. He asks me if I'd like to break in one of his young horses, and his assumption of my ability and nerve is gratifying – but I've had enough trouble controlling Leo today so perhaps not, and no thanks to his floor-mop dog as well, which is trying to give me a plastic hamburger. Hubert's brother Norbert appears, calm and hospitable, and it's not long before we're persuaded out of a fourth night in Bessie and into dinner and a room in the château, run by the family as *chambres d'hôtes*. We resolve this will be positively our last luxury.

Leo and Apollo take over the horse paddock, but it's been denuded of grass and they turn away disapprovingly from a pile of hay only to find that two opportunist peacocks are tucking into their concentrates. Our own dinner is expertly cooked by Norbert and we sit down at the family table with the brothers and their mother, the conversation drifting through French to English and back again; Norbert's very focused on the development of the business and the renovation of the château, and Hubert is equally enthusiastic about a TV documentary he hopes to make about an obscure breed of horse. His own heavy Boulonnais mare is away to be broken in for driving at an equestrian centre at Conty, about two days' ride away, and we decide to head there – a small diversion, and the first of many.

Tonight there are blissful baths, bubbles and white towels, and we take it in turns to soak and drowse in warm water up to the chin. In Bessie it's a case of boiling the kettle for hot water to wash in, brushing teeth and spitting out of the groom's door – life has already become very basic, and lying in bed at Béhen I have to remind myself that when I sit up I won't crack my head on the ceiling.

It's a late breakfast, another leisurely start; first there's a tour of the elegant dimensions of this eighteenth-century château with its wood-panelled reception rooms, and then a walk outside to stroke the flock of pygmy goats before we saddle up Leo and Apollo for a photograph with the family. An elderly Frenchman is persuaded to stamp our pilgrim passports with the Béhen church stamp – and I realise I've left mine in the kitchen at home. God knows how I'm going to get hold of it.

It's midday by the time we leave Béhen for Hornoy where Norbert has booked us into a gîte that caters specifically for riders, and we travel all the way from one side of a Série Bleue map to the other. This is our fourth consecutive day of riding and conversation dwindles and dies as aches set in, and the beautiful ribbon of country road ahead becomes just so many more miles to cover. Leo's still veering to the left and it's hard to steer with one hand – I need to keep the map open because there are cart tracks we can take if I don't miss them, but at least he takes no notice of the ocean of paper rustling on his shoulders. The one cart track I do pinpoint is the wrong one, and we plod wearily back again to ask directions from an academic in pebble glasses standing in his farmyard. He produces cider for all of us, to the horses' pleasure, and points down the road – we're almost in Hornoy, in fact, and Monsieur Academic invites us back tomorrow to look at his museum of local artefacts.

The gîte is wonderful – Susie has a dormitory for eight entirely to herself, and Leo and Apollo have their own walled garden complete with open stable and fruit trees, and enough lush grass to keep them happy for a couple of days. Bessie's parked out of the way on an uphill slope which leaves me in danger of falling out of bed, but I'm too tired to worry.

Rest day is anything but – it means doing all the accumulated washing by hand, as there's no launderette within miles, slinging it over Bessie's ramp gates to dry, and then sorting out the confusion when Susie and I discover that we've bought identical sets of six pairs of knickers from Tesco. In the afternoon we drive to Conty to book in to the equestrian centre for tomorrow night; the owner is Monsieur Macho personified and he whisks us away on a guided tour, stopping to kiss a child here, inject a horse there, and finally to requisition someone's carriage and pair to take us to the paddock where the horses will be turned out. We dread to think how much it will cost us to stay in such a smart place, but to our surprise Monsieur Macho says there'll be no charge for tomorrow's board and lodging.

We roar off to Amiens. We have an illegal emigrant with us: an English spider, fat bodied and patterned, who lives in the overhang above the windscreen. Every night she knits an enormous web right across the glass, and during the day the flies smack into it as Bessie trundles along, leaving the spider with satisfying evenings spent parcelling them up and moving them into her storeroom in the overhang. So far it hasn't rained, and Peter's forbidden to use the windscreen wipers. He thinks Susie and I are mad, but he patiently drives along peering myopically through net curtains.

Susie homes in on the cathedral while Peter and I go on to France Telecom to register our mobile phones with Orange sans Frontières, a lengthy and complicated procedure involving many computers – but we need to phone home, as our children must be wondering if we're still alive. When we collect Susie again she's so happily preoccupied with the discovery of a stone statue of St James that she directs us out of Amiens and back towards

Calais, and by the time we realise this mistake it's the rush hour and Bessie clogs up all the traffic crawling back through Amiens again. And rest day's not finished yet – we still have the visit to the farm near Hornoy to see Monsieur Academic's museum, where he gives us an erudite résumé of its history for the last seven hundred years to a noisy background accompaniment by Madame Academic, who's up a ladder with her hammer and chisel restoring the wattle and daub on one of the barns.

It's late evening by the time we get back to the gîte.

Our map doesn't cover Conty, so I steer there by compass with the result that we stray into the middle of crowded Poix de Picardie. In heavy traffic the horses react differently from each other: Apollo likes to be led, gluing himself to Susie's heels, but Leo shoves me in the back with his nose to hurry me up if I get off, and fidgets at traffic lights. He can't tell red from green. He prefers to be ridden, but because fear certainly runs along the reins I have to steel myself not to be scared witless when a double HGV lorry roars past eighteen inches from my stirrup.

Out in the country again neither horse turns a hair when we're deafeningly buzzed by a military jet, but Apollo has a phobia about cows as well as farriers, snorting loudly until we take to soft tracks and leave them behind, eating up the miles in a fraction of our normal time as the horses canter easily along. At the equestrian centre, Monsieur Macho's nowhere to be seen and instead we're met by his manager, Monsieur Lebègue, a wonderful horsy old boy with a mouth that droops mournfully at each corner. He speaks no English, but when we ask him in our rapidly improving French if he knows of anywhere we can stay tomorrow, he offers to accommodate the horses at his own farm at La Falaise. This isn't on our map either as it's another deviation from our general direction south-east of Paris, but Monsieur Lebègue is shyly insistent. I buy another map in Conty and tell him we'll be there, and he brightens up as he takes Susie off in his car for a dummy run of the route.

By ten o'clock in the morning we're *still* not ready to leave. Susie's walking round adding bounce to her chestnut hair with curlers, ignoring me when I suggest (hopping from one foot to another) that it's about to be squashed flat under her riding hat anyway – but while Leo's breathing fire like me, Apollo's as wonderfully unconcerned as Susie. As for Peter, he simply thinks we make far too much noise in the mornings and farts disapprovingly from his bed in the lorry.

The way's difficult to find; we have to rely on directions from old men in doorways, and now we're slowed by our first day of rain. The horses are huffy at being asked to trot through a downpour, swinging their hindquarters into the road as they try to keep their backs to the wind, until a bombardment of thumping hail sends us scuttling into a barn full of surprised calves. Apollo has to rethink this particular phobia as the alternative is a drenching: this is shivering reality and there's no going home to a warm stable and a centrally heated house now.

Monsieur Lebègue's wife is even more shy than he is, apologising for her gumboots and shaking our hands self-consciously. Monsieur has brought in his Highland ponies and penned them into stalls so that ours may go out to graze, and nothing's too much trouble – he's so intrigued by the story of our pilgrimage that he's tracked down an old man who's followed the Chemin de St Jacques, and we're packed into a battered Citroën to go and visit him. Monsieur Baticle is sprightly, loose limbed and 82 years old, and he's bicycled to Santiago several times on his smart *vélo* (racing bike). He gives us tumblers full of highly alcoholic Poire and, sitting gracefully cross-legged on the floor, he writes down the names and addresses of everyone we must visit on the way. When we leave, Monsieur Lebègue drives down the road like an eel, veering from one verge to the other.

Cacophony reigns in the farmyard – there are legions of chickens, cats, dogs and geese, and a cock pheasant exclaiming loudly from the top of a hay bale. Madame Lebègue was born here and has lived on the farm all her life; she's travelled no further than Boulogne, where her husband takes part in the biennial Route du Poisson race to Paris with heavy horse and cart, commemorating the days when fish were rushed from the coast to the restaurants of Paris. We drink copious amounts of Eau de Vie in their kitchen, fussed over by their elderly collie, and in the shadowy light we examine old maps of the area, and black-and-white photographs of the race. We must be a strange intrusion in their lives.

Tonight we're staying in a gîte that would give our local planners at home apoplexy. It's an old house, a skeleton of wooden struts and beams, preserved because the practical French planning committee has simply decreed that a glasshouse should be erected round it. The effect is startling and it's freezingly cold, but the morning's salvation is a boiling hot power shower that drums on the shoulders and batters the feet. Peter's been complaining that I'm starting to smell of horse all the time, but today at least it's Badedas.

In the neighbouring village of Folleville the church is dedicated to St Jacques, and here is Monsieur Baticle again, bright-eyed with anticipation at showing us round. The fact that the church is locked doesn't deter him – he tracks down the mayor who's already fully occupied getting ready for election day tomorrow, and coerces him into producing the key and another conducted tour to add to our collection. St James is here in triplicate: over the tomb, alongside other saints, and outside perched above the church door with his scallop shell on his hat. One of Monsieur Baticle's maps of the Chemin is pinned to the wall, proudly showing that Folleville is on the pilgrim route. The mayor's now edging out of the door but he's too slow: Susie's captured him, and he's not allowed to escape until he's stamped her pilgrim passport. I'm still trying to think how on earth I'm going to get mine, short of persuading Monsieur Lebègue that a Route du Poisson race in reverse would be fun, with a brief pause while I nip back to England on the ferry.

By the time we get back to the farm once again it's nearly

midday, and the Lebègues are waiting for us. Susie asks Monsieur how much we owe them for the night's lodging for the horses, and he says it is expensive. Very expensive, but he points to his cheek: a kiss will do. He flushes crimson as she obliges and then, as I kiss him too, Peter folds Madame Lebègue in a hug. It seems as though time pauses for an instant before surging on again through air that's shivery with emotion; we've bowled through the even tenor of their lives, and probably we won't meet again. Unexpected tears well up, and when we're far off down the lane they're still standing in the road, watching as we go.

I've decided to dispense with safety and my hard hat. My waxed Drizabone riding coat and Aussie leather hat with a floppy brim were presents from Peter, and the hat's wonderfully comfortable after my jockey's crash helmet. Leo's told to behave himself so I don't risk falling off, but we get on to our first Grande Randonnée route, on the grid of long-distance walking trails in France, and its grassy track has us galloping flat out. It's a brilliant blue sunshiny day of exuberance, of wide open spaces and miles of blinding yellow oilseed rape flowers, but Susie has her first real taste of vertigo when we have to cross over a narrow railway bridge – it's not a big drop to the line below, but she gets off Apollo and walks over by his side. I don't think much about it at the time, leaning back in my saddle to photograph their distinctive bottoms.

The Lebègues have booked the horses in at a farm where the sun-drenched road runs through the middle of the adjacent village, and there's no-one about. I feel like Clint Eastwood clopping through a one-horse town where the inhabitants have taken cover, but the reality is that they're all asleep after lunch. The gîte down the road is owned by a Frenchman who speaks English with an American accent, and he shows me his collection of Western saddles from Texas. His Uncle Gilbert ran the family's famous circus for 25 years and was the last of the great tiger trainers; Monsieur confides that Uncle Gilbert was the first to wear a Tarzan suit after the Second World War, and he produces creased photographs of him in his costume with the tigers. The circus kept going all through the war, he says, but on the day Paris was liberated the Germans killed 67 of the animals out of malice. The only animals owned by this generation of the family are two labradors and an old horse called Rocky, who's prone to bucking people off.

In the evening Peter, Susie and I sit round the table talking and drinking wine bought for one euro and 28 cents from the butcher in the village. We're comfortable so far in our threesome, with enough space and privacy not to step on each other's toes and the odd opportunity, like tonight, for Susie to sleep in a gîte. Peter and I are quite at home in the lorry although there wasn't time to finish everything before we left. The stereo's squashed at the end of our bed because it needs a shelf built next to a jack plug, most of the books are still in boxes and the carpet tacked to the ceiling in the Luton head has fallen off. I tried to help Peter put it back last night by lying on the mattress and holding up the replacement tacks for him to hammer in, but I fell asleep in seconds. When I wake up I dozily notice he has a glint in his eye, but it is no use, I am just too tired – what do you mean, you're bored and you've nothing else to think about? What about all those political biographies you've brought along?

I'm still anxious about our late starts and our flagging timetable, but I have to bear in mind that Leo's a more comfortable ride than Apollo, whose stride is shorter, so I probably ache less than Susie does. After five hours in the saddle she's had enough. Anyway, I think I've worked out that if we ride fifteen miles a day for four days and rest for one, rather than twenty miles for three days and then take a day off, the result will be roughly the same. The intellectual effort required for this probably erroneous calculation is enough to send me straight to sleep again.

Scores of children appear the next morning to drag us to the horse field, where some of them have camped for the night to make sure Leo and Apollo don't escape. The horses have already been tied up and groomed to perfection, and the morning's occupied by riding lessons and much patient trotting to and fro, until the midday sun's so hot we call a halt – this is supposed to be Leo and Apollo's rest day. It's also election day, but nobody in the village seems to be taking much notice. The radio's crackling with the news that Monsieur Le Pen is hot on the heels of Monsieur Chirac, but when we idle down to the hall to see how the voting's getting on the polling booth's deserted.

Our farmer host's father arrives in the morning, an impressive figure who's president of the Syndicat Agricole and who offers us his wrist to shake, saying his hands are dirty from driving his tractor. A billet has been arranged for us tonight with a friend of his at Le Metz, and he says he'll find us somewhere to stay further on in Chantilly, by which time Leo and Apollo will definitely need reshoeing as they've worn down the left side of each shoe to a sliver, thanks to the steep camber of the roads. We're told they've been much admired and every child in the village now wants an Appaloosa. No-one mentions the election, which was won by Monsieur Chirac even though Monsieur Le Pen unexpectedly gave him a fright.

Monsieur Circus hands out mugs of black coffee so strong it makes me grimace, and no doubt I'll be searching for a convenient ditch in half an hour. He's a religious man with earnest brown eyes who believes that God sent us pilgrims to his gîte. Unfortunately, I'm completely distracted from his limpid soliloquy; a terrible torrent of giggles wells up in my chest when I can't help but notice that his two male labradors behind him are practising blow jobs together all over his lawn.

It's time we left.

5. A FRIENDLY LOO FOR TWO

Leo and Apollo are tired after all the exercise on their rest day, and we need to resist imploring small children in future. We've been on the road for two weeks, and by my reckoning we've still got about thirteen hundred and fifty miles to go – a daunting thought, but at least we're getting into a routine. I'd wondered whether I'd be bored with riding every day, but there's no time to think about it – I'm completely preoccupied with finding tracks without getting lost and roads without too many lorries on them, with horse care and cooking and somewhere to stay the next night, and with hoping that Peter's playing enough golf to keep him happy. My supply of books is untouched; all I've had time to read so far are the small ads in an outdated magazine, and as for contemplating my immortal soul, there's no time for that either: I seem to have left it at home with my pilgrim passport.

It's balmy shirtsleeve weather, and Lady Aldington's canvas bucket is tied across the back of my saddle. It's several decades old, but as our search of army surplus stores for a collapsible bucket was completely fruitless, Susie and I are very grateful for the loan of it. As the weather warms up the horses need watering several times a day, and they're learning to suck up puddles and drink brackish water from bogs, both of which they seem to prefer to clean water from a tap. But today there are no puddles or bogs available, so the bucket has to be used for the first time.

The straight Roman road leads to an urban mess of main streets and intersections. Shielding Leo's and Apollo's eyes from the coarse-grained flesh in the horse butchers' windows, we dive up a side street and end up at the train station, where I untie Lady Aldington's bucket and take it into a bar, to a chorus of rude comments from idle old men about the Americans being in town. But I get my revenge: Monsieur behind the Pernod bottles reluctantly fills up the bucket, and as I carry it out again there's a sudden jet stream of water spouting all over the floor from a hole in it we haven't noticed. The horses are thirsty enough to be grateful for the rest.

At Le Metz a topless Peter's roasting with Bessie in a roadside field. Our farmer host isn't here but there's a message to make ourselves at home, and Leo and Apollo plunge rapturously into the long grass and dandelions and wind Peter up by galloping past and brushing against him as he sits in his chair before skidding to a halt, snuffling into his ears and gazing over his shoulder at John Major's autobiography. For a non-horsy man, he's remarkably tolerant. Monsieur Thibault arrives home full of apologies for his lateness, which is due to the sudden and unexpected birth of his daughter; he's tall and deep voiced and utterly accommodating, arranging tomorrow night's farm for us before rushing back to his wife and new baby in the hospital. He too refuses to let us pay for our lodging.

Today is Monday, and on Mondays the whole of France is closed – we still have trouble remembering this fact, and consequently no-one's done any shopping. Supper's an imaginative mixture of lorry rations: fried eggs and baked beans followed by Marmite sandwiches and yogurt, and a whole box of Peter's After Eights from our collection of leftover Easter eggs.

Surprisingly, no-one gets indigestion; in fact, apart from aching joints, we're all feeling very well. And so are the horses. Apollo's still disgracefully fat, supplementing his diet by grabbing grass out of the verges as we ride along and Leo, who's forbidden to follow his example, has become a chocoholic instead and bullies me into giving him his own Mars Bar at lunchtime. Because Apollo's body is completely round his saddle tends to slip and rub his back, and Susie pores anxiously over his coat looking for broken skin every evening. There isn't any, although he does develop lumps by the end of the riding day which are gone by the morning. The area isn't tender but we swap the saddle pads around to alter the pressure points, and hope that once we're in the heart of horse country at Chantilly some classy racehorse owner will produce a healing potion.

I'm up at dawn for an exploratory trip to a disused farm bathroom, richly redolent of decaying walls, but the rusting hip bath's full of empty spray containers and I decide not to try it out. It would be good to get under way early, but this time both horses are on strike – they lay down in unison ten minutes before Susie and I go to catch them and both are fast asleep, Leo stretched out flat with all his teeth showing. It's very hard to put a headcollar on half a ton of inert horse and drag it to its feet, so we're late again and Monsieur Thibault, like a disturbing number of people we meet, wishes us *bon courage* and looks sympathetically at Peter.

Now there's a problem of a different kind, and this time it's not a case of faulty map reading on my part – the track's not there at all, because it's been ploughed up. By the time a passing tractor driver points us in the right direction we've already added a deviation of three miles to our journey today, and three miles is almost an hour at a walk. When was this map published? Oh, great. Hidden in the small print are the figures 1977 – 25 years old, and it's still current. I have a horrible feeling the rest are the same; if so, following tracks is going to be risky, but the unattractive alternative is to stick to the roads. We decide to chance the tracks.

Away to the south the Thérain River flows into the Oise. Now there are long-legged hares and dappled deer lolloping through the young corn beside our path to three farms and a chapel in the middle of the woods. Monsieur seems vaguely surprised to see us and nothing's arranged for the horses, but he invites us to park them in his absent neighbour's half-fenced walnut tree orchard. We block the gaps with electric fencing, lugging the car battery into the field and clipping it to the tape. Leo and Apollo have a deep respect for electric fences and it's hardly worth turning it on, but Monsieur's nosy children have arrived en masse so perhaps it'll keep them out. An odious small boy is leading a depressed little dog in a pink harness. He's full of questions and pokes about in the lorry uninvited, examining all our belongings, until I manage to scare him by threatening to take off my breeches and change into my jeans in front of him if he doesn't clear off. He removes himself to the safety of a nearby wood pile from where he can gawp through Bessie's window instead.

We're shown a shed which contains a plank-covered trench. The plank has two large holes in it, and the black pit underneath doesn't bear description: this is the friendly farm loo for two, a real earth closet, with a bucket of water provided to encourage the soak-away process. The deep woods look preferable, but there are bottom-stinging nettles growing there alongside a wonderful profusion of Solomon's seal with rows of waxy flowers drooping on the underside of the stems, like Edward Lear's botanical illustration of Manypeeplia Upsidedownia from my childhood reading on the stairs. And there's also the problem of the boy, who by now is rampaging through the trees, so perhaps the plank with its likely population of spiders and woodlice is a better idea after all. Preferably in solitude.

It's warm enough for an outdoor supper, and the gas stove bought from Lena's Nautibits comes into its own, hissing delicately as it struggles to reach a heat that will fry the chips. The steak remains very rare as I run out of patience, but it's a romantic dinner by pale moonlight to the accompaniment of red wine and midges, and minus the odious child who's finally gone to bed. Poring over the maps, we plan tomorrow's route. This is becoming more and more difficult now we're so close to Paris – we need to cross the broad River Oise, but there are surprisingly few bridges, and numerous main roads and towns. There's no riding straight from A to B round here; we'll have to go west and cross the river to Outreleau using a bridge that looks small enough, at least on the map, not to be scary with lorries.

Monsieur le President of the Syndicat Agricole has arranged for us to stay close to Chantilly with someone who sounds like a very big noise. When Susie phones him he tells her casually that he may arrange for the press to be there when we arrive, but all I can say is they'll be greeting the great unwashed – we're relying on the cold farm tap here and we can't be bothered to boil a kettle for hot water tonight. It's straight to bed, to the sound of randy owls screeching in the darkness.

When the sun hoovers up the early morning mist, the heat dances on the road and bakes the track running between the Oise and the railway line. We stop and wave to the bargemen piloting their vast craft upstream, with their cars on deck and their satellite dishes screwed to the wheelhouses; Leo and Apollo don't mind the barges passing right beside them but when the wake follows on behind, fanning out in swishing ripples to the water's edge, they flash the whites of their eyes with the astonished expression peculiar to Appaloosas. The bargemen look equally staggered to see us, laughing and pointing as they chug by.

The bridge at Outreleau is certainly narrow, but what the map doesn't show is that it's made of metal, and so long that it has traffic lights. We cause havoc by clanking along at a walk and confusing the lights' sequence, with the result that scores of cars have to reverse to let us over, giving the horses the chance to breathe in a friendly way through their open windows and ask for peppermints. In the boiling afternoon we reach Chantilly's rich suburbia and ride along mown verges bordered by railings, where deadly Dobermanns froth safely in their gardens on the other side. Suddenly, this is the land of racehorses: it's tempting to divert for a quickie round the sand gallops, but Leo and Apollo don't really look as though they're in training for the French Derby and Susie and I, creaking along at a trot, doubt if we'd be mistaken for lithe young jockeys. We plod decorously round the public path until we reach the stud where we're staying and find Peter talking to Monsieur Babin in the sun-drenched yard.

Monsieur Babin breeds Barb Arabs, an ancient breed with distinctive Roman noses, and he owns dozens of mares and several stallions. He notes Leo's immediate interest in the ladies with a practised eye, and he and Apollo are relegated to a small paddock next to the foals. Monsieur Babin uses his stallions sometimes for endurance riding, and he comments disparagingly on the size of Apollo's stomach, telling us too much grass is *pas bon* for our horses. He's very down to earth and catches Susie's gloomy expression at the sight of the stableyard loo – a hole in the ground with a footprint in porcelain each side that is only a minor improvement on last night's loo for two, and sternly reminds her she's a pilgrim: what did she expect?

Luckily there's no sign of the press.

Rest day brings an essential visit from the farrier. Apollo's sedated in the special shoeing stall while Leo whirls in circles in a stable, outraged at being shut in, but he switches off the nonsense when it's his turn to be shod and offers each hoof in turn for a new shoe. Apollo looks as though he's had a beer too many as he sways off to the paddock to recover, but within half an hour the two are racing the foals up and down the fence and Leo's flirting with a little filly. I think Monsieur Babin's about to say something uncomplimentary about the capabilities of the English vet who gelded him, so I try to explain the story of Leo's unfortunate seduction by a nymphomaniac mare. Monsieur Babin looks sceptical, shaking his head at Susie's and my clear lack of expertise in equine matters; it's obvious we need all the help we can get, and after gently probing Apollo's back he gives Susie a tube of expensive cortisone cream and advises her to rub Vaseline into the lumps every night. The problem's under control.

Peter and Bessie depart to a golf course, thankfully discarding Susie and me in Chantilly on the way; calligrapher Susie's been looking forward to a trip to the Musée Condé all week as it's the home of *Les Très Riches Heures du Duc de Berry*, a very famous mediaeval illuminated book of hours (so she informs me), but the original's locked away and only a facsimile is on display. We console ourselves with ice creams and a visit to the dressage exhibition at the Grandes Écuries, and wait for Peter with our cafes au lait on the pavement as the sunshine fades and rain threatens.

A steady downpour drums on my Drizabone mac in the morning, but it has leg straps to anchor it in place and a wide pleat at the back that covers the saddle – it's completely waterproof, and Susie has a tartan-lined British equivalent. Peter, snug in Bessie, demolishes the spider's web with the windscreen wipers, but the spider's tucked up in the overhang and by now is used to occasional reconstruction work at the end of the day. Apollo and Leo are both in a temper about the comparative lack of grass for two days, and I can't say Apollo's noticeably thinner. They dance sideways for the first two miles, and when we canter my arms are pulled out of their sockets as I struggle to keep a close eye on our direction. We're riding through the Forêt de Chantilly and the map delineates 558 numbered parcels of land bordered by tracks. But for the rain it would be a beautiful ride, as we skirt a series of lakes past the Château de la Reine Blanche where the wraith of the white lady can be seen walking on the water. But not today. It's far too drizzly, far too cold, and even the tourists have legged it.

Madame Babin has arranged for us to stay at a farm, but Peter phones to say there are only stables there and no pasture. The horses need to be turned out because Leo's digestive problem means that he can develop cramp if he's been standing in a stable overnight, without his usual diet of grass, and taken out on exercise the next day his hindquarters can seize up within minutes; it's appropriately called tie-up, and when it's acute it can be dangerous. Leo's only had it mildly, and very occasionally, but it would mean resting him for several days, and I'm as paranoid about it as Susie is about Apollo's back. But as we skirt Parc Asterix, Peter phones again to say he's found an equestrian centre where the horses can roam loose in the manège. He's also tried to book a round of golf at the local course, but Madame at the snooty golf club took one look at seven-and-a-half grubby tons of Bessie and wouldn't even let them through the electric gates.

We divert south to the equestrian centre. Susie dismounts to lead Apollo over the motorway bridge and finds she's frozen so solid that she's walking bandy-legged in exactly the same position as if she was riding. We pass another fairy-tale château, the first of many I think I'd like to buy when I'm rich (whenever that may be) – at least the thought diverts me from my sodden feet and the petrified claws my fingers have become.

At the manège Leo's so wound up at the presence of all the other horses that he paces up and down in the sand, refusing to eat at all, and Apollo troughs his way through both their dinners and most of the hay. As for us, we feel we deserve a two-star hotel and, warming up at last under the shower, I try to banish thoughts of Leo with tie-up in the morning. It's Peter's and my turn for civilisation, but ironically Susie has a more comfortable night on Clara's mattress in Bessie than we do in a hard hotel bed.

We must be getting used to this gypsy life.

6. LEO GOES ON HONEYMOON

Male horses have a habit of letting it all hang out when they're resting, and Leo and Apollo are no exception, relaxing rudely every time we stop. The fastidious Susie offers to cook the dinners for a week if I'll wash Apollo's willy, but no thanks – it's bad enough having to deal with Leo. It's an unglamorous but necessary aspect of horse-keeping: passers-by who stop us are distracted at being waved at so obviously, just when Susie's trying to explain the religious significance of the pilgrimage and I'm trying to look holy and keep my mouth shut. Most people this far north have never heard of the Chemin de St Jacques, but they're extraordinarily generous when we tell them we're riding for charity, and already there's an envelope in Bessie bulging with euros for the hospices.

We need to travel east for a while to keep clear of Paris and Meaux. We're already too close to Charles de Gaulle Airport and avoiding the main roads is becoming so tricky that a recce in Bessie is necessary to see if we can find somewhere to stay tonight. I'm studying a map in the middle of the road at Oissery, eighteen miles away, when a man leans out of his window and asks if he can assist, so I'm deputed to drive off with this stranger in his car wearing my best smile. Luckily he heads straight to the town hall where he greets Olivier, who calls up Patrick, and Patrick has a farm right here with a *petit pâture* for the horses and a yard for Bessie and the rest of us.

First we have to negotiate several more miles of forest on two supercharged horses in the rain, and Leo shows no signs of tie-up, dancing athletically every time I stop to check the soggy map. Taking no chances with the weather today, Susie and I are swaddled in jumpers and ski socks under our macs, which metamorphose into tandoori ovens when the sun comes out in the afternoon and the temperature soars. The forest is a maze of tracks and Grandes Randonnées, or GRs, and we try to decipher the faded white cards that mark the land parcel numbers, the horses fizzing as we fly down first one wrong trail and then another. Emerging abruptly from the forest by compass direction and luck, we arrive in Oissery to hear Peter administering a loud dose of Anglo-Saxon to an oik he's caught letting Bessie's tyres down while he was putting up the electric fence – not that the horses need it; after two nights in manèges they're so desperate for grass they barely stir out of the first emerald patch they reach.

The genial Patrick directs us to put Bessie under cover in his barn, and we daren't abuse his hospitality by taking her out again when we discover that he farms onions, and they're all in there as well. When their cold-store refrigeration unit is humming away there's no problem, but it's thermostatically controlled, cutting out when the temperature drops, and as the temperature rises again we're overpowered by the stench of thousands of last year's onions. We spend the evening trying not to breathe.

Patrick invites us to make use of the bathroom in the rambling old farmhouse across the yard, and promptly retires to bed and locks the front door. No problem in theory: when planning the practicalities of the pilgrimage I went to the local garden centre and bought three trowels from the mystified manager, but this farm is in the middle of the village and it's all a bit public. Even extracting water from the tap in the chicken abattoir next to the house is hazardous – it's worked by a system of pumps and stopcocks, and I manage to drench Susie while washing my face. There's no spitting out of Bessie's door tonight, in case we pollute the stray onions on the floor with toothpaste, and as Peter and I stand out in the blackness of the midnight yard aiming simultaneously into the same puddle and hoping the scummy evidence has gone by the morning, he asks himself what on earth he's doing here.

After a night of snoring my way through thick layers of onion-flavoured air, I wake up to find the farm door's still locked and no-one's up. This seems surprising for a farming family, but today's Sunday and I have a feeling they're all having a lie-in. Finding somewhere with my trowel that isn't overlooked by the whole village isn't easy, and I meet Susie looking equally desperate, so we have to avoid each other as well. On my way back to the barn it's necessary to adopt an expression of nonchalance when I see Patrick approaching, and I edge him back towards the farmhouse so we don't risk tripping over Susie in the weeds. He's coming to tell me he's arranged for us to stay with a widow friend tomorrow night. He is *désolé* that he can find us nowhere closer for tonight, but I assure him that it's *pas de problème*: Peter will drive ahead in Bessie and arrange it all. Patrick refuses any payment for our lodging, so we sneak a bottle from our wine rations on to his kitchen table when he's not looking.

Peter's unimpressed when told he's going to be arranging it all for tonight – his French is still at the rudimentary grunting stage and he'd rather play golf. There's a nice little course just the other side of the Marne, and his pilgrimage terms were that he would drive the lorry in return for the opportunity to play as much as possible and for hot dinners every night, not cooked by him. I think of reminding him that those were unilateral terms and I hadn't agreed to them, but decide it would be wiser to try persuasion: as it's Sunday, I'm sure he'll find a crowded course, difficulty with a tee-off time, and anyway it's too risky in this relatively farmless area for us to turn up somewhere unannounced with the horses. If we do a dummy run with Bessie again, it's twice the diesel and half the day gone before we're even in the saddle. Eventually Peter agrees to try the only farm I can see to the south-east of us on the map, sandwiched between the main N3 and the autoroute into Paris.

Susie and I set off in a steady drizzle and such a biting wind that I decide on Drizabone and the ski socks again. Both horses are in dead-donkey mode after making up for lost time on last night's grass and leave a trail of crots for miles, but we push them on unsympathetically as they try to crab sideways to the wind, and whistle down to the town of Varreddes, caught between loops of the rivers Ourcq to the north and Marne to the south. The Marne is wide, sleepy and slow beneath the bridge, and on the other side lie the pretty town of Germigny-l'Évêque and the sprawling Forêt Domaniale de Montceaux.

Peter phones. He's drawn a blank. I manage to pinpoint one more farm below Montceaux on the map and plead with him to keep trying, and twenty minutes later my mobile rings again just when I've got off Leo to find a convenient tree, and have discovered (at a crucial moment) that the legstraps on Drizabone are still done up. It's a struggle to find the phone, and this time there's an extremely irate farmer on the line as well as Peter, and he tells me we can't stay with him because he's not going to mix our horses with his cows, it's Sunday and he was in the middle of his *déjeuner* when this stranger turned up, and he is *absolument* unable to help.

Well, I get the message, but in that case I can't understand why he's insisting on putting Peter in his car and driving him to the edge of the forest to meet us on the other side. He wants to know how long we'll be. I start to explain that we're two sisters on two horses, but he cuts me short. We can't be, he says. It's *pas possible*. This is perplexing but I try again, glossing over the fact that at the moment I don't have a clue where we are, and hazard we'll be about forty minutes. Monsieur le Farmer shouts at me that's a very long time. In the background I can hear Peter imploring me to hurry up. I haven't the heart to tell him we're lost and we set off, trying to ride by compass direction and with Peter phoning every five minutes sounding increasingly desperate. Susie asks some walkers in the forest how we get out of it again but they don't seem to know, so God knows how long *they've* been in here, and anyway they're far more interested in asking us for minute details of the Appaloosa breed and our exact route for the last two hundred miles.

And then the sun appears, and with it comes Dominic jogging through the forest on his old mare Honeymoon, his dressage whip poked casually down his riding boot. Susie would like to think he's really an elf come to our rescue, but in fact he's a driving instructor from Germigny-l'Évêque. Honeymoon is Swiss and in her younger days they used to ride long mountain trails together, but now they just amble round the forest, all of which he knows very well. He will show us the way.

The main track through the forest is perfectly straightforward. I can't imagine how we got lost. Dominic trots in front over two railway bridges at such a speed that Susie has no opportunity to think about vertigo and dismount, and within minutes we can see our rendezvous spot where the farmer and Peter are standing stiffly, as far away from each other as possible. Monsieur le Farmer has a flat cap and a rat-trap mouth, out of which columns of angry words are quick-marching, and Peter's ears have been battered by the word *merde* so often that he's switched off. Both look amazed to see us: Peter because we've suddenly sprouted another horse and rider, and Monsieur le Farmer because he wasn't expecting to see horses at all – he was expecting to see a car. When we told him we were on *deux chevaux*, he thought we meant a Citroën.

Dominic is peremptorily asked if he speaks French, and when he agrees rather faintly that he does, he gets an earful. The farmer has tried everywhere, everywhere (arms spread wide at the hopelessness of such a quest); he's abandoned his lunch, given up his Sunday afternoon to drive this Englishman to every farm he knows, but no-one can help and all their siestas have been interrupted. When he pauses for breath, Leo fills the silence by snickering into Honeymoon's ears and she instantly comes into season, spattering the path noisily with urine. Dominic observes that she loves anything with a bottom. Monsieur le Farmer is looking appalled, and my diversionary tactic of suggesting we might camp in the forest tonight brings another staccato torrent of exclamations: it is *absolument interdit*, no cars are allowed in the forest let alone lorries, and we shall undoubtedly be arrested by the police.

Dominic has an idea. We can return to Germigny-l'Évêque with him, and he'll find us somewhere to stay with a friend. It's a pity we have to retrace our steps, but it's a kind offer and there seems to be no other option. The farmer sets off with Peter to reunite him with Bessie, and we turn back into the forest with Leo nipping Honeymoon daintily on her neck whenever he can manoeuvre himself alongside. He is a very smooth operator.

As we're cantering down the track to keep up with Dominic, along comes a forest ranger in a van. He's huge, bearded, and grins broadly at us with teeth the size of piano keys. This time Susie thinks it's Hagrid from *Harry Potter*. What is our problem and can he help? *Mais oui*, he has the answer! His house is just down this track in the middle of the forest, and he has a *petit pâture* for the horses, a yard where we can park Bessie, an outside water tap and electricity if we want it. It's the perfect solution.

The only problem is that I have to contact Peter to tell him about this change of plan, and by now Monsieur le Farmer is in his car grimly escorting him in Bessie back to Germigny-l'Évêque. Peter's tried to explain that he knows the way as he's already been through the town at least twice, but it's no use: he's being furiously mollycoddled the whole way to the doorstep of Dominic's friend. Dominic stays with us, looping his rein through his stirrup and leaving Honeymoon to graze unattended, and Peter reappears having had to wait at least fifteen minutes in the town before he dared turn Bessie round and drive back the way he came. Then suddenly Dominic and Honeymoon are gone, an elf and his horse melting into the forest before we've thought to write down his full name and address.

The ranger's name has a poetic cadence: it's Hervé Le Droit. Like almost everyone else we've met he speaks no English, which seems surprising in northern France and so close to Paris, but perhaps it's just a conceit of the English that we think everyone else should speak our language. Susie's and my French is improving fast, and Peter's added several words to his vocabulary today, but although I'm now even dreaming in French I can still get tangled up. Fortunately Hervé is quite understanding when in my effort to reassure him that we don't want to inconvenience him in any way, I tell him that I hope he's not decomposed. The correct word, *dérangé*, doesn't sound much better.

Thoroughly unnerved by his day, Peter raids one of the whisky bottles wedged at the end of our mattress, and Susie and I decide we'd better try some forward planning. We consult our gîte directory and try to aim our route past gîtes that don't object to horses where we can book Susie in for a night, but several phone calls later we've drawn a blank – the horsy gîtes are linked to equestrian centres that are full and would need at least a month's notice. We take to the whisky as well. It won't be long before we have to implement Reserve Plan Two which is simply to turn up on doorsteps looking old and pathetic.

Thunderous rain during the night changes to gales and sparky sunshine by daybreak, the forest glittering with wet leaves and heavy with the scent of wild garlic. Hervé refuses to let us dispose of the horse crots in his field as he's glad of the manure for his garden, and he won't accept any payment for saving our skins. He wishes us *bon courage* and returns to ranger duties in his van as we cross the road that bisects the forest, and work our way down the track to Montceaux. The temperature drops as the road leaves the town and crosses empty unsheltered tracts of farmland, and all day we bowl along awkwardly cambered lanes, the telephone lines overhead clacking together in the wind as they loop between poles.

Patrick's widowed friend is shyly polite and hospitable. Her beautiful old farmhouse at La Grange Justin faces on to a courtyard where Bessie lumbers loudly through the electronic gates and shudders to a halt, shaking oil spots on to the cobblestones. We have the use of a mansion-sized converted barn, its hall dominated by an open stone fireplace, and the echoing kitchen has three cookers, two microwaves, and kilo pots of farm-produced honey stacked down all thirty feet of counter. Susie's in a big spooky room upstairs where the casual farmhands sleep during the harvest and where, next door, the distinctive pong of French drains rolls up through the basin plughole. Leo and Apollo have thick grass in a proper horse field, and Madame's offered us the use of her washing machine. Tomorrow will definitely be a rest day.

I've decided it's time I walked round a golf course with Peter, so we drop Susie in Meaux to find a cyber café, and drive to a course recommended by Madame which has an impossibly immaculate clubhouse. Hiding mud-splattered Bessie in the car park is a bit of a problem, and we attract some odd looks when we lower the ramp and wheel down a set of golf clubs on a trolley instead of a horse. Peter's invited to join Jerome the futures trader, a lanky man who works from home when he feels like it, but mostly plays golf. He lopes along like the Pink Panther, and I find myself puffing round the hilly course wondering whether this was such a good idea, but Peter wins their needle match and over a convivial drink in the clubhouse afterwards, where I'm trying to conceal my feet in dirty jodphur boots under a chair, I can see that some of his rapidly waning joie de vivre has been restored.

In Meaux, Susie's finally tracked down an internet café, which surprisingly is the first one we've found. We've promised to send regular despatches to the Pilgrims' Hospices' website, but after a silence of nearly four weeks they must be wondering if we've all fallen in the Marne. Susie and I are both computer illiterate, but as I can type reasonably fast I'm delegated to send the message, although she points out the first few sentences are gobbledegook owing to my failure to notice that the French keyboard has a completely alien layout. She's spent the day composing a handwritten draft the length of *Gone With the Wind*, and the effort of typing it plunges me into a lengthy menopausal hot flush at the end of which I miss the send key and press delete. The amended version is all of two lines long, and Susie takes some convincing that it says just as much as the original.

In the barn kitchen we pig out on steak and garlic mushrooms again, and attack the first of the wedges of local Brie bulging ripely in their waxed paper. The honk in our Frigo box knocks us backwards when we lift the lid and I'm not sure it's all due to cheese. Frigo drains Bessie's domestic battery at an alarming rate if the engine's not running, so Peter says we must economise and switch off the refrigeration when we're stationary. This may or may not result in unscheduled days off due to food poisoning but at the moment I haven't the energy to investigate some of the slimy-looking packages in the box.

Madame returns our washing beautifully dried and folded, and she's phoned her friends further south and has our next four nights' accommodation lined up. She says we're in hunting country now, and it should all be easier. She smiles deprecatingly when we thank her; she wants no payment, even in wine, and gives us each a kilo of the farm honey. Her teenage daughter Claire is looking forward to riding with us tomorrow on Bolero, her father's old racing trotter.

Meanwhile, the barometer in Bessie is dropping like a stone.

7. FLYING OVER THE TGV

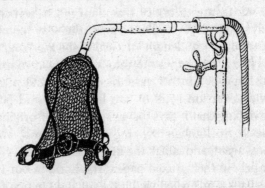

Heavy rain crashes down on Bessie in the night. The only way to sleep through the din is to pile pillows on my head, but the new fibreglass lorry roof is doing its job and there are no leaks. By morning the deluge has whirled off to the east leaving a blustery day in its wake, and I find Claire in the house telling her mother that of course she doesn't need a waterproof jacket. I catch a glimpse of the maid laying the long dining-room table for Madame's lunch, a solitary place setting with a crystal glass and a half-bottle of red wine, small beacons on an ocean of tablecloth.

Bolero wears a bitless bridle at a rakish angle and is mindful of his racing days, but Claire is completely relaxed on him, turning continually to chat to us with the result that we're lost within a mile – so she calls up her friend Gérard, who arrives on a three-year-old trotter filly who's never been out on the road in her life. At the main road junction the filly freaks out at the traffic and ties all her long legs in a knot, but Gérard is unflappable, soothing her across and leading us down grass tracks towards Mauperthuis where he and Claire will point us in the right direction and then return home.

But we can't ride through the village – there's a car boot fair going on, a *brocante*, and the street's full of old Peugeots and Citroëns disgorging ageing china and candlesticks on to the verge, their owners undeterred by the furious squalls now howling across the sky. Gérard and Claire are repeatedly soaked, which fact Claire doesn't mention to her anxious mother who by now is phoning her on her mobile to find out where she is, while Susie and I try not to look too snug and smug in our Drizabones. Bypassing the village centre, we reassure our escorts that we'll be able to find our own way from here to our next stop.

Le Plessis Farm consists of one wonderful shop by the road in the middle of nowhere that sells partridges, Brie and home-made ginger cake. Usually the owners lock up and go home at half-past six, but today they have to close late – the sight of two tired horses curled up in the grass with their noses in their dinner bowls attracts a convoy of passing cars, and there's an unexpected acceleration in business. Later we dine in style in the lorry on guinea fowl casseroled in local beer and crème fraîche, but for the first time I jam the groom's door shut from the inside when we go to bed. This is a very isolated place with no houses nearby, and only one starved tree whose exposed roots are now protected by a mound of potato peelings that Peter's thoughtfully dumped there, rather than stumble round in the darkness looking for the dustbins.

The night brings drizzle but no intruders, and the morning is the most unattractive so far: grey and flat, the countryside featureless. We've had instant success with accommodation, though – one telephone call to shy Madame's farming friends near Nangy has resulted in an invitation for several nights while Susie returns to England for the wedding party.

I have time this morning to highlight our intended route on the map in Day-Glo pink, but of course it isn't that simple – the town of Rozay-en-Brie is bypassed by a track that's marked straight across the N4, but when we get there the main road's a dual carriageway with double crash barriers on the central reservation. Even Harvey Smith would have to acknowledge it would be a difficult in-and-out combination to jump, enlivened by articulated lorries thundering past in both directions, and we have to divert to a giant roundabout, trot the whole way round it and then ride along a flyover spanning the motorway. At any rate, I ride over it before remembering that Susie's probably dismounted because of the height. When I look back, she's twinkling along at top speed towed by Apollo, and luckily I'm too far ahead to hear what she's saying.

Our day's further complicated by the need to circumnavigate an oil refinery. We have to get across the main railway line and long tentacles of its sidings first, and there's no obvious way to do it. The enormous Elf complex is right beside us, and we end up threading our way over the lines beside the rows of waiting tankers, and hoping no-one's looking. As the track disappears into half a mile of very rough ground and tall weeds, Susie decides this is the moment to take a photo of Leo and me, with the ugly refinery in the background. I manage to arrange us photogenically on the exact spot where a deer's trying to make itself invisibly flat in the undergrowth, and I don't know which of us gets the biggest fright: the deer bounding off to Fontainebleau or Leo and me, hurtling back to Calais. By the time Susie's camera has focused we're just a dot in the distance.

Monsieur and Madame Michel produce cups of Russian tea and sweet choux pastries while we're waiting for Peter to arrive from golf, and show us a little field with exactly enough grass to keep the horses occupied during their four days' rest. Susie books herself into the village hotel for the night, but it's surprising the owner doesn't ask her to leave again: she decides to use the shower to wash Apollo's saddle pad and the nose net he wears to keep the flies off his face, resulting in short black hairs stuck to the tiles from ceiling to floor, and something that looks suspiciously like a bondage accoutrement hanging from the shower head.

The train from Nangis to Paris runs only every three hours, and by the time Bessie's worked up enough energy to get to the station we've just missed one. We drop Susie at Melun instead, and Peter and I carry on to Fontainebleau to see the château, where Peter nudges Bessie conspicuously between the German tourist coaches outside, and we saunter off as two lady gendarmes come striding up the street. The château's a rich soup of impressions, from its intricate ceilings to the Long Gallery where François I had his crest engraved on every wooden panel, but it seems strange not to be under any constraints of time and we meander aimlessly through the tourist shop, feeling stodgy from a surfeit of ornate furniture and decorations.

But a visit to the château of Vaux-le-Vicomte on our way back to the hotel is a different story. This wonderful miniature Versailles was built between 1658 and 1661 by Nicholas Fouquet, the finance minister of Louis XIV, and unfortunately for Monsieur Fouquet (so the story goes) he made the mistake of finishing his château before the king had completed Versailles, and then rubbed it in by throwing a grandiose party there in Louis' honour. Three weeks later the king had his minister arrested on dubious charges of embezzlement, sequestered the estate and the château, and employed the designers of Vaux-le-Vicomte to finish off the palace at Versailles. As for poor old Fouquet, he was still in prison when he died twenty years later.

This château is much more intimate than Fontainebleau and it's imaginatively laid out, from the display of carriages in the stables, where I find a set of old English prints depicting grisly horse accidents entitled *Fores's Coaching Incidents*, to the little suites, the morning room with its perfect mediaeval backgammon set, and the grand library shrouded by elaborately painted window shutters. The formal gardens were restored to their original layout when the château was bought by a rich businessman in 1875 whose grandson is now the owner, and below stairs, life is portrayed just as it was centuries ago, with the kitchen table laid for a meal for the staff, perfect down to the last utensil.

Arriving back at our hotel, Bessie gets jammed under the arch over the entrance to the car park as we're driving in. My efforts to shin invisibly up the gatepost with an adjustable spanner in each hand to unbolt the arch before she drags the whole lot down don't go unnoticed. Monsieur and most of the staff arrive within seconds, but fortunately the arch is made of chipboard, and Monsieur assures us that the sizeable chunk missing from it by the time we've extricated the lorry is *pas grave*.

Peter and I have two cosy nights in the hotel. Well, the first night's cosy although we manage to home in on the television's soft-porn channel while flicking through the programmes, and the acting's so appalling that we're rolling about with laughter rather than lust. Various clips from various countries seem to be on offer, but there's only one soundtrack for all of them which consists of two words: 'ooh' and 'aah'. Ooh and aah are very soothing after a while and, thirteen hours later, I wake up from the longest and soundest sleep I've had for years.

On the second night, due to a misunderstanding with the hotel barman which results in my drinking an enormous amount of Campari, I have my first conversation with God. Unhappily it's on the great white telephone. Peter sleeps smoothly through the monkey howls issuing through the gap under the bathroom door, and I'm still feeling so hungover in the morning that Sunday lunch with the Michels is restricted to two small squares of bread. Peter politely eats my share of the feast as well as his own, and I'm still left looking like a greyhound.

Susie's back from England, disorientated by her return to civilisation, and she's collected my pilgrim passport as well as the post that's been piling up at home for the last month. It all seems to be junk mail, utterly irrelevant: I've stepped off the world here, and if my bank bothered to take a good look at the state of my account they certainly wouldn't be inviting me to apply for a platinum credit card. Real life for us now is saddling up the horses and travelling further and further into France.

On our map Monsieur Michel's marked out an incredibly convoluted route on tracks to another friend's farm. It's a beautiful way through the Forêt de Villefermoy, but disheartening to find at the end of it that it's taken us eighteen miles to travel the ten the crow flapping down the straight minor road would have flown. Leo's in super-march mode after his rest, which is just as well for me as I'm still feeling steamrollered by the Campari episode, but no fun for Susie as Apollo has to keep on jogging to keep up. If I slow Leo down he gets wound up and finds dangerous rocks to shy at, but both he and Apollo show considerable sangfroid when we pass a livery yard where the first two stables are occupied by horses, but the second two have hairy camels leaning out to say hello.

Monsieur Michel has warned us that his friend can be brusque, but we've no idea whether he is or not: we never meet him. We have nothing fixed up for tomorrow and both Peter's and my phone cards have run out, so it's another dummy run in Bessie to find somewhere to stay and to replenish the *mobicartes* at the same time. We trundle down the main road through Montereau-Fault-Yonne across a double bridge where the Seine's a forked serpent's tongue with the River Yonne, but there's absolutely no way we're going to ride over this bridge tomorrow – it's a constant stream of HGVs and nose-to-tail impatiently hooting cars all through the town. This is going to take some planning, and we drive south, still stuck on a major road. I'll be glad to leave Ile de France behind with its spider's web of motorways, as this is an equine navigational nightmare. Veering south-east for countless miles, we arrive in the tiny hamlet of Blennes which looks promising, except that the only gîte is full. We bounce off down a very rough lane.

There's a farmer stacking logs on the hillside, and when I smile warmly at him, to my relief he smiles back, revealing top teeth worn right down to the gum. When I ask diffidently whether he would be *dérangé* if we stayed with him tomorrow night (at least I've got that word right) he gestures expansively to show that all the land around here belongs to him, and we're welcome to put up our electric fence wherever we like. He will show us the *potable eau* tomorrow, by which he means the cold-water tap for the flower vases in the cemetery. He's pleased to hear we're pilgrims, and we get into a deep discussion about St James, but I've spotted a shrine in the hollow of a weeping willow tree in his garden with a little stone statue of the Virgin Mary in it, and I leave Susie to do the talking.

Over supper that night the debate rages between the three of us: what God? Isn't it just a case of humans needing a pack leader like wolves or indeed horses, so they've invented one with various different names depending on their religion? Susie's belief is very strong and Peter, a determined agnostic, is becoming adept at winding her up. As for me, sometimes I feel as though something's looking after me, and I could be fanciful and say that for all I know it's St James, but the more pressing problem is to work out how to get across both the Seine and the Yonne tomorrow. Peter and Susie are still arguing during the washing-up while I try to make sense of the map.

It looks simple as far as the Seine – there's a bridge across it to the south-east of us, the direction we want – but after that we'll have to travel west again to cross the second prong of the serpent's tongue, the Yonne, where there's only one suitable bridge and it's practically back in Montereau.

Arriving at the top of the escarpment above the Seine next morning, we can see a glittering plain of rivers and lakes spread out below us in the sunshine. The shiny snake of the TGV line is running right across the middle, but that's not all – the A5 motorway, which is vaguely recorded on the map as '*en construction*', is rubbing shoulders with it and solid with high-speed traffic. We have no choice but to follow a busy major road that rears up into an impossibly high flyover to clear both the A5 and the TGV. It dawns on us that the river bridges are the least of our problems.

The escarpment's bad enough. The drop from more than four hundred feet to sea level is achieved by one hairpin bend, and Susie looks very thoughtful as she walks down leading Apollo with her eyes fixed on the tarmac. Crossing the Seine is a doddle, but the flyover's another matter. Leo's completely calm as I begin riding him up the slope, but I daren't look behind to see how Susie's doing – she's totally silent and walking at Leo's heels with Apollo beside her. There's no comforting pavement to buffer us now: just a span of railings that I would sail over if Leo decided to shy.

But he doesn't. He flicks an ear back at me and plods solidly onwards. I can hear a lorry behind us but I'm not going to look round, and it passes so close that the side draught vacuums us towards it. My Aussie hat blows over my ear, and Leo shakes his head in annoyance at the sudden gale, but he keeps going, his steady footfalls echoing on the bridge. By now I'm singing 'It's a Long Way to Tipperary' in a banal sort of way – anything to keep myself defused and stop Leo realising that I'm absolutely shit scared. There are HGVs coming the other way whose drivers kindly slow down when they see us, but this is even worse: the whoosh of air brakes is deafeningly added to the roar of the traffic on the motorway below and the gusting of the wind as we reach the apex of the flyover.

But then we're over, down on the plain again, and both Susie and I are wringing with sweat. It's the most terrifying piece of riding I've ever done, but the horses don't know what all the fuss is about. Leo casually rests one hind leg while we're waiting for Susie to climb on a milestone so she can get on Apollo again and he, ever the opportunist, has buried his nose in the grass. We cross the quiet little bridge over the Yonne.

Further south the countryside is friendlier, the traffic far less, and there's an opportunity for a burst of canter on a track – but both horses brake violently at the end of it. Huge lorries are one thing, but a flock of loony ostriches flapping round a field is quite another, and Leo and Apollo prance past in a slow Spanish trot, picking their feet up very high and snorting with amazement.

The hot afternoon is wearing on. It's one of those rides that's just too long: more than twenty miles this time. As the horses tire, so Susie and I have to exert more effort to keep them going, and we're already feeling completely drained after this morning's adventure. At Blennes we flop on the farmer's grass with our shirts sticking to our backs while Leo and Apollo roll and roll the sweatiness off theirs.

Tomorrow is VE Day, 8 May, and Monsieur invites us to attend the village ceremony at 11 a.m. when he will read out the names of the dead in the two world wars. Tonight his eyes are sparkling with mischief: Bessie's parked next to our improvised horse field and one side of it consists of the cemetery wall – Monsieur tells us to sleep well, and hopes that our neighbours don't keep us awake.

8. COLD DUCK AND HOLY WATER

Blennes has only three hundred inhabitants, and it's mostly the oldies who are assembled outside the tiny town hall in the morning. The eight members of the fire brigade are in marching order in their uniforms; four are carrying elderly trumpets so highly polished that the sun reflects at odd angles in their dents and scratches, and one is cuddling a drum. They manage the 'Last Post' but the 'Marseillaise' is beyond them, and someone pushes the button of the stereo strategically perched on the windowsill. We proceed to the cemetery to pay our respects to the soldiers who gave their lives in the two world wars, passing sad little headstones for dead children. Leo and Apollo are peering over the wall, pop-eyed at the trumpets.

Back at the town hall again our farmer friend reads out the name of every man who died, and a dignitary follows him with: '*Mort pour la France.*' The words sigh away into solemnity, and in the minute's silence afterwards the only sound is the soft stirring of the four national flags on their tall poles.

We're invited for a drink – or five, in Peter's case; Ricard is heady stuff at eleven in the morning, and I'm not sure he's taken in our host's directions to a farm some miles away. Susie and I set off, slavishly following the map, but Apollo's dawdling so much that at lunch-time alarm bells start ringing: he isn't interested in the grass, or even a piece of Susie's apple. He just stands there, motionless, and we can't begin to guess what the problem might be. The most usual sudden horsy complaint is colic, yet he's showing none of the signs: no kicking at his belly, looking round at his sides or trying to roll. But the fact that he doesn't want to eat is for him the clearest distress signal possible, and Susie immediately feels guilty for calling him an arsehole when he stumbled over a pebble for the umpteenth time this morning.

We're about nine miles short of where we want to be, but there's no question of going further, and we're still debating what to do when three passing riders stop to help. They're from a nearby equestrian centre, and there the staff are all worried commiseration, lending us two loose-boxes where Leo stews and sweats in his, and Apollo lies down in the straw with a sigh of relief. Dr Bompy the vet is telephoned but it's 9 p.m. by the time he arrives, still in his jodhpurs, straight from an afternoon's showjumping. Apollo puts up with enough undignified examinations to make his eyes water, his lower lip drooping mournfully, and Dr Bompy tells us he has a very high temperature and a headache, and the problem is probably tick fever. He pumps him full of antibiotics and vitamin B, and we're told he'll need to be rested for several days.

This is a real setback. We'd thought the horses might be troubled by lameness, or Leo by tie-up, but tick fever had never occurred to us – there are no malignant ticks in England. But apparently there's been an unusual spate of cases in France this spring, although not every tick causes problems; Apollo has none on him now and although Leo had one on his neck a week ago, it disembarked without causing him any ill effects. I examine him minutely all the same, and Dr Bompy says we need some precautionary tick pincers which we can buy from his surgery in Nemours. Some hasty rearrangements are made so the horses can be moved to a farm within walking distance of the equestrian centre tomorrow, and we have to unscramble tonight's accommodation and find somewhere nearer.

It's boiled eggs at midnight.

Apollo's a little brighter in the morning. At the neighbouring farm we're greeted by Jaws, who has metal teeth on the left-hand side of his mouth and none on the right. He looks speculatively at Susie and is so very, very helpful that she decides to take the so-far useless bike to visit the nearest town, St Valérien, while Peter trundles me off to the golf course. Within three holes I decide this wifely duty is going to have to cease – my trainers are acting like blotting paper, soaking up every last residue of energy from my plodding feet, and the velvet sward of the fourth green is an inviting mattress for a nap. It's a very dull course, and I count the avenues of trees bordering the fairways up and back, up and back, par four, par five, par four again, and pray for the eighteenth tee to appear.

By the following day Apollo's definitely on the mend, and while we're waiting for Dr Bompy to arrive with more medicine we get into meaningful conversation with Jaws, whose name is actually Maurice. Turning to Susie, he tells her plaintively that he's celibate and ideally would like a nice English wife, or at least one from further south than St Valérien – and when we relay to Dr Bompy that Maurice would like a good woman, he says he wouldn't mind one either. Peter explains that Susie's already spoken for but that we're meeting up with our sister Tessa (further south than St Valérien) who isn't, and he suggests helpfully that she'd do instead. Maurice looks hopeful. So does Dr Bompy, but he's quickly distracted when Susie and I show him a tick embedded under Apollo's chin that we've smothered in surgical spirit in an effort to dislodge it. He points out that it's actually a nodule and part of Apollo, so it's just as well we didn't implement Plan B which was to burn it off with Peter's cigar.

We have two more days to wait before Apollo's fit enough to carry on, so Susie takes me on an educational tour of Sens cathedral. I'm a frustrating subject – I can appreciate its clean lines in a general sort of way, and some similarities to Canterbury cathedral which is based on the same design, but words like narthex and transept are a foreign language to me, and I thought a tympanum was something to do with the percussion section of an orchestra. Susie crushingly tells me that's exactly where it came from, in architectural terms – it's the semicircular space between the lintel and the arch over a church door. Sort of drumlike, I suppose. I'm suitably chastened for being a facetious smart-arse and remove myself to buy some maps so I can plan a more direct route to Vézelay, and we lug another load of washing to the *laverie*. We're developing a sure instinct for tracking down launderettes with tumble dryers so hot that our clothes are violently baked to half their normal size in fifteen minutes.

In the evening sunshine the flowering chestnut tree outside our gîte hums with bees, and during the night I can hear a nightingale singing at full throttle in the woods across the road, but we're glad not to be riding the following day: it pours with rain. The barometer in the lorry seems to be forecasting a hurricane, and Bessie's spider is having a difficult time – she's knitting larger and larger webs every night that stretch right across the windscreen, but the rain droops them into sad loops that collapse on top of the wipers by the morning. We drive to Nemours to pay Dr Bompy's bill and buy a pair of tick pincers – apparently you squeeze the tick round the neck with them while deftly rotating your wrist, and it lets go of your horse. Get it wrong and you're left holding the severed rear end of the tick while the mouth parts are still embedded, and then it's you that's let go of your horse, which has leaped backwards in irritation.

Apollo's back to his normal jocular self which means we can move on tomorrow, and tonight Susie has her head in the Vézelay books while I have mine in the Vézelay map. This is a real explorer's map, almost three dimensional, for although it shows the soft valley of the River Cure down the middle, on each side the contour lines crowd together on dark-shaded hills and in woods that merge into a vast forest. It's still a long way away in equine travel terms, but it renews our sense of purpose: it's the true start to the pilgrimage.

We have an invitation for English tea in the morning at ten o'clock with Maurice, his elderly farmer brother and comfortably rounded wife. Madame's in a flap because the baker's an hour and a half late, and I have an inkling it wasn't so sensible to eat my cornflakes in the lorry first. When the baker appears, Madame's arms are overflowing with croissants and in seconds the kitchen table is groaning with cheese and ham and cake for English tea. Susie's family photographs are minutely pored over and her sheep discussed in great detail, but the garrulous Maurice is *désolé* that we're going, and hardly says a word. Madame is rummaging in the fridge. She produces a cold cooked duck wrapped in foil which she insists we take with us, just in case we haven't had enough breakfast, and we pile out into the farmyard for a group photograph. Madame flirts with Peter, confessing coyly that her name is Marie-Antoinette, and exchanges her slippers for stout boots for the photo call. She is the boss around here.

We're taking the horses to our gîte at Domats for the night, a short ride for the convalescent Apollo; Domats shouldn't be on our route and we've lost several days, but I try to tell myself there's no point worrying. Clara telephones, sounding so ecstatically hungover after a surprise twenty-first birthday party organised by her friends that I don't feel so guilty about abandoning my children, but she asks me when we'll be home again, and I have to tell her I haven't a clue.

It's another dummy run in Bessie to try to find somewhere to stay tomorrow. We drive south down the Autoroute du Soleil, divert to the village of Cudot close beside it, and ask at the bar. Although it's late on Sunday afternoon, the mayor, a man with a stomach of considerable gravitas, is summoned to show us a holy glade with holy trees where we can camp; legend has it that centuries ago a shepherd with leprosy drove his staff into the ground here, and a spring welled up and he was cured. The mayor assures us the water still heals skin diseases, and people come from as far away as the United States to try it as it pours from a pipe now into a pool covered by a barn with an impressive domed roof. You can paddle in it, wash in it and it's fine for drinking, so it'll be cold duck and holy water for supper tomorrow.

The barometer's still forecasting disaster, but it doesn't arrive, and we conclude optimistically that it's so shaken up by the rattling Bessie that the needle's stuck at the lowest point on a doom-ridden 940 millibars. In the sunshiny morning a cheerful Apollo skips up the road pretending to be scared of a dog hunting in the hedge; there's no-one about when we get to Cudot so we help ourselves to the holy glade, winding the electric fencing tape carefully round the young trees planted by the villagers to create a field. The horses are very happy with their dinner washed down with holy water in a bucket, but there's no relaxing for the rest of us yet, because the usual niggling problem is raising its head: we've nowhere to stay tomorrow, although several phone calls result in a booking at a gîte below Auxerre for the two following nights. At least we're finally approaching Burgundy.

Peter and I are back in the lorry again, ranging further south in a wide circle. He manoeuvres Bessie easily down tiny country lanes. I've only driven her once in France and found her wooden body wobbled alarmingly without the horses to weigh her down, and there was so much play in the steering I couldn't stop her behaving like a snake. But Bessie is Peter's faithful companion, just as the horses are Susie's and mine, and his books and maps and cigars are neatly arranged in boxes on the parcel shelf to mark his territory.

The impressively named St-Aubin-Château-Neuf is a straggly village with a gîte *d'étape* that's been abandoned, and *chambres d'hôte* that are closed, like everything else on a Monday. It's getting later and later, and the heat has gone out of the day. I knock on the door of the largest house I can see and an old lady opens it, accompanied by a Yorkshire terrier with its jaws clamped round a multicoloured glove. She's sorry to say she has no land but she calls out to Georges, wandering by, and he phones the mayor who says we may use the communal land at Le Moulin tomorrow, where there's an abandoned water mill next to a huge field. This field has everything in it from a football pitch to a manège for schooling our horses, should we be so inclined, and it'll do fine, although it's quite a long way. It's nearly nine o'clock by the time we get back to Cudot to find Susie wrapped in a horse rug, huddled like an abandoned orphan on the doorstep of the shrine.

The water goes down well with the duck, which we've lavishly plastered in a hot sticky sauce of cider, oranges and honey; they aptly represent the spiritual and practical sides of our pilgrimage so far, and Susie and I joke that she may be the holy water, but I'm definitely the cold duck.

It's not a holy night. A gale and lashing rain arrive from nowhere, screaming through the trees and spooking the horses, so perhaps the barometer was right after all. The mayor appears promptly at 8.15 a.m. and we all notice simultaneously that Apollo's spent an industrious night chewing the bark off the holy trees. Worse, Monsieur le Mayor turns out to be an agricultural expert, fully aware of the potentially lasting damage, but although we've stretched his goodwill to the limit he assures us that it's *de rien*, and something healing will be put on the trees. Leo meanwhile is looking positively saintly and sticking to the grass – fortunately for him he has no history of tree-chewing and Apollo, who does, gets all the blame.

The mayor takes us to see the church, dedicated to St Alpaïs who we conclude is female as the stone statue is wearing a large skirt. Susie has her camera out and is clicking away, but I'm looking at my watch: it's gone ten o'clock and we've got a long ride ahead, and the mayor's in a hurry, too – but he can't leave until he's fetched a special stamp for Susie's passport and has written in it at length. I daren't ask for mayoral writings and another stamp in mine for fear of delaying the poor bloke further, and it's nearly midday by the time we set off, both of us grumpy and tired after a disturbed night and because I'm itching to go while Susie's untroubled by any sense of time passing.

We grouch off down the road and bicker our way through the first ten miles in excellent time, stopping when we reach the end of my map to buy some pork chops and receive some dodgy directions from the garage man. I'm too tired to concentrate properly on what he says and miss a right turn over the river, resulting in a complete circle of five miles before I realise what's happening. By the time we reach St Aubin we're tight-lipped with fatigue, the horses have run out of steam, Peter's exhausted from waiting for us and the chops are sweating nicely in my pocket.

But it's peaceful at the water-mill field. The rain and wind have flown away leaving a pale blue evening, and the river murmurs near the derelict mill with its stilled water wheel. The mill pond is silent, cloudy with algae, but the river still bursts exuberantly down the water steps below it. We decide to risk the chops, stewed to death in the last of the cider, and eat supper outside to the lively accompaniment of dive-bombing May bugs.

Peter shakes his head in disbelief when Susie and I, in harmony again, turn to face the first sliver of the new moon and bow to it gravely, seven times each, for good luck.

9. AN INVISIBLE COMPANION

My mother eats custard with a fork,
Carrots with a spoon,
She thinks she'll be home again
Soon.

The nursing home's a church,
Mice singing in the choir
(Or gerbils, she's not sure)
And my father has returned
From the war.

In alternative dimension
She knows it's all a joke,
A dream created randomly
From which she never woke;

She laughs at herself,
Her mind a hotch-potch;
The only ones who suffer
Are those who watch.

She would have loved to ride with Susie and me if she'd been twenty years younger, if Alzheimer's hadn't crawled insidiously into her brain to eat away at her memory. She used to be an enthusiastic traveller as well as a prolific writer, flying alone to Jordan in the 1960s to research a book about horses at the invitation of King Hussain. There she camped with the Bedouin in the desert with a royal bodyguard to look after her, waking each morning to the thump and rush of goat kids leaping up one side of her tent and sliding down the other. Not long afterwards she went with our father to Iran, where they stayed as guests of the Shah and where she rode an ebony stallion across the mountains. She persuaded her reluctant cameraman to get on another one, but she failed with our father. He, no more horsy than Peter, insisted that he would only ride a nice, safe gelding which caused some worried head scratching – there was scarcely such an animal in Iran, and the one that was eventually found for him was understandably depressed.

In the year before Susie and I left to ride the Way of St James, our mother insisted periodically that she was going to accompany us. In her mind her old Connemara pony was still alive and ready for anything, and so was she, but by the time we went she was preoccupied with the confusing new environment of a home peopled by strangers, her husband of 66 years now just a visitor, and it was hard to tell whether she registered our departure or not. But we're taking her in our minds, all the same, and no more so than on this part of our journey into Burgundy.

I'm woken at three in the morning by the sheer stillness in the water-mill meadow. It's magical outside: the horses are lying down in the long grass, creatures of the night, all pewter spots and dark dapples, and not even a rabbit stirs in the silver field. In the morning, the sun's a peaceful orb hanging in the sky, and it's altogether a better day. I photograph Susie tramping through the dew in her nightie and gumboots, trowel in hand, and we eat our croissants outside on Bessie's ramp, dribbling honey on to the coir matting.

The countryside is changing to deep valleys and woods, and today we ride a long chalk track on the crest of the hills, as the landscape undulates into the distance. We're flower hunting, as we did in our childhood days with our parents, struggling on short legs over the steep Kentish downs in search of orchids, which our mother made us record laboriously in an exercise book. She would have been lit up with excitement at what we find today: early purple orchids, milkwort and a group of 33 lady orchids, one a foot high. On the same bank, we see vivid bee and rare green man orchids with little hanging legs, and a handsome grass snake sliding by beneath them. There are butterflies everywhere, swallowtails and fritillaries and tortoiseshells, and a red and black cinnabar moth – which is poisonous to birds – looking for a yellow ragwort plant – which is poisonous to horses – where it will lay eggs. Ragwort's the scourge of the equine world but it has a Latin name that intrigues us – it roughly translates as St James's Weed.

We make very slow progress because Susie's off Apollo with her camera every few yards, but such a perfect day needs recording and, anyway, Peter's playing a lengthy game of golf somewhere. Lunch-time's spent in the sneezy pollen of the hedgerow, using the saddles as backrests and waving our melting Marmite sandwiches at a passing motorist who winds down his window to shout 'Bon appétit!'

Monsieur Political runs the gîte near Auxerre. He's an ardent supporter of Le Pen and his first name is also Jean-Marie. He's also the president of the local gîte association, which solves our accommodation problem for later in the week. Today is 15 May and it's Leo's ninth birthday. His present is the equine equivalent of two days in a luxury hotel, courtesy of Jean-Marie: a valley with a clear cold stream rippling along it, and an adventure trail through a wood if he happens to be bored. Predictably enough both horses ignore these desirable features, and Apollo's head is straight down into the grass without pausing to admire the view, while smooth mover Leo strolls over to the far fence to beam at the fillies queuing up to greet him on the other side.

There's no sign of Peter and no mobile signal where we are either, but I scramble up a hill behind the gîte with my phone as Bessie comes into sight, winding her way down the valley, Peter shiny with sweat at the wheel after a heavy game of golf and two wrong turnings on the way here. It's ten o'clock by the time the day cools down, and we eat supper on the verandah as the light sinks out of the sky and all that's left is the moon, a bigger sliver tonight, equidistant between two stars.

Jean-Marie's chickens arrive on Bessie's ramp early in the morning to demand pretzel crumbs. I'm tempted to lay a Hansel and Gretel trail through the lorry and up on to our duvet where Peter's invisibly snoring underneath it, but it probably wouldn't be good for marital harmony, and eventually the clucking's so loud that he's forced to get up anyway and register his displeasure at the hens' fat feathery presence. We drive off to Auxerre in the boiling heat, squeezing Bessie into a car-sized slot in the city centre car park next to the notice telling us that vehicles over 3.5 tons are strictly *interdit*. The traffic wardens advise us to ignore the sign.

The soaring cathedral of Saint-Etienne dominates the town, and down in the eleventh-century crypt there's the only known painting of Christ on a horse of the Apocalypse. He's trotting contentedly across the wall with no visible means of control such as a bridle or reins, and the other four horsemen are eyeing Him speculatively. While Susie inspects the cathedral in greater detail, Peter and I pig out on florentines and strawberry tart in the narrow mediaeval street outside. Afterwards, the effort involved in extricating Bessie from the car park down a similar street with overhanging gables has Peter in even more of a sweat than yesterday.

We need to find a garage. Bessie's reduced to Cyclops as one of her headlights has been broken by a flying stone, and there's a chain of connection from Bedford through Vauxhall to Opel, but the Auxerre Opel salesmen are flummoxed. The showroom's shiny with new cars multicoated in metallic paint, but an old

Bedford lorry has never lumbered on to their forecourt before. Needless to say, they don't have a headlamp, but they manage to order the most expensive one in the world to be forwarded to Nevers, which hopefully we shall reach next week. Back at the gîte, Jean-Marie revives us all, and Peter in particular, with unlabelled bottles of Chablis and measured arguments in favour of Le Pen, and in wine-inspired enthusiasm I mark out a way across three whole maps that's almost straight.

When Susie and I were originally planning our route I'd hoped to divert to Chablis if only to get pissed on horseback on my favourite white wine, but the reality is that there isn't time. We settle down to the miles of tracks I've earmarked to Mailly-le-Château and the only bridge across the Yonne that looks horse friendly, but they're impossible to follow and we could do with a machete. Faint trails thread through tangled woods that haven't been cleared for years, and the horses jump fallen logs and stop dead the other side to avoid cannoning head first into the next tree, catapulting Susie and me on to their necks as we duck low branches and creepy-crawlies are showered inside our shirts. The flies descend in clouds from a sullen sultry sky. This normally results in Apollo repeatedly shaking his head, but thanks to the nose net attached to his bridle no insects can fly up his nostrils, and it has the added advantage of thwarting his efforts to snack his way from one end of the day to the other.

Mailly-le-Château is built on a precipice. The signpost at the top of the town tells us that Vézelay is 23 kilometres away, but after a short descent and a clop over the Yonne along an old stone bridge, the next sign says 16 kilometres. Either way the sight of the name finally set out in solid black letters on wood is enough to make us feel like proper pilgrims on a mission, and fatigue vanishes as we reach the pig farm where we're booked in for tonight, the clouds finally rolling up as we spot the farmer in tiny shorts cycling up and down the road at tremendous speed.

Spurred on by a skinful each of Bourgogne ratafia, Susie and I embark on a hated task of sewing, attaching pilgrim scallop shells to random bits of clothing, my Aussie hat and a replacement for the broken shell on Apollo's browband, because tomorrow, finally tomorrow, we shall reach Vézelay. We go to bed in a state of repressed excitement even though the constant rain promises a wet day. Peter's looking hopeful that some of my elation will be directed at him, and I have to admit that there's nothing so cosy these days as curling up with one's lover in a lorry when there's a downpour raging on the roof.

The final stretch to Vézelay takes longer than expected, thanks to my son Oliver phoning us when we're in the middle of a wet wood. Because he's deaf he has to use the Typetalk service, laboriously typing what he wants to say on to a minicom which the operator relays verbally to me and my replies are typed to him. My pay-as-you-go phone runs out of euros almost before the conversation has begun.

'Hello, this is Oliver. Is that Mum? Go ahead.'

'Hello, Oliver, this is Mum. Go ahead.'

'Hello, Mum, how are you? Go ahead.'

'I'm fine, thank you. You'll have to be quick. I'm in a wood in the middle of France and the money's running out. Go ahead.'

'How's Leo? Go ahead.'

'Leo's *fine*. Hurry up. Go ahead.'

'Well, I thought you'd like to know I've collected the post. Go ahead.'

'Thank you, Oliver. Very much. Please can you ask John to forward it to, er … (Where shall we get it forwarded to, Susie? Leo! Get your head up.) Nevers. N. E. V. E. R. S. Poste Restante. Go ahead.'

'Never what? Go ahead.'

'N. E. V. E. R. S! It's a place. John will know. Hurry up. Go ahead.'

The Typetalk lady sounds as though she's suppressing giggles.

'OK, OK, OK. Well, I'm well as well. Go ahead.'

'*Il ne reste que soixante-sept cents.*'

'What?'

'Mum, are you there? Go ahead.'

'That's terrific. Give my love to Clara. Oliver, I've got to go, the money's gone, lots of love, go ahead.'

The phone's conked out.

We get slower and slower. This is the true Chemin de St Jacques but it's designed for foot pilgrims, and the tunnel of trees is at pedestrian height. After last night's rain the sodden branches are hanging so low that our backs are soaked, but it seems a shame to dismount, and after ducking and diving for an hour we're through the wood and suddenly the basilica of Vézelay is straight ahead, a sprawly sphinx far away on a hill. In between there's an ocean of tall green corn and the River Cure, burbling quietly along the valley floor. When we reach the foot of the hill the horses fly up the steep track, and suddenly we pop out right beside the basilica.

I've had to bone up on some history about Vézelay, starting with the fact that the Benedictine monks settled in the town in about 860; after that there's questionable information that the relics of Mary Magdalene were brought to the monastery, and the first church there was dedicated to her. That church was later burned down by the Normans, and there was no great destiny for Vézelay in the offing until 1037 when the abbot actually displayed the relics, a shrewd move resulting in an abundance of miracles, pilgrim visitors and much wealth for the region in general and the monastery in particular. Thousands poured through every year, many from the east on their way to Santiago de Compostela; a huge church had to be built to shelter everyone, and the basilica was dedicated in 1104. It had an unfortunate start because a few years later the nave was destroyed by fire and twelve hundred people were incinerated as well, but it was reconstructed and the narthex was built – and by now I've gathered that a narthex is a giant ante-room to the church, where smelly pilgrims can be parked.

Then came days of glory for Vézelay when Thomas à Becket preached here and Richard Lionheart set off on the third crusade.

However, unfortunately for the monastery, at the beginning of the thirteenth century the complete body of Mary Magdalene was apparently discovered in a sarcophagus at Saint-Maximin in Provence, which rather dented the credibility of the relics in the basilica in Burgundy, and by the time King Saint-Louis visited Vézelay in 1267 with the papal legate to declare that the relics were authentic after all, the pilgrim trade had dried up.

The basilica fell into decline; it was secularised, mutilated, the apse used by the Huguenots as a riding school, and finally it was abandoned. It wasn't until the middle of the nineteenth century that it was realised that this was a dangerous ruin that would have to be demolished if something wasn't done, and over the next twenty years it was painstakingly restored. Pilgrims began to reappear, in 1946 forty thousand of them on a Crusade for Peace, and the trickle of those on their way to Santiago became a flood.

By the time Susie and I catch up with Peter, he's been parked with Bessie for two hours and is just observing the preliminaries to the third wedding he's watched take place today. Overwhelmed by the effort of galloping up the hill, Apollo dumps a huge crot under the noses of the bride, groom and all the guests posing in top hats and tails on the basilica steps. We quickly disappear to the car park to tie the horses to a tree, and creep back to see what's going on. Despite the wedding there are tourists still pouring into the church and we join them, passing below the exterior tympanum, which Susie tells me is showing Christ in glory at the Last Judgment, sitting on a throne with His arms extended. He's weighing up souls to left and right: those on the left are being removed by demons to hell, while helpful angels point those on the right in the direction of St Peter and the Pearly Gates.

I'm on tiptoe, trying to stop my riding boots echoing on the stone slabs of the narthex floor. Huge doors are ahead of me and another tympanum, this time showing Christ with hands opened in benediction. Rays spill out from His fingers and fantastical figures surround Him: Jews, Cappodocians, dog-headed Indians, Ethiopians, and Pygmies struggling to get on a horse using a ladder. I would need a week to take it all in, and we've only got a couple of hours.

When I look through the portal into the nave what I see there takes my breath away; there is no stained glass in this church and the voices of the choir singing the Catholic Mass rise through layers of light. The rounded Romanesque arches in the nave are set with alternate slabs of dark and pale stone, their curves repeating the vault of the sky, and the positions and size of the windows were carefully calculated by the mediaeval monks so that the nave is a luminous path leading to heaven. At the far end, the pointed Gothic arches of the chancel are awash with light even on this dull day, and everywhere the capitals on top of the pillars that support the arches are riotous with carvings: saints, demons, lions, legends, the deadly sins, signs of the zodiac, the four winds and St Eustachius perched on a cross-looking pony with its ears flat back.

The choir abruptly abandons Bach and launches into the Beatles. The effect is startling, but Mass is over and the bride and groom who've been standing stiffly through two hours of it relax visibly. I scamper down to the crypt, the oldest part of the church where the relics of St Mary Magdalene lie; the crypt is silent and mysterious, and in its tiny chapel the flagstones are worn into uneven shapes by hundreds of years of feet.

The newly married couple are riding away down the hillside on horses: he on a fizzy Arab and she riding sidesaddle on a steady mare, the delicate white train of her dress drifting against the horse's side. It's time for us to leave as well, but we go the other way, down through the town's main street, as Leo's trumpeting under his breath and thinking of joining the wedding party. The old town is higgledy-piggledy with stone houses piled up the steep hill against tourist shops, cafés and restaurants while brass scallop shells are sunk in a shining line down the middle of the street to mark the Chemin de St Jacques. It's a slow walk down as curious tourists stop us to pat the horses and ask us where we've come from: now, we can say we're *pèlerins* without tripping over the word, and everyone understands exactly what we mean.

10. THIRTEEN HAIRY FRENCH LADIES

Foissy-lès-Vézelay lies below the town – at the foot of a precipice, in fact, where the horses have to scramble down the overgrown track, Leo tobogganing on his haunches with me still on board, and Apollo sliding into Susie who's walking in front of him. Their reward at the bottom is a lush field for the night, and ours is a parking spot for Bessie in a deserted buttercup lane, with the municipal dustbins to the left and a cemetery to the right – ideal for us, now that we've discovered the usefulness of a cemetery tap.

For now we're trying to rely on a French book of maps to follow the proper Chemin de St Jacques. Susie's keen to try the authentic GR route marked out in this book with a broad red squiggle; one of our English guidebooks suggests it's up to the pilgrims to select their own paths and quiet roads, because several have evolved on the Vézelay route to Santiago, but we decide to give the French version a go. Susie reckons it will be straightforward, and I'm just hoping she's right. I like the idea, but I'm beginning to wonder if we'll make it home by Christmas.

Within minutes we're on the wrong road and then the wrong

track, heading in the wrong direction in thick woodland. The book says we should be on a marked trail heading north-west (odd, when we're trying to go south-west in the general direction of Biarritz) so I try using the compass, and unexpectedly a modern Santiago sign is in front of us nailed to a tree – not a defined scallop shell, but the first Council of Europe version we've seen, all yellow lines, royal blue background and obligatory EU stars. The Chemin itself becomes easier to follow but the book isn't. Susie needs her glasses to read the directions and it's a perplexing day of stops and starts, with an unexpectedly early post-lunch-time start by Leo and Apollo on their own until they pause, deeply embarrassed, and wait for Susie and me to come pounding up the road with their bridles.

There's the usual problem of nowhere to stay when we ride into Tannay – and all round it and out again, and back. In our search for the *terrain communale* that we're sure must be somewhere, we manage to interrupt first a game of boules and then a tea dance, where vague gestures are made towards the top of the town, and someone says the communal land is near the police station. We find the police station all right but it's locked up from its barred gate to its slammed shutters, and when I ring the bell, Leo and I jump out of our skins: there's a voice piping up in the concrete post beside us. I have a detailed conversation with this post but it turns out that the disembodied gendarme who's responded to the entryphone isn't entombed in the police station but is putting his feet up at Clamecy, several miles to the north. The Tannay gendarme, he says, is out in his patrol car and won't be back for hours.

Back in the town we come across a football match that we missed on our circumnavigation. Most of the citizens of Tannay are here and no doubt their policeman is as well, and a man in a yellow shirt who may or may not be the mayor gives us permission to put up our electric fence on the empty land opposite the police station. We toil up the hill again, both horses now in dead-donkey mode. The *terrain communale* is unfenced;

one side has spindly grass and huge lizard orchids, and the other is plushly green with clover leaves, so naturally Susie and I encircle this part with our electric fence. We've just turned the horses out when Peter backs into view round Bessie's cab, making placatory gestures at a furiously advancing arm-waving Frenchman.

We're on his land, he says, and the communal bit is several metres to the right and can't we see the boundary and we have to move our fence immediately because he's due to cut his clover for his four horses and two donkeys (who can indeed be heard neighing and braying in the background) as they're short of food. Fortunately, by the time he's said all this he's short of breath, and I ask him if he could possibly, possibly let us have some water for our poor tired horses (best smile switched on), and he calms down and invites us to use his tap. But we still have to move the fence first.

At Monsieur's house down the hill, his wife's surprised to see us with our assorted buckets, but she's swiftly hospitable, producing an extra container and a ramshackle handcart. The cart's loaded with a huge amount of water and Monsieur peremptorily instructs Peter to wheel it back to the field, as he wishes to take me on a conducted tour of the four horses, two donkeys and several sad dogs chained to posts. Afterwards Madame has a sticky bottle of home-made blackcurrant syrup for me, and Monsieur courteously accompanies me back up the road, carrying the final bucket. Peter's face is a study when we reappear: he's convinced his arms have been elongated, his golf swing ruined by having to drag forty gallons of water uphill in a cart like a recalcitrant supermarket trolley, all stubborn wheels setting off in different directions. The final insult was when Susie took his photograph.

We're back on a more direct route to Nevers the next day – yesterday's GR was picturesque but very slow, and it took us five hours to cover less than fifteen miles. Unfortunately, Tannay is just off our IGN map but we set off in hope, steering by compass and fortified by hot fresh croissants from the bakery, while Peter's still in bed asleep, trying to retract his arms to their normal length.

Susie and I take an educated guess at a short cut to Talon via a well-defined track, but it peters out in a wood imaginatively named Le Crot Sauvage, where an attempt to follow flagged trees fails when it finally dawns on us that the flags indicate trees for felling and not a signposted path for dumb foreigners. We break all our self-imposed rules by plunging off into the undergrowth in what we hope is the right direction, Leo and Apollo scrabbling up a cliff at breakneck speed, and five minutes later emerge above Talon into the hot midday stupor of another typical French public holiday.

I phone Peter. The tracks on our next map are impossible, blocked off to create cow pastures, and we follow his road directions to the mediaeval Château Chanteloup which doubles as a gîte, its grounds crowded with peacocks, hens, cockerels, pheasants, cats and ponies. Apollo comes face to face with his double in miniature, with exactly the same coat pattern – the first Appaloosa we've seen – but he and Leo are more interested in pulling shark faces at the peacocks, beak-down in their bowls, and trying to salvage some of their dinner.

Peter and I are to sleep in the château tonight, which has an eerie little twelfth-century chapel at one end that's still consecrated. It's only the fifth night we haven't been in the lorry and it seems strange to be in a proper bedroom again, one with a four-poster bed. We take a photograph of Bessie-by-the-château (elegant stone statue in the foreground) to counteract yesterday morning's photo of Bessie-by-the-municipal-dustbins, and depart to neighbouring Corbigny for a blow-out dinner in a restaurant. It's late when we leave there, and Bessie's spider is taken by surprise. Normally, we never drive at night, and she's out in the middle of her web across the windscreen collecting the day's takings; as Peter starts the engine she clutches a parcel of flies to her bulbous stomach and legs it into the overhang. Our journey is accompanied by a lot of peering, as Bessie still has only one headlight, and we skulk slowly down the back roads to the château to find we're locked out.

A Dutch couple have arrived this evening but obviously they haven't realised any other guests are staying, let alone absentee ones. They don't hear us calling, nor the howling from one of the many cats who also wants to go in. We press the intercom button guiltily because by now it's eleven o'clock, and eventually the manageress answers – but when we implore her to let us in, she's ominously silent. It turns out that she's not upstairs in some cosy turret, but five miles away in her own home, and she'll have to get up, get dressed, get in her car and get here. There's no-one else in residence except the Dutch couple and presumably the rest of the cats.

Five minutes later the Dutchman hears us trying to work out the code on the front door. Unhappily we've wrecked the handles by turning the outside one out of synchronisation with the inside one, but he manages to force the door open and let us in, along with the cat and a large bat which both disappear up the stone staircase. The Dutchman is pale, fraught and hungry. His wife booked them into the château, he says, thinking it was the château of the same name where they'd previously stayed in Le Mans. When they finally arrived in Le Mans from Rotterdam after a long hot drive they were told they weren't booked in and anyway the place was full, so they were sent on their way for another four hours' drive to a château where they didn't want to stay, in an area they didn't want to visit.

He has the drained look of a man who's been apoplectic with rage all day and has now run out of energy, and he obviously thinks that we, his wife and also the manageress are all mad. A scribbled note was left to tell the couple where they were sleeping, but it didn't include instructions not to lock the front door because there were English guests who'd gone out to dinner in their horsebox.

When Madame arrives, we keep quiet about the state of the

door. She removes the cat, which has come downstairs again, minus the bat which can't be found, and the Dutchman disappears to bed; but while she's throwing the cat in the general direction of the garden she shuts the door while we're all outside, and then none of us can open it again. She mutters that it's *très bizarre*, unlocks the staff door, tells us that it's of no consequence that this rambling château (full of priceless antiques) is completely insecure for the night, and roars off in her car before anything else can happen.

Peter opens the staff door and there's a ginger flash as the cat flies in again while a teenage cat, underage mother of one tiny black kitten, rushes out into the night. Peter's had quite enough; he's completely unmoved by the pathetic mewing of the deserted kitten, and heads for where he thinks our bedroom might be. Susie's asleep in the lorry, but I can visualise the kitten stiff on the cold kitchen flagstones by the morning so I spend ten minutes hunting round in the bushes for its delinquent mother. In the end she strolls up purring, but as soon as I've reunited her with her baby, chucked out the other cat, shut the staff door, opened an internal door and gazed at a metal staircase spiralling into infinity, the young cat's streaked up it to the second floor.

As I follow her, my childhood fear of the dark grips me firmly by the back of the neck. Ahead of me in the long dim corridor the curtains stir at their casement windows, and I can just make out the slipping shadow of the cat. She stops dead in a doorway and as I catch up with her I can see why: the bat is there, hanging by one sticky foot from the stone lintel, its ears flickering with fleas and radar messages. When it swoops down into a black pit I realise I'm teetering at the top of the central stairway.

I've now had enough as well. As the teenage cat launches herself into the void, I manage to wedge her, yowling, under my arm and march her back to her kitten in the kitchen. My feet are thundering on the floorboards, scaring the spooks away, but even so when eventually I find our bedroom I lock the door and hope that nothing supernatural can melt through it. I'd like to regale Peter with all this excitement, but he's a snoring starfish in the middle of the bed.

By morning the front door has mysteriously returned to normal function, so no confessions are necessary. The manageress shakes her head at the strangeness of it all. Outside in the garden there's a wan woman walking who's either the owner of the château or the ghost of the owner; there's no sign of the Dutch, and the cats have barricaded a chicken into the kitchen.

The horses are in dead-donkey mode again. We've been riding for five days without a break but tomorrow will be a rest day, so we're booked into a gîte for two nights. Today's a hot headachy day for me, thanks to too much of the seductively soft Tannay wine last night and not enough sleep, as every creak of the four-poster bed had me bolt upright looking for poltergeists moving the furniture. We have to dawdle down the roads because the first track, clearly marked on the map, leads us into a farmyard where the farmer tells us there's been no way through for 25 years. The horses' shoes are paper thin after 350 miles, and both have lost their front toeclips, but the gîte is advertised as a *ferme equestre* so hopefully we'll be able to track down a farrier.

Monsieur from Paris who owns the farm is very laissez-faire – he's far more relaxed about his own horses than we are about ours. Having turned Leo and Apollo out into a vast acreage of grass and hedges, I'm suddenly diverted from the imposing spectacle of the huge ruined château next door by the appearance of a little palomino mare who looks suspiciously like a scout. She seems to be in the same field and, luckily, Leo has his back to her as she disappears again round the corner. Where's the fence? Monsieur Paris looks amazed. What fence? They'll all be fine together; there are, er, thirteen mares and four geldings in there as well, he thinks. Thirteen mares! Even Leo's going to be overwhelmed. Susie and I run round subdividing the field with our electric fence, squabbling like children over the best way to unravel two miles of tape in thirty seconds.

We've only just finished when Mademoiselle Palomino, her blonde mane flowing, reappears at a gallop at the head of the Heavy Brigade. They screech to a halt to check the new arrivals over our fence, and Leo and Apollo are beside themselves with excitement, pluming their tails over their backs and showing off, until Leo's extravagant extended trot takes him through a bog and his hooves get stuck. We're entertained all through supper by the sight of him elegantly flirting with all the mares bar Mademoiselle Thunder Thighs, a grey Percheron who's taken a shine to Apollo although she's twice his height. Apollo's quite bashful, retiring behind a tree now and again, and all the while Mademoiselle Palomino is snaking up and down, seeing off the competition. Who needs television?

By morning, the hot weather has vanished, and the day settles into a continuous depressing downpour. Monsieur Paris invites us to use the main gîte sitting room for free, where we guiltily turn on the electric fire, and I check our maps only to find that crossings over the Loire River, our next major obstacle, are few and far between. Susie's beginning to worry about the Auvergne, now not so far away, and I repeat unconvincingly that I won't take her over any mountain passes. It seems politic to go out for a wet walk in gumboots before she can question me more closely.

The neighbouring château has been bought as a holiday home and it's in the middle of renovation; the right-hand side's complete, but on the left the drab daylight gawps through bare rafters and broken tiles on the turret roofs. You'd need to have at least thirty children to fill up such an enormous building. There are too many workmen paddling around in ponds of wet cement for me to risk an extensive snoop, so I decide to check out the boundaries of the horse field instead and spend half an hour slopping through the wet grass in ten ruined fields of about forty acres in all.

There are fallen trees and marshes and bramble forests and broken barbed wire in tangled heaps; every imaginable hazard, in fact, to trap two unwary English Appaloosas whose minds are on romance with thirteen hairy French ladies. Thunder Thighs plods up to greet me with her tickly whiskers, her iron grey coat sleek in the rain, ignoring the fox beside her who's pinging the elastic guts out of a dead sheep. I cut back to the gîte across the soaked land on the other side of the château, which is even worse than the first, though it has a certain grandeur. I can only hope the Dutch owner's wife likes having babies.

Darkness is creeping down by the time the farrier and several acolytes arrive to shoe the horses. The sombre vet who accompanies them looks as though he's closely related to Rasputin, and he sedates Apollo with such an overdose that the poor horse slips over in the clammy horse shit in the shed where we're sheltering from the rain. The blacksmith's assistants are students in the middle of their final exams, horrified at the prospect of shoeing one horse that's so wobbly it can hardly stand up, and a second that would rather be gazing into Mademoiselle Palomino's brown eyes. Leo fidgets continuously for the two hours they take to put new shoes on him, with a lot of Gallic swearing and squinting in the light thrown by a single bulb.

The shoes are cheap. Very cheap. Leo's stepping out gingerly, and Apollo's managed to lock his legs so he can sleep standing up, and isn't stepping out at all. I'm convinced they'll both be footsore tomorrow, and we won't be going anywhere.

11. COITUS INTERRUPTUS

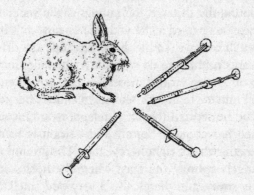

At least the rain's stopped. Leo potters on to the tarmac like a tentative teenager in new stilettos, but he obstinately refuses to stick to the soft verge and still moves to the left whenever I take a hand off the rein to unfold the map. Every track across country that we try is blocked, and we're forced to stay on the road at a walk all day. When Susie charms a village mayor into showing her the communal land we stop with a sigh of relief, although it's a narrow strip by the River Ixeure where our overtired imaginations conjure up visions of horses falling in the water. There's a field next door, though, and the lady who lives opposite invites us to put them in there, not that it's hers to lend. Having solved that problem, my imagination switches to possible spectral nuns in the ruined convent beside us. At 11 p.m. the crickets are still making such a racket that Peter observes they must have sore knees, but they and Bessie's spider, who's busily knitting after yet another web has been demolished by the windscreen wipers, are the only signs of activity in the moonlight and there are no roaming ghosts.

Even so, Peter sleeps badly and grumps off to find a golf

course, while Susie and I embark on another day of stately plodding along the roads, the horses slightly more at ease in their new shoes. We cross the Loire at Imphy on a long bridge, where I try to photograph the wide shallow river from Leo's back while he looks doubtfully through the railings at the water far below. Peter phones: he's passed a gîte with horses next to it on his way to golf, but when we amble hopefully up the drive, smart Madame wants nothing to do with us. A few miles further on, a Dutchman on an egg farm is more obliging, but when I contact Peter to tell him we're in luck and to give him directions I'm in disgrace: I've committed the sin of telephoning him on the golf course when he's about to tee off. He's obviously having a bad round. Something's not right here, either. The ground under our feet is strangely springy, the grass where the horses are grazing only loosely sown, and there's also a very odd smell. When we poke the earth with the toes of our boots, Susie and I realise that the entire egg farm is sitting on thick layers of chicken shit. Great. This is really going to make Peter's day.

When Bessie crawls through the gateway, to my consternation Peter drives her off the concrete hard-standing and she sinks gracefully into the grass up to her mudflaps, releasing indescribable waves of honk. He extricates her for a trip to Nevers to collect the new headlight in total silence. The headlight costs more than £60, five times the price it would be in England, and Peter's raised eyebrows speak volumes about Susie and me, the French and the whole expedition, as he wordlessly downs a beer at a bar. Susie's so unnerved she daren't spend time inspecting the flamboyant Gothic cathedral of St Cyr, and I decide this isn't an appropriate moment to do the rounds of the estate agents, window-shopping for châteaux. Even our efforts to buy more maps are unsuccessful: we need some for Allier but it's the next district and *non*, Mesdames, we don't stock them here.

Our host at the egg farm admires the new headlamp and produces an identical one from his garage, cobwebby but serviceable, which we may have for free.

But after a good night's sleep despite the smelly fog round the lorry, Peter's almost able to raise a smile, particularly when Susie and I decide that a comfortable hostelry this evening would be politic. It's a day of trotting on wide verges, eating up the miles, and we have no trouble in finding a field to lodge the horses. The elderly owner joins us for a glass of wine in Bessie and tells us he used to be a pilgrim before he had trouble with his colon. Peter and I look suitably sympathetic and imagine his colon writhing angrily, but Susie tells us he probably means *colonne*, as in slipped disc, which doesn't sound nearly so exotic. Anyway, he still reads the *Pilgrim News* magazine every week, and he refuses to charge us for the horses, pressing twenty euros into our hands instead for the Hospices.

The comfortable hostelry is a hotel right on the river at Villeneuve-sur-Allier, where the beds are wide and soft and we're kept awake by a lonesome dog barking hopefully at ten-second intervals. In the morning we leave hastily, on discovering that Peter drove Bessie straight through the hotel flowerbed last night. We cross the Allier River in high winds and flapping macs to reach a long sheltered track through the woods and another Dutch farm where the horses can stay.

Géri's happy to be of help and we turn the horses out into five acres of field, but their immediate enthusiasm at the expanse of grass disappears in seconds – it's been grazed down to the earth by his sheep. Géri invites us in for tea. His wife's away in Holland but his nine-year-old blonde daughter is looking after him, and she politely deals with the teapot before returning to her task of arranging hundreds of syringes into artistic patterns on the kitchen table. What are they for? Well, they're waiting to be used for the artificial insemination of Géri's five hundred rabbits, of course. The sperm will arrive fresh from Normandy on Tuesday because apparently rabbit semen doesn't freeze. When I weakly suggest that perhaps the doe rabbits might prefer a nice buck (or 500) Géri says they don't – they're very choosy, and if they don't like the buck they see him off growling. So they get upended and artificially inseminated instead, all on the same day, so they produce litters simultaneously, 32 days later. There's not much one can contribute to a conversation like this so I look around the room, lost for words, and notice that the eight clocks ticking away on the wall are all showing different times.

I'm not going to ask any more questions.

There's a campsite nearby run by another transplanted Dutchman, where we can use the showers and washing machine. A marauding mass of tabby cats intent on raiding Frigo have to be evicted from the lorry before we can go to sleep, but in fact we should have kept a few as hot-water bottles – the campsite's on high ground, and the wind whistling through Bessie's freeze-dried shrunken planks leads to a teeth-chattering night. We wake to flying clouds, the occasional downpour, and the realisation that this is Day 50, 27 May, and we're not even halfway through France. I wonder idly at what point I shall have to send an email to work to let them know I'm going to be back just slightly later than I thought. In the meantime Freek, our latest Dutch host, kindly offers me a racing bike so that Susie and I can go and visit the horses without disturbing Peter, who's still asleep. I had thought of posting one of the tabbies under the duvet to wake him up, but it's probably too soon after doldrum day at Nevers for him to appreciate a purring pussy joke.

It's about two miles to Géri's farm, and the first part is on a switchback of a stony track. With no sense of balance on a bike, I daren't unglue my bottom from the narrow seat and stand up on the pedals in case I fall off, and the first vertical descent of the switchback, minus brakes because I can't get a grip on the levers, rattles my eyes out of their sockets and leaves me unable to focus for the rest of the day. There's no sign of Susie, who's riding her own bike to make it feel useful, and when eventually she comes into sight it's got a puncture, and she's pushing it. By the time we get back, Peter's looking at his watch and wanting to play golf, but Susie and I delay him further by having a minor panic because there's no web over Bessie's windscreen and we're worried the spider's fallen off. In fact she's sensibly decided it wasn't worth constructing one yesterday evening as it was too cold and windy for flies, and is tucked up in the overhang.

The trip to the golf course near Moulins is spent in heated discussion on the subject of Géri's rabbits. Susie and I have had a conducted tour of their sheds as they wait in their wire boxes, attentively listening to a CD of *Eine Kleine Nachtmusik*, for insemination or to be sent for slaughter. I can't say I'm keen on eating rabbit, although Clara's one-time pet named Killer was threatened with the chop several times for good reason, but Géri's are obviously clean and healthy, and he says there's a good market for them – the French are prepared to eat horses, so they're hardly going to have a crisis of conscience about little legs in stews. Susie thinks it's disgusting and reckons she'll end up a vegetarian, but when Peter indignantly joins in to ask who's going to speak up for the screaming sprouts, we decide it's time to change the subject. As I'm in dutiful-wife mode I walk meekly round the golf course, suppressing a giggle at Peter's frustration at the fairways, which are so full of puffballs sprouting out of the turf that he can't tell what's his magnificent 300-yard drive and what's fungus.

Freek wants to show us his population of non-productive animals – the exception is his roan Appaloosa mare, who unexpectedly gave birth to a black mule baby a few weeks ago. One of Freek's donkeys is the father, although he was assured when he bought them that they were all castrated, and I'm invited to double-check to see if, in my opinion, any of them has testicles – but the donkeys are discreetly keeping their distance, and it's impossible to tell. Anyway, Freek isn't displeased by events, as a good working mule is more valuable than a horse around here.

The cats have taken over Bessie again, sleeping comfortably on the boat cushions or begging for cheese, and supper outside at the campsite table is spent batting them out of our plates and pushing dribbling Labradors off our laps.

In the morning Freek accepts the 33 euros we owe him but returns eighteen of them as his contribution to the Hospices and, when we go to collect the horses, Géri, who's just finishing inseminating the rabbits, so to speak, refuses to accept any payment at all.

Susie's in the mood for churches, so we stop at Autry-Issards and I wait outside with the horses while she walks round. She persuades the owner of the café next door to stamp our pilgrim passports, and I don't know why we assume the stamp will have the church on it – of course it doesn't, and underneath the Vézelay stamp we now each have one with the name of the café in large letters and the words '*Bon Courage*'. At Souvigny we stop again so Susie can look around the enormous church there. We're on the first leg of our diversion from the main Vézelay route to a minor pilgrim trail through the Auvergne, and Souvigny was an important pilgrim centre with a Cluny monastery in the twelfth century. Apparently the church is filled with the tombs of dead Dukes of Bourbon and its organ is world famous, but there's not enough time to inspect it – we have no accommodation arranged for tonight, and umpteen miles to cover. Apollo's as curious as Susie about the church, peeping through the doorway and snuffling at the flagstones. He seems to be more amenable to religious education than I am, although the reality is that he probably thinks the church is a large and luxurious stable.

The horses settle into long comfortable strides that eat up the ground, and navigation's easy on the minor roads heading south. We home in on some fat Percherons, but their owner ignores our very heavy hint that he might like us to stay the night with him and directs us to a horse stud down the road at a place that sounds as though it's called Château Zero. There, the aristocratic owner looks completely stunned when I ask him whether we can all stay the night. He says it's a most unusual request, but having been put on the spot he can think of no obvious reason to refuse. Leo and Apollo can't be turned out because all his fields are occupied by his pure-bred beauties, but he has plenty of hay and we tell him they'll be perfectly happy with that in the enclosed sand manège. In fact they're both disgusted, having just spent two days scratching around in Géri's naked field, and they stamp round the perimeter in the dusk staring glumly at the thistles just out of reach, ignoring the coloratura nightingale singing soprano over their heads in the hedge.

The stallions at the stud start roaring for breakfast at 6 a.m. That's the end of sleep, and there's no sign of Monsieur Aristocrat, who I need to ask where we're supposed to put the crots from the cleaned-up manège. There's a commotion going on in the indoor arena, so perhaps there's someone in there. There is, but what on earth … strewth! It's a frothing stallion, enthusiastically humping the badly constructed back end of a headless plastic mare, while the groom holds what looks like one of Monsieur Aristocrat's waders underneath to catch the semen. She glares at me, and I disappear in case I cause a case of coitus interruptus – even the horses don't get to do it naturally any more, it seems. Such is technology.

Today's supposed to be a day of tracks, but the very first one is blocked after half a mile and we have to stick to the tarmac again, our disappointment tempered by the succession of mellow stone châteaux in varying states of disrepair at the roadside. From the back of a horse you get an excellent view into walled gardens and through mullioned windows, and Susie and I are away in fantasy land buying them up, restoring them and uprooting our grateful families to France.

The Romanesque church at Fleuriel, dedicated to St James, tempts me inside as well as Susie, but as always there's only time for a brief look before we have to focus on the problem of somewhere to stay. However, we're getting quite blasé about going into local Mairies and demanding to see the mayor, and when a farmer's unwise enough to wander into Fleuriel's town hall behind us, the helpful mayor tells him he's got us for the night.

Pierre is a Belgian widower whose wife died of cancer, I would guess recently, leaving him with two teenage daughters who are away at school. He invites us to use his house and bathroom as we wish; the house is spotlessly tidy and polished, and achingly filled with the presence of someone no longer there. Pierre farms a herd of black-and-white Holsteins and tiger-striped Normandy cows, and we fence off part of their field where the horses are in heaven: it has real rich grass and they scarcely bother with their dinner of concentrates. After a good roll, Apollo's head is thickly clothed in cowpats and we rug them both for the night, on the basis that it'll be quicker in the morning to wash a horse rug than a horse.

I'm busy looking at tomorrow's map, wary now because so many of the tracks are no longer open. We have to cross the river, the bubbling Bouble, and there's a footbridge I need to check.

It turns out to be made of wire mesh and it's far too narrow for horses, but the walk's worthwhile anyway in the luminous evening, and I'm accompanied by stout calves overcome by curiosity and a dignified stag beetle, three inches long, who's marshalling his legs for a trek uphill through the woods.

The riotous French spring is ripening into summer now, into gangling meadow grasses top heavy with flower-heads for haymaking. The countryside is changing again, the skyline today punctuated by the silhouettes of three volcanoes, and ahead of us in the distance are the long, long hills of the Auvergne.

12. THE DEMON GRIP OF VERTIGO

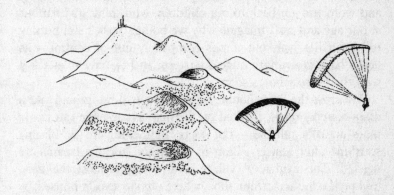

Are those volcanoes extinct or just dormant? Susie wonders if she can see smoke coming out of the highest, which we've worked out is the Puy de Dôme, but whatever else they are I know they're not active and it must be a wisp of cloud. At least I think so. I'm trying to keep Susie away from the Chaîne des Puys map which fills me with a surge of excitement but her with a surge of apprehension. We won't need it for a couple of days but, like the Vézelay map, it's three dimensional, and it's full of tightly packed contours and dramatic grey shading on the soaring sides of the volcanoes. There's a GR route that rides the ridges and teeters round the lips of the craters, but we certainly won't be going that way.

By morning Leo's managed to plaster his head and neck with gluey cow dung. He smells revolting. They're the only exposed bits of him and his rug of course is completely clean, but I can't face riding him like that all day so he endures a hot hairwash in the waste water left over from sluicing out Pierre's milking machine. He hasn't had to have a shower before, but Susie and I groom the horses thoroughly every day and oil their hooves.

The latter is more to do with common sense and an attempt to stop them cracking than keeping up appearances, thanks to Jason the blacksmith's very sound advice, but applying mascara to our eyelashes when we get up each morning is pure vanity and word has got back to our children, who think it's hilarious at our age and can't imagine why we bother. Susie's still putting rollers in her hair, but mine's completely out of control – its layers have grown into huge doorsteps, and I'll have to attack it with the horse scissors soon.

We cross the River Bouble by a sturdy road bridge and take a cross-country route, marked on the map as a double cart track, that's actually reliable – but we're all melting in the blazing sunshine after a steep climb to Charroux, and ice creams are needed. The mediaeval village is shuttered against the heat, except for the ice-cream shop where Apollo excels himself by dropping a steaming pile of crots outside the door, but the proprietor's wreathed in smiles – it's just what she needs for her geraniums. She waves away Susie's apologies and hands out Magnums, but I don't get much of a look in with mine because we bump into Peter, and he and Leo decide they deserve it more than I do.

A long grass path leads down the escarpment out of the village; you can see for miles in the clear air, and we watch Peter and Bessie below us snaking away across the glowing green plain towards Ebreuil, where we're booked into an equestrian centre for the night. There's a whisper of a breeze this side of the hill, a sun-soaked old château I would definitely like to buy, and more off-road tracks down to the tunnel under the motorway and the river Sioule, where Leo and Apollo pause in the ford to cool their ankles and drink the crystal water in leisurely gulps. It's a long time since Apollo freaked out at the thought of wading through water.

Rush hour in Ebreuil means there are at least twelve cars in the high street, and we squeeze the horses into a single parking space outside the Mairie while Susie goes inside to get our pilgrim passports stamped. The equestrian centre's down a rough road just out of town and its fields have been grazed bare by the school horses, so ours are crossly back on hay again. Susie's assiduously rubbing Vaseline every evening into Apollo's coat where his saddle has worn away the fur, and there's no broken skin; he remains enormously fat in spite of the recent lack of protein-rich grass, and he has meaty pads either side of his spine which is probably why the problem persists, but I have a feeling the lean days of Spain will sort him out. By the time we get to the high plains, the *mesetas*, it's going to be breathless boiling summer and green grass will be a distant dream.

Among the riding-school horses there's a leopard-spotted Appaloosa called Tigre who stands out from the rest, and I threaten to take him with us. It's only a joke, of course, but I have to eat my words when our host says he'll give him to us anyway. Despite his beauty and charisma, Tigre's unpredictable and he can't be turned out with other horses – at eleven years old he'd been a stallion all his life until last year, when he was gelded, and now the poor fellow doesn't know what he is, and fights with every horse that comes near him. Peter's full of horrified sympathy.

No-one lives on site but our host gives us the key to the Pony Club and disappears in his car. We sit outside with our supper and a plentiful supply of wine as the sun goes down and discuss the next few days, deciding to travel for five days and pause for two near Puy de Dôme – having persuaded Susie to come this way, which she suspects is against her better judgement, we might as well stop to explore. I'm just trying to avoid giving her the maps to look at when there's a timely diversion: a thin man walks towards us up the lane and after several minutes' conversation in French we discover he's English, he owns the campsite opposite and he's come to invite us to use his bath.

What a treat! A real, real hot bath in an old-fashioned Victorian tub on legs. Peter and I pile into it together, and whip up the last of the Badedas shower gel into a froth for flicking at each other like toddlers. Strolling back to Bessie afterwards, warm and relaxed, I get a terrible fright: as we walk under a dead tree at the campsite entrance, I realise there are six vultures roosting thirty feet up in its scarecrow branches, hunched silhouettes against the silver starry sky. Some more wine seems like a good idea.

Mr Campsite has offered to mend the puncture on Susie's bike, and when we wheel it over in the morning I realise the vultures in the tree are only peacocks. Susie props the bike up so awkwardly that it falls over, and Mrs Campsite tells her that she can see she doesn't know much about bikes. The well-meaning Mr Campsite doesn't seem to know a lot about bikes either – he spends considerable time and trouble locating an old inner tube, patching it and inserting it into the front wheel, and by the time Susie's wheeled the bike the fifty yards or so back to the equestrian centre the tyre's flat again.

Yesterday evening I carefully plotted a route on tracks through a river valley for today – or so I thought. But we come badly unstuck, rounding a corner to see, far below us, not the river and the shallow ford marked on the map but the intense blue of a very deep lake. It's very deep because it's dammed, and the only way round is over the top of the dam whose sheer side rises a 150 feet out of the water. Susie's off Apollo in seconds, walking on the inside so that he's between her and the edge of the track that skirts the lake. She's absolutely green, almost hyperventilating with fear. What now?

I can understand vertigo to some extent: when I have to go up *Jorrocks*'s mast sitting on a bo'sun's chair to sort out some tangle in the rigging, I have to be extremely careful to focus only on the problem and never to look down, but what Susie is experiencing is something else. Her legs look as though they're made of cotton wool, and I can't begin to imagine the turmoil going on in her head. We grind to a halt and I scour the map for an alternative route, but the shortest diversion is at least six miles, probably another two hours' slog in the heat. I point out a car driving over the dam, but Susie says she can't cross it. And that's that.

The horses stand quietly, waiting to see what we decide. Let's just go and look at it, Susie, a bit closer. It mightn't be so bad. It's obviously got a road over the top. I get off Leo and we all walk together with Susie jammed on the inside against the hill, creeping up to the end of the track to find the road beyond is metalled, though no wider than the swing bridge over Faversham Creek. From here I can see that the perpendicular drop falls even further to the river on the far side, and both sides are clearly visible through the low railings bordering the dam. But Susie's still moving forwards: her eyes are down, fixed on the road. She's going to do it.

I move in front and Leo follows me. Susie holds his tail with one hand and leads Apollo with the other, watching only Leo's heels as he slowly walks across. It's a 150 yards of resonant hoofbeats, and when we reach the other side she and I are both feeling faint, she with fright and me because I forgot to breathe; but the horses are completely calm until they spot some luscious bushes and drag us up the scrabbly track to get at them.

We're into the Parc des Volcans now and it's real hiking country over the hills, scrambling up cart tracks and slithering down the other side. The horses' front shoes are already starting to slew sideways, and the toes are wearing out because we're riding on pumice and it's literally filing down the metal. Peter's ahead of us at Chanteloup, but there's nowhere to stay there and we push on to Loubeyrat in the hot afternoon, tired and heady from the scent of new-mown hay and too much excitement. Leo and Apollo plunge their noses into a roadside horse trough and Peter already has his in a beer at the bar, chatting up the owner so successfully that her son and daughter-in-law volunteer to have us all to stay in the paddock behind their house. I spend the evening trying to hammer Leo's shoes on more tightly while he's rooted to the spot munching, and Susie unfortunately spends the evening studying the Chaîne des Puys map, which we'll need tomorrow: she's spotted the word Col and, after today's adventure, she simply doesn't believe me when I say it's not a mountain pass but the entrance to a valley.

The Chaîne des Puys is a north–south ribbon of about eighty volcanoes, roughly 25 miles long and two miles wide. The first eruptions date back seventy thousand years but the most recent only about seven thousand and, as there've been dormant phases in between lasting several thousand years, I hope it's realistic as well as more exciting to believe that these volcanoes are only sleeping and not extinct. Most have cones and craters, some have rounded domes and a few of the lower ones have cobalt blue lakes in them. The Puy de Dôme is the most striking on the skyline because, at almost five thousand feet, it's by far the highest and it has a double dome. Susie and I photograph it at intervals the next day as it looms closer and closer.

We have such an enchanted ride there's not much room for thoughts of vertigo, although I do modify our route to avoid the Col de la Nugère. We're climbing all the time, but it's a gentle ascent through clumps of violet and blue heartsease and spotted orchids, and on the way we find twelve herb Paris plants, each with its distinctive black berrylike flower in the middle of four broad leaves. We haven't seen herb Paris for forty years, not since our flower-hunting days near home in the sonorously named Spong woods, and we have a debate with our consciences as to whether we should pick just one and take it with us. Our consciences lose, and then we have a row over who's going to keep it, until Susie presses it decisively between the pages of her diary, and I never see it again. I'm back in my Youngest Sister rock-bottom position in the family pecking order.

Although we've deviated away from the Col de la Nugère, the Puy of the same name is still quite close. Its crater's filled by a solid lake of lava, and lava flowed into the Volvic valley below it periodically over thousands of years – the local water filters through it, accounting for its purity and popularity in every supermarket. We ride past sad little Volvic station, which is miles from the town, and an equally sad little train passes us, one engine, one carriage, with flaking pale blue paint and the fading initials SNCF. We're so close to the Puy de Dôme now that we can see the paragliders jumping off the top.

Back on the GR route, some bicyclists steam by unexpectedly, scaring Apollo who didn't hear them coming, but Susie and I take childish revenge as we canter effortlessly past them again on a steep uphill slope as they sweat along, all muscly legs and shiny shorts. Leo and Apollo rise to the occasion and show off madly, pricking their ears and noisily grinding their teeth in their eagerness to race, and we're so busy feeling superior that I miss the turning to the Pony Club at Orcines and we head straight up the Puy de Dôme.

Another track opens up to the left just as Susie realises we're on our way to the summit, leading us through a flock of long-legged Limousin sheep and straight across the golf course. We pause to let a player tee off at the tenth to a background accompaniment of equine snorts and farts, and then suddenly we're outside the club house in the middle of all the golf buggies. This can't be right – I'm thankful Peter's not here to have to disown us. The management are only too pleased to redirect us to the Pony Club whose organisers have kindly agreed to let the horses stay for three nights, and there they're installed in a buttercup field while we find a campsite close to the village. Clearing out the back of the lorry, there seem to be horse food crumbs everywhere, but when I count the bags they're diminishing at an alarming rate. No wonder Leo and Apollo still look like barrels on legs.

Exploration day means a trip up the Puy de Dôme for me, a good book on the grass at the bottom for vertiginous Susie and a game of golf for Peter. It's a three-mile trek up the Puy, and I chicken out of walking it and take the bus. The view from the top across the green velvet volcanoes marching north and south is staggering, but the main source of entertainment is neither them nor the windswept ruins of the temple to Mercury – it's the paragliders, accelerating uncontrollably on their paddling feet down the bank. They launch themselves into the air and instantly they're transformed into graceful birds soaring on the thermals, to raucous cheers and clapping from the spectators, many of whom have dragged their panting pugs and poodles up the hikers' route. When I get down to the bottom again Susie's looking marginally put out – a speedily descending paraglider has just missed landing on her head.

Our second rest day is one of fitful sunshine and sudden downpours, and we visit Clermont-Ferrand where the cathedral rises blackly out of the middle of a mound that's all that's left of the oldest of the volcanoes in the Chaîne des Puys. I'm reminded of the Houses of Parliament before they were cleaned up, but it turns out that this is the natural colour of the Volvic stone used to build the cathedral in the thirteenth century. It used to be prized as a building material, but now it's been demoted to the sculpting of suitably sober funeral monuments. We park Bessie behind the equally black Hôtel de Ville, and head off with a double load of washing to a *laverie* with the slowest machine in France. There's plenty of time to fill ourselves up with almond croissants and hot chocolate, and although there's an internet café nearby, I'm in too much of a fat catatonic trance to get round to sending an email to my employers.

By the time we get back to the Pony Club, the rain's hosing down, and we ponder the dilemma of Leo's and Apollo's worn out front shoes with the blacksmith while the thunder cracks overhead. We're sheltering in a shed and Apollo's so distracted by the noise that he forgets to be phobic about leather aprons and hammers. The horses were shod only twelve days ago and their feet were cut back further than they should have been by the student farriers, so they can't be trimmed any more, but if the same nail holes are used again on untrimmed feet, new shoes will work loose in days. The blacksmith solves the problem temporarily by leaving the old front shoes on but replacing just some of their standard nails with more substantial tungsten ones, hard-wearing and bright as bronze; the hind shoes aren't in such a bad state, and they'll just have to last a while longer.

There's still time for a visit to Vulcania, the underground volcano exhibition up the road from Orcines, which apparently is impressively full of fire and brimstone. Bessie laboriously chugs back up the hairpin bends, lurching to a stop when we spot a red rag by the side of the road. Susie thinks it's her knickers, and she's right – she left them on the lorry's indicator to dry, and they must have flown off when we drove to a restaurant for dinner last night. A querulous queue of motorists behind us has to wait while she jumps out to pick them up, and Peter idly wonders how she's going to explain away the tyre marks across them to John.

Vulcania's closed, and we point out to the departing ticket lady that it's only 4.20 p.m. and the brochure says it's open until six o'clock. It is, she says, but it takes two hours to go round, so they don't let anyone in after four o'clock. The brochure doesn't say that and, while she's shrugging her way through this conversation, another fourteen cars turn up and drive away again.

At the campsite a thick sun is glimmering through the humidity. I just have time to clear two hundred dead flies out of our pillowcases and turn the tacky mattress when round globules of rain start thumping down again, and as the lorry's only partly sheltered it's soon sputtering in through the seams. Storms rampage across the sky all evening in one long drumming tribal dance, but the Frenchmen camping next to us simply ignore the weather and carry on playing boules, rolling the metal balls along the sodden grass as the lightning jumps and sizzles in the power lines behind us. Peter refuses to rescue the bicycle, which is outside shuddering underneath an incandescent pylon, and at nightfall we turn off the electricity and huddle together by gaslight, listening to the eerie sound of the old wartime siren on top of the Mairie at Orcines wailing to the firemen to deal with the floods.

Susie and I make a mental list of all the metal items that clink along with us when we're riding: bits, buckles, stirrups, horseshoes. If it's doing this tomorrow we'll have to stay put.

13. SHOCKS AND SURPRISES

The volcanoes are sleekly subdued in the stillness after the storm. Or is it the stillness before the storm? I have a suspicion the sun's leering at us out of the brittle sky, but we're taking precautions – we're wearing the green crackly blousons and trousers donated by suppliers who told Susie they're completely waterproof. Well, she thinks that's what they said. On the strength of that information, we've left our Drizabone macs in the lorry with Peter, who's decided to visit Vulcania while we ride to a gîte at Montlosier, our next stop. As the Vulcania exhibition is somewhere in the bowels of the earth, there'll be no mobile signal and he'll be out of touch, but we only have about twelve miles to ride so it should be a short day. We're due for a trek through thick forest where there's a maze of GR paths and cart tracks, but it's also full of volcanoes, and finding a Susie-friendly route kept me awake half the night. As we skirt round the foot of the Puy de Dôme and into the trees, the sky slithers from blue to grey and a fine drizzle caresses the horses' haunches.

Susie, it looks a bit black over there.

Rolling thunder, hissing rain pounce on the Puy de Dôme, and instantly our lightweight suits are transformed into pea-green sieves. We go smash-crash-thrashing through the undergrowth, accelerating deeper into the woods, but the trees with their slappy wet leaves are no protection from the rain, although at least the lightning shouldn't find us here. The forest is so thick it's hard to see where we're going, but we make a snap decision to carry on: I don't fancy becoming target practice for a lightning bolt out in the open. The drenched map in my pocket is disintegrating and I have to guess which is the right cart track to follow.

Wrong. We're in deep tractor ruts when a flash flood comes hurtling down the track behind us. It catches up, overtakes, boiling over the horses' knees and hocks as they struggle to keep their balance. Hail hammers down, staining Leo's neck bright red as the colour leaches out of his headcollar rope, and the sheepskin over Susie's saddle turns green from her sodden suit, but it doesn't occur to the horses to say bugger this, let's go back. They stumble patiently on, ignoring the cracking thunder that makes Susie and me jump in our saddles with shock.

We pop out unexpectedly on the main road. We're in the wrong place, but we've missed the Col de Ceyssat, to Susie's relief – it's that dreaded word again. The storm's easing away behind us, taking its lightning with it, but now there's another problem: we meet a cloud rolling down the road, and it contains cars. All the yellow fluorescent browbands, tail guards and tabards are in the pockets of the Drizabones, and Leo becomes an invisible white horse in a white fog as we tuck into the right-hand verge. Apollo, with his black tail, is walking at the back. By the time we reach Laschamps, the rain's stopped, and we turn off on to the GR route again. Miles back, the Puy de Dôme is still wearing an angry black cloud on its head, its own private thunderstorm.

There's no point in stopping for lunch: we're soaked through, with no hope of drying out, and we just want to get to

Montlosier and out of these cloying wetsuits. In the afternoon, the thunder starts up again all around us but there's no lightning this time, and the horses remain completely blasé about the noise. The GR runs along the foot of the Puy de Lassolas and then the Puy de la Vache, each with a horseshoe-shaped crater open on one side where the lava flows burst out thousands of years ago and swept down the valley, and we stop briefly to photograph each other posing inside the horseshoes, my face invisible because the rain-gorged brim of my floppy Aussie hat has flopped to my chin.

The gîte's in an outbuilding of an elegant château which forms part of the Maison du Parc des Volcans, a study centre in extensive grounds. Susie and I can't wait to get rid of our clothes. The gîte is empty, its sitting room lined with long tables and benches for the absent students, and we home in on the cavernous fireplace, raiding the wood supply to build an inferno and cram our hats, shirts, gaiters and breeches on the mantelpiece in steaming heaps. My soaked skin's crinkled up and Susie's is an interesting colour from her suit, and when Peter arrives, fresh from an educational not to mention sheltered trip to Vulcania, he's surprised to be confronted by the unappetising sight of a wife as wrinkled as a Shar-Pei in wet knickers, and a nude green sister-in-law wrapped in a blanket in front of the fire.

We have no food. Peter's and my search for a supermarket in Bessie takes us on a round trip of forty miles, by which time I've warmed up again because the lorry heater is as fierce as dragon's breath. As we circle west we stumble across the little town of Orcival; unfortunately it's not on the route we need to follow on the horses, but Susie would love it. It has a Romanesque basilica dedicated to Notre-Dame right in the middle and, judging by the coaches parked in the square, it's a big pilgrimage destination. It doesn't have a supermarket, though, so we carry on to Rochefort-Montagne, which isn't nearly so pretty but at least has a large shop.

There's something missing from Bessie. I can't work out what it is until we get back to the gîte, when I walk round to the front of the lorry and realise there's no vestige of web on the windscreen. Susie and I search the overhang, but Bessie's spider has gone. We're ridiculously put out about it, and have to console ourselves with the belief that she hasn't dropped off on some rainy road, but simply decamped to a more desirable home at Orcines in a tree whose leaves were whispering along the lorry's roof. When Peter and I snuggle into our bed in Bessie, resigned to a rackety night as the storms start up again, I can see there's a spider spinning a fragile web across the window above the stove. But it's only a small and inferior French one.

Susie spends a creepy night alone in the gîte full of empty bunks, but we can't all afford to stay in it and, anyway, it has no double beds. She has my hot-water bottle but I don't need one; in the lorry I have a warm radiator of a husband. It requires a real effort to slide out of bed in the morning to face grey skies and heavy drizzle, and now the wind is getting up, moaning round the château, as Susie and I go in to speak to Eva who organises the equestrian *randonnées*.

Susie's in the all-pervading grip of apprehension about heights, drops, mountains and gorges. I'd been hoping we could stay with our minor pilgrim route south and then south-west via Aurillac and Rocamadour in the Dordogne, which we both want to visit, but it's out of the question: it's far too mountainous. We've agreed instead to travel south-west straight away to Mauriac, heading out of the side of the Parc des Volcans instead of the bottom of it, but even that's going to be problematic. We'll still have to cross a high plateau beyond the Lac de Guéry to get to the spa town of La Bourboule, and then pass uncomfortably close to the towering Monts Dore and the Puy de Sancy, the highest peak of all.

Eva, of course, knows this area extremely well and has good advice about the trails, but when she phones the owner of the gîte at the Lac de Guéry to find out what the weather's doing there, he tells her it's too dangerous to try to reach it today –

there are storms, fog on the road and the rain is *absolument énorme*. If we try to go on the roads rather than tracks, he says, the lorry will have to drive in front with its headlights on. Susie's speechless, and I'm racked with guilt at making her come this way instead of sticking to the gentle undulations of Limoges and Bordeaux. I can think of a carrot, though, and that's to go west via Orcival and its basilica after all. It's only ten miles on the winding but flat GR30. Well, it's comparatively flat, and it's better than sitting out the weather here, worrying.

We're firmly back in our Drizabones.

When the rain eases and the visibility clears, it's not entirely a blessing as it means Susie can search the horizon for precipices. There aren't any, although the track's a bit steep in places, but she reminds me of a spooky horse looking for trouble: she's sensitised and demoralised by vertigo, and it's far worse than either of us thought it would be. When we reach Orcival, though, her face lights up at the sight of the sturdy basilica, and we tie the horses to the lorry and go inside.

I'm confused by the layout – my newly acquired knowledge says we should come in through the narthex, but we don't: the entrance is in the south transept and the narthex is on our left. The original entrance through the heavy wooden St John's door, with its elaborate latch and hinges, is also on the south side. In fact the pilgrims have never been able to enter through the narthex because it's jammed against the hill at the western end, allowing the apse at the other to be exactly orientated to let the rising summer sun flood through the windows into the sanctuary. There's not much light on this grey day, but it's enough to see the figures that dominate the whole basilica: the carved Romanesque Virgin in Majesty with the child Christ sitting on her lap.

Christ has the face of an adult, which Susie tells me is because it's the Day of Judgment, and Mary radiates serenity, as her long arms with their big hands encircle the child protectively but do not touch him. The statue's carved from wood but plated in silver, the faces painted, restored some decades ago, and only in existence still because it was saved from the Revolution by someone who walled it up in a gallery in the narthex. The whole church is heavy with history, but as usual there's not enough time to find out more because we've nowhere to stay, and Peter and the horses are still waiting in the square.

There's nobody at the gîte up the road at La Croix, so Susie strides purposefully into the Mairie. The mayor obligingly whisks her off in his car to the only other gîte in the area; the owner isn't there either, but her son is, and the mayor tells him we shall all be staying until the weather clears. So that's arranged.

The son is very uncommunicative. Wordlessly, he opens the gate into a field on a precipitous hillside so we can turn the horses loose, and he points to the gîte perched beside it above the farmhouse. Kneeling on the icy stone hearth, I coax a small flame out of some brushwood, but the chimney's so cold it refuses to draw for half an hour, by which time the sitting room's filled with smoke and Susie's prudently gone back to the village to get her hair cut. I spread out all the maps on the long table, and pore over them with stinging eyes and a sinking heart as I delineate possible routes and alternative routes with a highlighter. There's no painless way out of the Auvergne for someone with crippling vertigo, and the Dordogne looks just as bad: high mountain passes are simply replaced by steep-sided gorges running for miles. And in the back of my mind I'm feeling uneasy for another reason – I didn't check the horse field properly to see where it went over the hill.

The horses have disappeared. I grumble into my boots and follow a track, catching sight of them on the other side of the hill trotting enthusiastically away from me and stopping at intervals to gaze down the valley, eyes wide with delight at all this space. The field's riddled with tiny terraces and sheep paths and bad-tempered brambles, becoming steeper and steeper, and after half a mile I've overtaken Leo and Apollo, but I still haven't reached the perimeter fence. A climb further up the slope to try to get a view is even more alarming: I'm scrambling over rocks, and suddenly I'm perched on the edge of a cliff. There's a sheer seventy-foot drop right in front of my nose. Shit!

Leo, Apollo, follow me, be good boys. Let's go back to the gate. Come on, it's dinner time. Yes, my pockets are full of oats. Yes, I'm lying.

What an idiot! Why didn't I check? I'm running back towards the gîte and luckily the horses think it would be fun to race me. We crash into a dip and simultaneously straight into a bog; its black mud sucks loudly at their thrashing legs and, as for me, I'm going to jump straight out of my boots in a minute. We lurch through, the horses now so unnerved that they do wait anxiously by the gate while Peter and I puff up and down the hill with the electric fence, reducing the pasture to a small safe corner. By the time we've finished, the rain's sheeting down the valley and everyone's drenched again.

Madame returns home, furious to find uninvited guests staying at her gîte, which is actually closed, as the mayor knows perfectly well, because her husband's been in hospital for the last ten days after a fall and he's broken several bones and has Parkinson's disease and we shall doubtless burn the gîte down with our fire, and the field is entirely unsuitable for horses. *That* is certainly true.

Even I am praying for a better day tomorrow, but in the morning it's still gloomily raining and when I try to check the *météo* on my mobile for the weather forecast there's no signal: we're in *un trou*, a hole, due to the hill behind us. By the time I've climbed to the top, I'm completely out of breath but at least the phone's showing signs of life, and a recorded voice says the weather will improve tomorrow. That's no good – Madame wants us out of here today. Still out of breath, I leave a pathetic-sounding message on the answerphone at La Croix explaining our dilemma: we can't stay where we are and we can't move on either. The valley is shrouded in fog.

Madame's just been persuaded to let us leave the horses in

their microscopic field, on the assurance that we shall take ourselves and our arsonist tendencies to some other billet in the village, when Monsieur Dabin at La Croix phones her: he's picked up my message, and we and the horses are invited to stay with his family. We don't even stop to saddle up, and Leo and Apollo tow us up the valley on the ends of their headcollar ropes, as eager to leave their ski-slope field as we are to remove them. Peter glances back at the farm in time to see Madame's monosyllabic son running clumsily after his dog, which has rounded up all the sheep and is disappearing with them over the horizon. Suddenly the hills are alive to the sound of swearing.

Madame Dabin is a picture of hospitality and her gîte pulsates with warmth, with comfortable old armchairs pulled up in front of a roaring fire and her dogs curled up on the hearth. It's the most welcoming place we've been in yet, or maybe it just seems like that after Cold Comfort Farm. We decide to hell with the expense, we'll all sleep indoors tonight.

Bessie rumbles up the twelve miles on the main road to Lac de Guéry on a dummy run, meeting only six cars on the way. The lake is a cold slate grey, reflecting the clouds. We're very high up but there don't appear to be any sudden drops. However, it's difficult to tell when the horizon's blurred by woolly fog, and I don't know if Susie's reassured or not. We carry on to La Bourboule and book the horses into the equestrian centre for tomorrow, and ourselves into a cheap and gently decaying hotel. The town has the Dordogne River rushing loudly through the middle of it and there are three spa centres, so Susie and I focus on a relaxing trip to the thermal baths tomorrow evening, although it's slightly disconcerting to find that arsenic seems to be the main constituent of the water. Next stop is a proper bicycle shop, where the proprietor mends the puncture for seven euros – and by the time we get back to Orcival, the tyre's flat again.

Monsieur Dabin has returned home. He's a squat flirty farrier and Madame Dabin is his third wife. He says his wives are getting younger all the time. He shows us his own horses, out in their electrically fenced field close to ours and, as I'm carrying a metal bucket full of water past it, my thigh accidentally brushes against the tape. Christ! The shock's appalling, a giant's clutching fist, shooting from thigh to hand to metal bucket as I reel backwards, water sploshing everywhere. Unfortunately, my other hand is stroking one of Monsieur Dabin's foals on the nose, and its eyes pop out of its head as it jumps off across the field like a squib. It'll probably never come near anyone again. Monsieur Dabin says yes, the fence is *très fort*. How *fort* is that? He proudly produces his voltmeter, which shows I absorbed 10,000 volts. Our own electric fence has just twelve flicking feebly through it. No wonder I nearly exploded.

Anyway, I've survived, but now I'm wondering how Susie and I will survive tomorrow, riding across the rooftop of the Auvergne.

14. MARCHING UP TO THE TOP OF THE HILL

My best day. Susie's worst.

The rain's washed the views clean, and we can see the Puy de Dôme to the north as we leave Orcival on a GR that runs along the valley floor. There are spiky pinnacles jutting high above us, buzzards on the thermals, and Susie's eyes are fixed on Leo's tail in front. She relaxes briefly when the rough track takes us through enclosed woodland but then we start to climb, picking our way past huge boulders that have fallen off the mountain, until we come out on the D80 road where hairpin bend after hairpin bend winds up to the Col de Guéry at four thousand feet. There's a drop to one side, partly hidden by Guéry Forest, but the pinnacles are suddenly beside us, sharks' teeth poking out of the trees. My cheerful chatter falls on deaf ears.

There's a viewing platform at the *col* where I daren't even suggest that we should pause so I can take a look, and we push on along a cart track that runs parallel to the Lac de Guéry, a shining plate below us reflecting icy blue today. The track runs straight for three miles across a wide empty plateau and the views open out spectacularly, the Puy Loup to our right and the

Puy May to our left and, far beyond that, the peaks of the Sancy range, streaked with snow. We're riding five thousand feet up with the cold wind blowing, and I'm filled with euphoria at the height, the space, the parade of mountains and my companion Leo who's sniffing the air with delight as we traverse the plain, moving dots under an infinite sky. But Susie hates it all. Paralysed by vertigo, she rides the whole way in tense and nervous silence, feeling ill. I ricochet between sympathy for her and frustration that I feel so guilty about enjoying myself I hardly dare stop to take a photograph.

There are other little dots ahead of us: disorientated cows scattering in different directions at an unco-ordinated gallop, their tails kinked. Their empty HGV transporters rattle past as we ride by the abandoned farm of Puy May, its derelict doors banging, and into the lee of the chunky peak at La Banne d'Ordanche. The wind drops abruptly. A fenced path leads gently down to the civilisation of a public car park, and we skirt round the first two people we've seen up here, dragging their low-slung dachshunds along by their leads.

La Bourboule lies far below, its tall buildings rubbing shoulders in the valley, a ski lift running up a swathe cut through the trees on the mountain behind it. On the map I've highlighted a convoluted trail to the equestrian centre that winds safely along the sides of hills, but sod it, I've just noticed there's a double cart track marked out that cuts out about five miles. Susie decides in favour of the short cut, but this one bisects the close contours and has all the vertical characteristics of a run-in to a ski jump, as we discover when it's too late to turn back. It's also stony and narrow, but Susie isn't worried – there are suffocating bushes crowding us, and she can hardly see a thing. Leo and Apollo never doubt our judgement, picking their way carefully down behind us and tobogganing where necessary. Cascading pebbles bombard the backs of my riding boots.

It looks as though there's some further tricky map reading to be done in the town, but we solve it quite simply by riding straight up the busy main street, where we get some strange looks but no-one tries to stop us. There's a pause at the tourist office to get our pilgrim passports stamped, another at our hotel where Leo breathes warmly on the proprietor's baby, and finally we clop into the equestrian centre. It's been another exhausting day.

Peter's day, on the other hand, has been stress free, spent perambulating twice round the nine-hole golf course thousands of feet up at Mont-Dore where the ball flies for miles in the thin air, and where he fully expected to meet Julie Andrews skipping down the fairway. There was no-one else playing, which meant he was able to stroll back to the luxurious empty clubhouse every three holes to watch England thrash Argentina in the football World Cup.

Treat for the day for Susie and me is our promised trip to the thermal baths. We present ourselves expectantly with our scraggy towels, and are turned away sympathetically but firmly by the staff. There's no idling the hours away in a blissful hot pool here because this is big business for the Americans and Australians – this is medicinal, not recreational, and unless I arrive with a referral letter from my doctor requesting a stream of gas up my nose, I'm not going to get through the door. We pad disconsolately back via the bicycle shop to complain about the flat tyre, but overnight the proprietor has shut up shop for ever and retired.

At the thin hotel, where Peter and I are staying while Susie sleeps in the lorry tonight outside the front door, Monsieur tells us that he's just bought the place and is doing it up. Certain things don't work yet, such as the power socket in our room which won't take my hairdryer plug, but I find an unearthed socket that does in an unlocked bedroom on the teetering top floor. It's a tiny servant's room pushed under the eaves that Monsieur probably hasn't even discovered yet; the iron bedstead's propped against the peeling brown wallpaper, and I can imagine generations of housemaid Juliets leaning out over the cracked paint of the windowsill to look down on their Romeos in the street far below.

My evening's spent working out two different routes to our next stop at Caux for Susie to consider. One goes straight up through the woods to the cross-country ski station behind La Bourboule before wandering through the high forest, close to the source of the Dordogne River and the ski lifts to the Puy de Sancy peaks, while the other is far lower and takes the winding metalled road to the west through La Tour d'Auvergne. Susie unhesitatingly chooses the ski-lift way. I'm stumped. Why? She says it's because there's less likely to be a drop to either side in the woods, and hopefully no view either. As I don't want to ride all day on the road, I'm certainly not complaining.

La Bourboule's pavements are glistening with rain by the time we go to bed; it carries on all night and all the next day. The path through the woods is slippery with mud, and it's me that gets the fright when Leo shies away from a noisy waterfall and hops close to the edge of the track. There's nothing to stop him falling thirty feet before he's buffered by the first line of trees, but I thump him uncharacteristically in the ribs with my heels and he leaps away again, while Susie's able to ignore the drop because she's keeping her eyes fixed on the ground straight ahead of her.

We're up at four thousand feet again but Susie doesn't seem to be bothered, partly because there's a dense curtain of trees on either side, but also perhaps because she knows this is our last day riding in the mountains of the Auvergne. Today would be a much better day for her than yesterday if it wasn't for the persistent downpour: we get colder and colder as we climb to the deserted ski station at La Stèle and begin the long descent towards Caux. We pass below the purpose-built resort at Chastreix-Sancy, drippily depressing as only an out-of-season ski resort can be, and beyond it the Puy de Sancy is jagged on the skyline, majestic even in the rain.

We're out on the road now on the south side of the mountains, and they're subsiding to rolling hills. By the time we reach the village of Chastreix, we're both shaking with cold. My expensive riding gloves are anything but waterproof, and when I try to warm my hands under Leo's thick mane against his fur coat, he too is wet through to the skin. We decide to call it a day at St-Donat, if we can find somewhere to stay, even though it's several miles short of Caux. Susie and I have a debate outside a farmhouse as to who's going to get off her horse and knock on the door, which on remounting is going to result in a soaked undercarriage from a rain-sodden sheepskin. Susie says that if she gets off, her legs are too short to get on again without a mounting block, so I lose. The farmer says he can't help us anyway, but his *frère le maire* can, and his brother's house is easy to find owing to a flagpole in the garden with two flags flapping limply, which announce that the mayor lives here.

He runs the campsite in the village, which is closed, but he says we may stay there as long as we clear up the crots and forbid our horses to eat his trees and hedges. We'd agree to anything by now, and in their new field, snakily fenced to avoid all trees and hedges, Leo and Apollo settle down in their warm rugs to some serious grazing, while the rest of us have the use of unlimited cold water and one working electric socket where I spend hours blasting hot air at my mac, hat, gloves and myself with the hairdryer.

A herd of cows splatters through the village, their owner hurrying home without his Charolais bull, which has stopped to eye us up before sauntering on in his own good time. St-Donat at the beginning of June is a ghost town, and you could make a good horror film here: most of the houses are shuttered, and the Providence Hotel is closed and up for sale, its horse-hitching rings rusting in the wall. By nightfall every building's in darkness, apart from the Mairie at the other end of town where there's a Fathers' Day knees-up going on. Through the orange square of window I can see a squeezy-box band and people making awkward gestures at each other, as though they're not used to socialising, and beside me a malamute husky on a long chain sighs softly from deep inside its kennel, ignoring my requests to come out so I can pat it. It's not into socialising, either.

We clear up every crot before we leave, and the mayor has no cause to complain; indeed, he applies the mayoral stamp to our pilgrim passports and writes 'Bravo!' beside each one, heavily underlined. The sun's struggling to come out, but it's not long before it gives up, and thin tendrils of cold trickle across my shoulders and round my ribs again as we wind round drizzly roads, with no warming up by trotting because it's all downhill. We leave Caux behind and wiggle slowly towards today's destination at Le Chambon, but first the River Rhue comes into sight, sunk in a gorge with a high stone bridge over it. Susie takes one look, and turns green again.

It's late afternoon on another grey day, and there's no point in tackling the bridge when she's tired. Peter drives off to a campsite this side of the river, where Susie and I find him trapped in the middle of a fan club of pygmy goats in shag-pile coats, clamouring at him on their hind legs, while their Dutch owner's happy for us to put up our fence round several empty pitches. Campsites are turning out to be good news: cheap, with running water and empty enough this early in the season for there to be plenty of space for Leo and Apollo – and it's far easier for us to turn up at a site on spec than to try to book ourselves into a gîte in advance. We have every *Gîtes de France* reference book that's been published, but most places insist on at least a month's notice if we want to stay, and they're not impressed by phone calls from scruffy English travellers on foreign horses threatening to arrive in six hours' time.

The horseshoes need replacing again. Leo's very patient with my attempts to persuade the nails to keep his shoes attached to his feet but it's a back-breaking job, not helped by him closing his eyes and leaning heavily on me every time I pick up a hoof. There are no blacksmiths in Monsieur's Yellow Pages, but there's an equestrian centre two days' ride away at Le Vigean, close to

Mauriac, where a doubtful-sounding lady thinks she may be able to accommodate us, and I decide not to push my luck at this stage by demanding a farrier and a vet for Apollo as well. Plotting a route there is a complete nightmare – the area's riddled with rivers that we shall have to cross, no doubt all running in gorges with high bridges over them like the one at Le Chambon we need to face tomorrow.

Leo has a tick on his stomach in the morning which refuses to be dislodged by my efforts with Dr Bompy's tick pincers, a dollop of surgical spirit and half a can of flyspray in quick succession. I'm preoccupied because we're running late, and light a match without thinking. It's lucky his coat is slightly damp with dew or the result would be instant roast horse, but the tick hangs on grimly for another four hours, despite being baked to a crisp. I'm sensing that Leo's not feeling 100 per cent at the moment: there's nothing specific except that he's losing his sparkle, but I certainly don't want to risk tick fever.

There are workmen on the Chambon Bridge mending the railings where it looks as though some suicidal motorist has taken a long plunge, but Susie has no opportunity to let her imagination dwell on it because they engage her in inquisitive conversation. She responds in polite French through gritted teeth and then we're over, round the next hairpin bend and off on a narrow muddy road that peters out to cart track through the middle of a fenceless farm, where the cows glance at us casually from their open-plan field and a lonely donkey threatens to join the pilgrimage, frightening Apollo with its twitchy outsize ears. It draws breath to bray, but shuts its mouth again when Susie threatens it with divine punishment.

The farmer's staring at us as though we've just rocketed in from Mars. Apart from the cattle, he has just one of each kind of farm animal: a feverish collie, an effortlessly flying chestnut chicken, a spotted pig that lurches out to watch us go by, and a horse half a mile away that he decides urgently needs feeding. He waits until we've passed before poking his crumbling Peugeot truck into life and roaring past us in a squirt of liquid mud and black smoke.

There are no straight roads for us today, and we have to loop and weave through every point on the compass. Leo's getting more dull, more unenthusiastic and, as we plod through Saignes, barely noting its little puy with a chapel on top, I sometimes wonder if we're ever going to leave the Auvergne behind. Peter's ahead of us investigating a campsite, but it's closed, which means another change of direction to Auzers, with a long haul up the final hill to the top of the escarpment where the village sits. Both horses have had enough. So have we, although Susie's worries are subsiding now we're not looking at mountains. The horses are parked in an overgrown garden, but Leo's not interested in the grass and I have to hand feed him his dinner to stop Apollo helping him out. Our own dinner at the local auberge looks suspiciously like offal, which Peter can't stand, but he pretends to believe Susie and me when we tell him it's a pork speciality of the region, cooked with nourishing cabbage.

When I check the horses at dusk, Apollo's enthusiastically trying to reach one of the garden fruit trees and Leo's at last nibbling at the grass. He stops to lean his tired head against me, my patient friend who's mutely asking for a rest. At any rate we should reach Le Vigean tomorrow, where doubtful Madame has now been persuaded to let the horses stay for two nights.

Bessie's parked alongside a stone wall with a drop the other side into a field. There's a katabatic wind howling through the lorry and down the wall, and it's freezing again. My brain's addled with fatigue, and all I can see are acres of IGN maps with minor roads wandering in the wrong direction. I'm worried: it's already 10 June and we're not making the distances we should, and there's no way we're going to be at the Spanish border by the end of the month. Navigation's becoming more and more difficult as I try to keep us on reasonably level land, away from the Dordogne River crashing down its gorges, but even without the problem of Susie's vertigo and the switchback trails, we would still be slow: the horses are tired and their shoes keep wearing out. We're going to have to take the most direct route to Cahors, whatever that may be. For the first time I'm feeling fed up, and I wish it would stop pissing with rain and the sun would come out.

Still, at any rate, Susie's sleeping in the auberge tonight, which means I can have a bath. This is my fourth one in two months. And life's so honed to simple pleasures that it's all it takes to cheer me up again: to savour the langorous slide in silky water, the warm cocoon; to lean back, close eyes, doze.

15. DISASTER ON A SUNSHINE ROAD

Grouchy French blokes are stomping into the auberge to watch France play in the World Cup on the deafening television – France hasn't won a single match yet, and to judge by the downturned mouths they're not expecting victory today. Susie and I depart for Le Vigan leaving Peter in a flood of black coffee and epithets in the bar.

Only thirteen miles to go today, our fifth consecutive day of riding. Leo's small spark of rekindled energy wears off and he's only marginally cheered by chocolate when Peter catches us up early on, France predictably having lost their game again, and hands out Mars Bars and Smarties through Bessie's window as he overtakes. At the equestrian centre, Madame Doubtful's now wearing a smile: a blacksmith and a vet are *pas de problème*, and are instantly arranged for tomorrow. The horses potter out into a big field with a sigh of relief, and Leo's far too tired to think of flirting with any of the bright-eyed occupants of the stables as he passes by.

The clouds are finally lifting, the forecast is sunshine, and we find a brilliant campsite with a lake, a beach, a luxury swimming pool and an internet café. I still can't get to grips with a French computer keyboard, though, which is a good enough excuse to avoid contacting my work to tell them I'll be at least a month late and probably six. There are other campers staying here and now we can add our own touch of authenticity: it's warm enough for Susie to sleep in the tent. She digs it out of the back of the lorry, upends it out of its bag, and looks at Peter. He looks speculatively back at her.

I think I'll just slide off now for a shower, taking the horse scissors so I can cut my hair and be gone a good long time. As I leave the scene, Peter's reading out the instructions to Susie and she's sitting on the grass in the middle of multiple sections of tent. In the shower block I manage the tricky job of layering the mirror image of my hair into a reasonable imitation of a thatched dovecote, which I think is a marked improvement, but when I get back to the lorry nobody notices. The tent's up, and Susie's on hands and knees inside it, arranging her large suitcase of clothes into a bedside table. Peter's immersed in his book, and I can't work out whether they're still speaking to each other or not.

The sun comes out for our day off, but this isn't an opportunity to laze on the beach or in the pool – instead it's a chance to heave all the bedclothes off to the *laverie* in Mauriac, where I spend a grubby ten minutes grovelling under the washing machine looking for my wrist compass, which has pinged off its strap and disappeared. I find it before panic sets in, and it's thumped back in place with superglue. I'm still trying to work out the best route to Cahors so that we can pick up the Chemin de St Jacques on the main Le Puy route, and to lose the compass would be a disaster.

On the way back to the campsite we call in at Le Vigean Church where there's a reliquary box of Thomas à Becket, all rich blue and gold paint and enamel. It depicts the assassins' horses patiently tied to a tree, oblivious of the savage killing, the brain flicked out of the shattered skull on the point of a sword, the smeared flagstones. Le Vigean seems an unlikely place to find a piece of someone I thought was safely lying in his entirety in a tomb in Canterbury Cathedral, but apparently his bones vanished from there in the sixteenth century. I can't think why such a box should be here and neither can Susie, but when she asks the otherwise chatty lady in charge why it's in Le Vigean, she just replies: because it is. And that's it. As it turns out, there are St Thomas reliquary boxes all over Europe, and he must have had at least forty fingers.

The weather's anxious to make up for its recent bad behaviour and, by the time we move on from the campsite, it's 35°C. An SOS to England for more horse food has resulted in a friend, who's travelling down this way, offering to bring some in his car. He's trying to track us down today, but contacting us by phone has proved to be near impossible. We seem to be permanently in *un trou* with no mobile signal, and it's hours before I manage to speak to him to arrange a rendezvous this evening in Pleaux.

There are no available tracks or even minor roads that we can take today – at least the main road's level and straight, but the sun blares down on the tarmac and both horses run out of steam early on. We sneak into the grounds of a château for lunch, and Susie and I collapse with our backs against the trunk of an oak tree while Leo and Apollo doze in its shade, too hot and tired to eat. At Pleaux, the mayor takes me off in his car to inspect a potentially suitable field, but there are three donkeys in it already, notorious for their horse-biting tendencies. But back in the main square, his friend Chassan is standing outside the only hotel in the town – he owns driving horses, and his mother owns the hotel. Our friend Chris is hastily booked in, and Chassan provides luxury accommodation for Leo and Apollo: sixty acres of pasture in the valley. It's at the end of a near vertical track and there's no question of getting Bessie there, so we lug all the electric fencing down to the bottom with water buckets and horse food, and pant back up to the top again on foot – we're not going to make the mistake of leaving the horses loose in a field *sans frontières* again. Peter's starting to count the number of times he pulls the still-punctured bicycle out of the lorry along with the electric fence, puts them all back in the morning and heaves them out again in the evening.

Chris is here with the horse food, ready to be entertained over supper with our tales of adventure. It seems very strange to be talking English to an outsider. When I'm asleep I dream in French all the time these days, holding nocturnal conversations about heavy-duty batteries and clearing up crots. Nothing too metaphysical. We have the distinct impression from Chris that many of our friends are surprised we've made it as far as we have, but it's disconcerting to think that it's taken us over two months to get to Mauriac, when it's taken Chris just a day in his car. Susie's best friend Jill is due to join us for a few days soon, and she'll probably arrive in a matter of minutes as her husband Michael will be flying her out in his aeroplane – I can't say I've noticed a single airfield so far, but no doubt there's one somewhere. Chris is asked to give Jill an urgent plea for more books – Peter's finished all his, and he's also run out of golf courses.

Leo spends the night crunching chunks out of his salt lick, and when we leave Pleaux he's more cheerful, so maybe a salt deficiency has been compounding his lack of energy. The map shows an inviting track that runs alongside the main road down to the river, bypassing the hairpin bends, but in reality it ends in a bog and we rejoin the road in time to catch all the bends snaking down the side of the gorge on a surface like a skating rink. The river slips smoothly along under the bridge to flow into the Dordogne to the west, and I have more success with the track up the other side of the ravine, which cuts out the reciprocal set of bends, although the ascent leaves us all sweating. It's 35°C again, a rise of more than 20° in three days. Now there are miles and miles of D2 wiggling round the contours, according to the map, but the road signs indicated on it turn out to be perplexingly absent, and the road itself is straight. It takes me two hours to realise that we're on a new road, built since the map was published.

There's another inherent difference between Susie and me bubbling to the surface, and it's me that's complaining: we've been riding for five hours in boiling heat and Leo and I are dripping, and want to stop. Susie wants to go on – she's better suited to the heat than I am, despite my shady hat; my brain's frying and it's difficult to concentrate on navigation. We keep going for another two and a half miles, but it takes nearly an hour and I'm full of menopausal mutterings of discontent. I'll have to get used to it, though – it'll be hotter still in Spain. But finally we grind to a stop in the tiny village of Montvert where the Mairie, complete with a gîte on the top floor, is decidedly shut.

My phone rings.

'Mu … u … um …'

It's my daughter. She sounds in a terrible state.

'Clara! What on earth's the matter?'

Loud sobs pour out of the phone. 'I got my results …'

Oh dear.

'And?'

'*I got a first!*'

Good grief!

'That's fantastic! Why on earth are you crying?'

'I can't believe it. I wasn't expecting it … I looked at the 2.1 list and the 2.2 list and I couldn't see my name, and I thought … I thought –' sound of daughter being suffocatingly bear-hugged by her friends in the background '– I thought I must have failed.'

I'm off the startled Leo, dancing on the road, heat and fatigue forgotten, shouting the news to Peter, Susie, the absent mayor and all the village.

Clara interjects. 'You will be back for my graduation?'

Swift calculation. Graduation day is on 10 July. We'll be nowhere near Santiago, let alone home again. We probably won't even have reached Spain. 'We'll be there. We'll fly back. I promise.'

The mayor's a farmer, two farms back in the direction from where we've come, so Peter and I abandon Susie by the side of the road with both horses, and drive there in Bessie. The mayor's out making hay, but his hospitable sister invites us in for a cold drink and we consume her entire supply of orange juice from the fridge, too overwhelmingly thirsty to be polite. She isn't sure whether the horses can stay at the farm or if we can stay in the gîte; she'd like to help us, but the decision is her brother's. Every mayor we've approached so far has been utterly helpful, but today I have a rude shock – my efforts to charm this one are spectacularly unsuccessful.

He says it's all too difficult. He doesn't know where he's put the key to the gîte; he has no pasture on his farm, not even a corner where we could park the horses; water is a big problem – and so on. He's completely unimpressed by my account of a pilgrimage for charity. His sister meanwhile is coming to the boil: she shouts at him furiously, he shouts back and an ugly family row develops. It's difficult to sound dignified at full volume above all the noise, but eventually I manage to get through with an apology for interrupting his haymaking, and an assurance that I shan't derange him further: we shall try another farm.

The mayor stops abruptly. Suddenly it's no problem at all. He whisks me back down the road in his car to the Mairie and, miraculously, the key to the gîte is found. It's a beautiful apartment with three bedrooms and we may stay there, but of course! – for free. He owns another farm right opposite, with a field knee-deep in grass and buttercups, and he shows me the water tap by a deep dark stable the horses may use if they want to keep cool. I thank him profusely, at the same time noticing out of the corner of my eye that the black-bearded tenant of this farm is walking away up the road to talk to Peter and Susie. Later, they tell me the tenant used an expression they didn't understand, but the dictionary translates it graphically. The mayor's a brute.

The horses are streaked black with grease and sweat and, as we sponge them down and turn them out, Susie notices that

Apollo's back is threatening to be sore after the long hot ride. Tomorrow we must, must leave early, cover as many miles as possible and stop before the stifling afternoon heat annihilates us. We drive into Laroquebrou to buy some more maps, as we're moving on into Cantal on a different route from the one we'd planned. The town is particularly pretty, the houses roofed with the curving stone tiles typical of this region, and there's a château perched on a rock on the River Cère where we shall cross tomorrow. This river flows through dramatic gorges on its way to the Dordogne, and I fervently hope they're far to the west of us. As it is, our drive back to Montvert on the road we'll ride along tomorrow proves to be a mistake – there's a drop to one side down to the river and an ominous crash barrier, which triggers Susie into vertigo and a decision that she'll have to walk the whole four miles on her own feet.

It's too beautiful an evening for apprehension, though; as the sun sets and the heat fades, the sweet smell of cut hay drifts in the air. An elderly madame in the tiny field below the apartment shoos her five hens into their house, and scrapes up her minute hay crop with a wooden rake. The view from the sitting room window is of misty hills rolling away to east and west, and I could stay here for a week.

But we're away before nine o'clock in the relative coolness of the morning, crossing the main N120 on to a grassy track over the hill towards Laroquebrou. When we come out on the road above the river, true to her word, Susie dismounts and leads Apollo slowly all the way to the town. As we walk round the final corner, the château on its rock comes into sight, a fairy castle this morning, ringed by the mist rising off the somnolent water.

We're climbing again as the day heats up. My temper's also heating up as I attempt to contact the bank in England on my mobile – our Santiago account is refusing to cough out any money, although John's checked and there's more than £2500 in it. The call-centre lady is completely nonplussed by my failure to co-operate with her questions.

'Please could you put me through to the Canterbury branch?'

'May I have your account number, please?'

I don't have it. I describe the account and, after a long silence, I get the impression she's found it. But she won't tell me anything.

'I need some proof of your identity, madam. The last movement in the account, or details of a household bill you've paid would be sufficient.'

'I don't know. I'm not in England, I'm riding a horse in France. I haven't paid any household bills out of this account. I'm not living in a house.'

'Well, I'm afraid I can't access your account for you if you aren't able to tell me about a recent bill you've paid: electricity, gas, something like that will do.'

'*I'm not living in a house*! I'm living in a lorry. We use camping gas.'

There's a further long pause while she digests this information. I can hear the money draining out of my pay-as-you-go phone at £3.50 per minute.

'I'm sorry. I can't give you any information if you're not able to tell me what was the last bill paid out of this account.'

'Well, could you transfer me to the Canterbury branch, please? They'll be able to help.'

'I'm afraid I can't do that without the account number.'

Blandishments, then threats. Eventually she agrees to ask the Canterbury branch to contact me, and when the manager phones she's all apologies. She doesn't know why the account is blocked, but the administrative equivalent of Dyno-Rod is applied to clear it. I'd be tempted to keep her talking for a good long time at the bank's expense, but it's also costing me £1.50 per minute just to receive the call.

We trudge on towards Sousceyrac. It gets hotter and hotter on the unending new sticky tarmac, and there are no tracks, no trees, no shade. I don't think we're going to get there today; Susie reckons it's only another four miles, but it seems a long way to me, when we've already covered eighteen miles and the temperature's hovering round 35°C again. It's two o'clock and the sensible French are kipping indoors. We pull into the verge so I can scour the map for a track, anything other than this baking road, and listless Leo puts his head down to snuffle at a blade of tired grass. Well, there aren't any tracks, so we'll just have to carry on as we are. But when I ask Leo to move on again he pulls his head up sharply, and suddenly he's sinking, buckling at the knees as Susie shouts needlessly at me to get off, and in slow motion I pull my feet out of the stirrups and step off him as he collapses in the road, rolls on his side and is still. Anguish, horror, guilt stab through my head.

I have killed my horse.

16. EYES AS BIG AS DINNER PLATES

'Leo! Get up at once!'

I must sound shrill, scolding him in panic for dropping dead. But his ears twitch guiltily and he sits up like a dog, gazes benignly down the road and scrambles to his feet. He hasn't a clue what's happened. Susie and I haven't either – we've never heard of a horse fainting. He has a graze on his shoulder, there's a scratch on the saddle, but he's checking my pocket for chocolate. I'm absolutely faint with shock myself, but Leo seems to be fine, and I can only think that, hot and tired, the sudden flinging up of his head had the same effect as a person springing up from a crouching position: the blood gets left behind. We used to experiment, as children, to see which of us would keel over first.

I'm cross and snappy with fright. We're not going any further today. I stay on the ground, just in case he passes out again, and we walk to the nearest farm – I don't care whose it is, we're going to stay there. We ask a sunburnt boy of about fourteen who's dextrously manoeuvring a monster tractor and trailer round a hayfield; I think he says it isn't a problem, but he speaks with such resonantly rolling Rs that I can't understand him. I catch the word '*patrrrrrron*', said with a smile, and we perch on the fence to wait for the farmer to come home. I'm just starting to relax when the sound of low-flying aircraft heralds something the size of a small helicopter homing in on me. It's a stag beetle lumbering vertically through the air, its wing cases paddling desperately, and needless to say it chooses my leg for a crash landing. I'm still trying to remove its six sticky feet off my shorts one by one and transfer it to the gatepost when *le patron* appears. He pats Leo sympathetically and shows us a little clover-carpeted yard for the horses that's full of farm machinery and Muscovy ducks. We have some electrolytes with us, evil-smelling golden liquid to be added to the drinking water, but neither horse will drink anything until it's poured away and the plain stuff substituted, when each gratefully consumes several gallons and turns his attention back to the greenery. So much for sophisticated and expensive equine nutritional care: they'd rather have their solid lump of rock salt, bought for a couple of euros.

The municipal campsite in Sousceyrac is closed, although the gates are open, and there's no-one to object if we stay. I'm still jumpy after today's mishap, and tired enough to be disproportionately put out when I find that three of our six teaspoons are missing – someone (not me, of course) must have been throwing them out with the washing-up water. And we could all do with a shower, but they're locked. There's abundant hot water for washing clothes, though, and I find I can just fit nicely into one of the stone butler's sinks outside for a bubble bath. It seems advisable to wait for darkness to fall before climbing in but Susie, the rat, who's had quite enough of me today, appears with her flash camera just as I'm trying to recline with my chin on my knees. In the resulting photograph I'm wearing a bubbly soap coat and look completely unhinged.

Apparently this is now the hottest part of France, having been the coldest last week. We have a tacky night in Bessie, whose wooden planks hold the day's heat long after dusk; noisy, too, thanks to the squadrons of bullfrogs in the campsite pond, but Leo's quite restored by morning even though it promises to be another boiling day. The young boy, Fabien, comes to say *au revoirrrr* and to direct us down a footpath to Sousceyrac; later we see him bicycling into the village with his sister's guinea pigs tucked under his arm, the haymaking done for this year.

Leo strides along all morning unperturbed by the escalating temperature, and by early afternoon we're in a hamlet on top of a hill where there's a tiny zephyr of a breeze. It's a good place to spend our rest day tomorrow, when Jill and Michael are flying out to join us, and Peter's found a little hotel here with a horse trailer in the car park, from which he's correctly deduced that *le patron* must have a field for his children's ponies. According to our host it's going to be 40°C tomorrow, but no problem – the hotel has a cool blue swimming pool.

It's Peter's and my turn for the hotel, and Susie's to sleep in Bessie in the public car park, and she's woken up early by a crocodile of rackety children and the realisation that she's next to the primary school. The headmaster persuades us to give a talk to the pupils on mediaeval history in general and the pilgrimage in particular, all in French, of course, which calls for some imaginative guesswork on obscure words. The children don't seem to be paying much attention. Susie and I are sympathetic: a history lesson outside in the searing heat is probably not their idea of fun. But that's not the reason – we realise that all the little girls' fingers are pointing at the horses, and all the little boys are purple with embarrassment. Leo and Apollo, snoozing quietly behind us in the sunshine, have their willies hanging out impressively at full stretch. The lesson's hastily moved to the school steps.

Peter finally gets round to putting up a shelf in the lorry for the stereo. It runs off a twelve-volt jack plug, but when we load it with some heroic Beethoven it's not running at all. I lug the whole lot to the garage, and some fiddly work is done by an obliging mechanic, involving split wires and insulating tape, but it's no good: it needs another plug, probably impossible to obtain in France. So much for our balmy evenings of music. I can't find the missing teaspoons, either, despite turning out the whole lorry, and having run out of things to do I really have no alternative but to join Susie at the swimming pool with a book. An hour's pure relaxation for the first time leaves me feeling very guilty. I'm sure I should be doing something.

Michael and Jill arrive by taxi from an airfield fifteen miles away, in time for an enormous hotel dinner featuring lamb and haricot beans squelching with garlic. Oceans of red wine later, Peter digs out his bottle of Irish poteen from Bessie's lockers – a bottle that was mouldering in the kitchen cupboard at home for several years. It's ferocious stuff, as powerful as the bleach bottle next to it and probably just as effective at cleaning the sink. Peter catches the warning glint in my eye and decides to try it out on *le patron* instead and, after a generous wineglass full, our host is to be seen taking himself off down the corridor to bed, walking in a straight line with great dignity and care.

The horses are dismayed when I go and catch them at 6.30 a.m., but Susie and I are away in the early morning before the heat rolls in again. The others are still asleep, but *le patron's* here to say goodbye, his face sweatily pale as he assures us they've all been delighted we could stay. We make excellent time to Le Bourg where we've arranged to meet the others, but they don't appear in Bessie for another hour and a half, by which time we're asleep on a bench outside the church while Leo and Apollo keep trying to go inside with the tourists.

Susie's bike is having a rare moment of fully inflated tyres, and now the procession consists of two horses, one bike and four people. Back at home, Michael's the skipper of his own classic yacht and a vastly more experienced sailor than me; I'd like to impress him with my navigational skills with today's IGN map, but no chance – I manage a wrong turn within a mile of leaving Le Bourg, and we have to backtrack almost into the village again.

But Leo's a diversionary tactic, and the two of them go trotting off happily together while I wobble along precariously on the bicycle. Michael's obviously used to riding and Jill, who isn't, is being carefully nannied by Apollo while Susie walks beside her.

We fall foul of the map again, thanks to a new road still under construction. The trail narrows, reduced to loose rocks thrown up by the diggers, and comes to a dead end thirty feet up on a shaky embankment. There's barely room to turn the horses round to backtrack once again, and by the time we reach Livernon we've been travelling for nearly eight hours and everyone's half-cooked, including the chicken for supper which has gone disgustingly off. Michael soars away in his aeroplane back to England, where he'll probably arrive in less than an hour, leaving the elegant Jill to rough it with the rest of us.

Humidity pours out of a suffocating sky the next day. There are only two more maps to cross before we reach Cahors and get on to the main Chemin again, but the way there isn't easy – we can go on the road or cut across country (I think), but the track marked is a single black wavering line, and I'm not convinced it even exists. Jill's in for a lurching day in Bessie, and Susie and I, drenched in sweat within half an hour, stop at a house to ask for directions. There's a cherry tree hanging its branches over the garden wall beside us and it's all lascivious temptation, bulging with shiny black fruit; we haven't a hope of resisting but the owner appears from nowhere, grabs handfuls and presents them to us. He pretends not to notice our transparently guilty expressions as he assures us that yes, there's a well-marked path over the hill to the village of Clavel. No need to go round by the road at all.

He's wrong. After several miles the straight cart track fades to grass, to stones and finally to bare rock. It's too far to go all the way back, and impossible to go on. We're on the perimeter of some long-dead estate, and Susie stays with the horses while I go off to explore on foot, keeping within earshot in case I come face to face with a *sanglier*, a wild boar, which no doubt will be female, protecting its piglets, all bristling tusks and mad yellow eyes, and much faster than me. But there's nothing but scrub and deer tracks, though when I crash back through the undergrowth Susie's craning her neck in alarm in case I've metamorphosed into a pig, and there's nothing for it but to lead the horses back roughly the way we came, through thickets of saddle-scoring thorns. The map shows a cobweb of black tracks through the woods apparently leading nowhere, and Susie's so unnerved by now that she just wants to hit the road somewhere, never mind where – but by the time we've taken a circuitous tarmac route to Clavel, where Peter and Jill are patiently waiting with Bessie, we've ridden thirteen miles to achieve eight.

Peter and I drive off to try to find somewhere to stay tonight. At the next village there's a statue of an uncomfortable Christ with a throbbing swarm of bees attached to His loincloth, a church that's dedicated to St James and a field that belongs to Christophe who isn't around but who would be delighted to lend it to the horses, according to his neighbours. I'm not so sure – it looks like an uncut hay field to me. Enquiries are made: Christophe is tracked down and indeed the hay is reserved, already sold, and Leo and Apollo are about to deprive him of a large chunk of his income. The villagers are *désolés*, and we're despatched to the mayor of another village that's so far off our route we might as well go back to Clavel and call it a day.

Susie and Jill have been observed by the only farmer at Clavel, and we're glad to accept his offer of a cut hay field, and an empty cowshed where there's a cold-water tap. There's a storm coming, and we run the fencing tape from harrows to plough to cowshed wall under a flat bronze sky. Monsieur and Madame invite us to their house for ratafia and home-made terrine, and offer us their walk-in wardrobe fridge where we're welcome to store the contents of Frigo and so save the battery. Frigo has only a small piece of cheese in it at the moment, which is excuse enough to decline this offer – we've noticed the meat hooks hanging from the ceiling, and the black bloodstains ingrained in the floor, which Monsieur assures us come from last season's slaughtered deer.

So it's cheese and salad in the cavernous cowshed, where electricity's provided by the lightning's blinding illuminations every few minutes. Susie and Jill dive through the curtain of rain and into their tent for the night, zipping it up at speed behind them, and I have a strobe light strip wash in a bucket of cold water in the shed before joining Peter in Bessie for the final entertainment of the evening: a competition to see who can pick up the greatest number of thunderflies crawling over our duvet, and fling them out of the door to drown.

Not far to Cahors now, but it's still not straightforward – the area's laced with rivers, and there's no Susie-friendly route. We have to turn south on a precipitous road that mirrors the convolutions of the River Vers far below us in a gorge, hugging the edge of the chasm, and Susie dismounts in dread and leads Apollo while I ride Leo slowly in front. But Jill, who's survived a torrential night in the tent with equanimity, comes into her own on the bike. Peter's waiting at the bottom of the hill, and he's treated to the sight of Susie's now far from elegant but exhilarated friend flying past with her tangled hair streaming out behind her, her eyes as big as dinner plates.

Susie's wobbling on jelly legs by the time we get down the hill, and a short stretch on the busy main road leaves her even more jittery. There's a proper horse route signposted beside the Vers, now slipping quietly along at the same level as us, but it's not marked on my map and I'm in trouble for painstakingly double-checking that it's where we want to go. Then Apollo's in trouble for jumping out of his skin when some horses come galloping up in their field behind us. We follow the horse trail anyway, a stumbling stony track through the woods where I can't see the water, but the town of Vers itself is bustling, cheerful and has an immaculate campsite at the junction of its river with the much wider Lot, flowing peacefully to Cahors.

This is our first experience of a campsite that's busy, but it's not full of tents – it's full of polished caravans, plastic tables, little gas barbecues and gin palaces bobbing in the marina on the river. Leo and Apollo are amazed at the boats, and the occupants of the caravans in their ironed shorts and snow-white trainers are amazed to see equine campers, not to mention a muddy horsebox and one man with three women. We take in two pitches with the electric fence and turn the horses loose, and when Leo releases two gallons of urine and an overpowering smell of ammonia with a sigh of relief, the affronted German next door tells us he hates horses, and our electricity is interfering with his radio.

After a scratchy afternoon, Susie and I are in no mood to be placatory. We're tempted to shove him into our fence, but settle for telling him it's just as well we like dogs, as he has something the size of a small rat yapping hysterically on the end of its lead. Our sarcasm goes unnoticed. A little later Herr German starts making friendly overtures, offering sugar to the horses – he's had time to report us to Monsieur Health and Safety, who arrives at a canter to tell us we must move them to the other side of the river. They are *pas sanitaire*. We argue in vain that horse crots are a lot more *sanitaire* than Herr German's dog's turds.

The diplomatic Jill treats us all to dinner in the town, and in the morning she leaves to catch a train back to England. Her taxi driver is full of good advice about the little roads south of the Lot, which he says are no good for horses: they're single track, they wind dangerously over steep hills, and we shall undoubtedly meet cars on blind bends. So there's no real choice but to take a deep breath, join the D653 main road we couldn't wait to leave yesterday and plod doggedly along with the HGVs and assorted speeding traffic for the whole ten miles to Cahors.

17. THE DONKEY FROM HELL

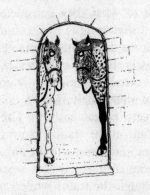

The Devil dropped in to Cahors several centuries ago and made a pact with the architect of the mediaeval Valentré Bridge, who was fed up that it was taking so long to build. He promised his soul to Satan in return for his help, and then panicked when the bridge, with its six massive arches, was almost complete and he was going to have to honour the bargain. But he came up with a plan to cheat the Devil, who must have been remarkably thick because when the architect asked him to fetch water to mix the last of the mortar, he didn't notice he'd been handed a sieve. Not surprisingly, the job couldn't be done, but in revenge he tore out the final loose stone in the last of the three fortified towers each night after the masons had gone home, so the bridge was never quite finished. When it was restored in the nineteenth century, a little stone Devil was sculpted and perched in the niche where the stone should have been, and it clings there still.

The Valentré Bridge is out of bounds to horses, and Susie and I are eyeing the other bridges as we ride into Cahors. Having taken the main road from Vers, we have no choice but to ride right into the city itself, where it hugs a tongue of land caught in a coil of the Lot, which we need to cross. The traffic's solid, slowing to a crawl up to a set of lights that appear to be permanently on red. It hasn't been an easy ride on the frenetic major road and Leo and Apollo, hungry after their ejection from the Vers campsite to what they considered was very inferior pasture, have been shying quite unnecessarily most of the way. Leo's found numerous dangerous stones at the side of the road that might suddenly fling themselves at him, and Apollo's pretended to be scared witless by a succession of pint-sized squeaky dogs that were safely behind their garden gates. We arrive at the largest roundabout in Cahors, which has an enthusiastic fountain in the middle throwing water at passing cars – and horses. Freaking out at this unexpected power shower, Leo prances over the bridge beyond it at top speed, lacing his way through the traffic while I manage to catch one wing mirror after another with my stirrup irons. Susie's left panting along behind, led by Apollo, and we only manage to pull up by diverting into the municipal car park on the other side.

There's a broad band of grass among the parked cars. Saddles off, the horses throw themselves ecstatically on the ground for a voluptuously wriggly, back-scratching roll, watched by a young girl from an attic window in one of the tall houses lining the river, who comes downstairs with a pink bucket full of water. While Leo and Apollo are squabbling over who's going to have a drink first, I check the map and find that, through pure luck and no good judgement on my part, we're smack on the GR65, the Chemin de St Jacques from Le Puy. In fact, now I come to look around me, there are two pilgrims on the zebra crossing next to us, recognisable by their huge sandals. These are the first we've seen since Vézelay, and instantly we're refocused, re-energised, and I've suddenly acclimatised to the searing heat of the last two weeks.

The Chemin runs alongside the Lot, and we pass the lofty Valentré Bridge and then the sacred spring that the original town of Cahors was built around, the Fontaine des Chartreux, where maybe the Devil was once to be seen trying to fill his sieve. There's a tiny bridge here, barely wide enough to take a horse, and the water is darkly, eerily green.

Susie consults her French guide to the Chemin, and it's completely different from my IGN map; we seem to be caught in a network of lanes, but the Chemin turns up on a flint track that leads to the village of La Rozière, with its church and cemetery jostling on a hill. The horses are sweaty and thirsty again, and so are we. Several insouciant Frenchmen, setting up the village hall for a party that evening, unwisely instigate a conversation by offering us water, and they're immediately asked if any of them would like to have us all to stay for two nights. An unshaven Monsieur with gold teeth and a deep suntan says we can use his field, his outbuildings, his cold tap and the driveway to his house close by at Bessières. He's sure his wife won't mind. He himself has to attend a dinner at his hunting club this evening because today is Midsummer Day, 21 June, and tonight there's a celebration all over France: the glorious Fête de la Musique.

The horse field's at the bottom of a long slippery bank where buckets of water have to be carted from Monsieur's tap on his house wall. Cooling off in the breeze on a hilltop afterwards, I come across a gîte. There's an elderly Dutch couple staying in it who see me pausing by the gate in curiosity: I must look as though I've reached meltdown, because when I explain why we're here they offer us all the use of their shower. They're in their late seventies and they come to this remote place every year, she to paint and he to read. The house is tranquil, full of deep rooms, the bathroom window opening on to a far view across the valley to green summer woods; paintbrushes crowd the dining room table, and the faint sound of Gregorian chant threads through the house.

The couple are playing Scrabble together, using an old set with wooden letters, and instantly I'm transported back to my childhood again when, as a family, we played with just such a set on winter evenings, cooking ourselves over the open fire before the scamper to bed up the arctic stairs and into icy sheets. My father still has the set buried somewhere in the house but my mother, removed by Alzheimer's, will never be able to play Scrabble with him again.

Supper's late, eaten outside in the wine-dark night. Madame's daughter brings us redcurrants and raspberries from the garden, and an invitation to drive with them into Cahors for the Midsummer Night celebrations since Monsieur's out getting pissed at his hunting club dinner.

We park on the perimeter of the city, where the Lot flows past like ink and the Valentré Bridge is looped from tower to tower with fairy lights. There's no traffic allowed in here tonight and at three in the morning the air's still silky and warm, the streets crowded with people in shirtsleeves walking, drinking, laughing, talking, listening. In Saint-Etienne cathedral, the choir's united voice is a hymn of pure thanksgiving to God – but outside in the streets the music's an earthy paean to a pagan festival. Kettledrums are thumping in one alleyway, mediaeval oboes wailing in another; a folk band has revellers stumbling in a drunken two-step in the square, and on the other side of the street, a girl with a world-weary voice lingers over the songs of Edith Piaf.

I'm out for the count with fatigue, asleep on my feet, and moulded to the mellow happiness of midsummer in this beautiful city. There's candyfloss for sale, its spun stickiness frosty in the lamplight; there's tooth-cracking nougat, coffee strong enough to stand a spoon in, but most of all the black wine of Cahors, plummy, persuasive, beloved of the Romans long ago, and potent enough to have Madame steering her car erratically back to the farm at high speed while our lolling heads lurch on every corner.

The impervious French are still strolling round the sun-baked streets, apparently none the worse for last night's over-indulgence, when we return to the city on our day off. My stomach feels like lead and so does my conscience, which is telling me to find an internet café, since I haven't sent any postcards let alone emails for weeks. I launch an extremely brief resumé of our journey in the general direction of Fred's computer at work, which includes a short sentence to the effect that I probably won't be back until mid-August, and depart to the *laverie* with the washing before I can receive a response.

Susie and I have decided on a policy of staying with the Chemin while it's reasonably straight, but of not being too purist about it: the GR65 has wiggly variations and hilly detours, and if it's quicker for us to take to the verge of a minor road then we shall do that, in the interests of arriving home again sometime before winter. Our first attempt at this is very successful, and we cross an entire map in a day having negotiated a steep shale track out of La Rozière. It changes to smooth chalk, and now it's regularly signposted as Le Chemin de St Jacques, which means I don't have to watch the map all the time.

We start to meet other pilgrims puffing along in the morning sunshine. There are butterflies again in profusion – peacock, marbled white and tortoiseshell – and there are horseflies, zooming beside Leo and Apollo and homing in on their sweaty bits. Our progress is punctuated by an unseating series of cow kicks as the horses try to swat them off their stomachs, and when those fail they simply increase their pace until we're flying along under horsefly power. We switch to the straighter road and arrive in St-Cyprien by lunch-time.

The first man we see is foolish enough to make a gallant comment about two beautiful ladies on two beautiful horses. Susie offers to hoist him up behind her on Apollo and, when his expression changes rapidly to alarm, she suggests the easier option of inviting us to stay with him. That's no problem – he's just cut his hay, and we may all park ourselves in his stubble field, sandwiched between an oak wood and the football ground.

We've finished our day's journey so early for once that there's time to heave the air mattresses out of Bessie for an afternoon siesta. As I'm drifting off to sleep, I'm aware that there's quite a lot of six-footed livestock about, from the ants mountaineering up the side of the mattress to clamp their mandibles into my shins to the shiny green flies buzzing round Leo's saddle. After fifteen minutes, I'm awake again, covered in blotchy red ant bites. My saddle could do with a clean, so I might as well get on with it. Where's the saddle soap? And what's that white stuff on my sheepskin seat saver? Strewth! Those flies must have thought it was a dead sheep (well, it is, I suppose). They've laid thousands of sticky white eggs right in the wool.

It takes me half an hour to scrape them off with my fingernails, but I'm going to get every last one: the consequence of them hatching into pale squirming squishy maggots while I'm riding along sitting on the sheepskin tomorrow doesn't bear thinking about. With mashed eggs under my nails and reeking of flyspray, it's a relief to find that the football stadium is unlocked, and at nightfall I sneak off to the visiting team's shower block and have eleven cold showers simultaneously to get rid of the revolting mess. The sheepskin gets scrubbed with bubble bath as well, and I just hope it'll be dry by the morning.

The next day starts badly: the D7 was so quiet yesterday that we've decided to stay with it, but Leo and I have a close shave with a speeding van almost at once. Travelling too fast behind us, it screeches into a skid when the driver realises there isn't time to pass us before he meets a car coming in the other direction. As usual I'm riding with my reins in a loop, and the noise sends Leo galloping up the road before I can stop him, but the van driver decides to overtake us anyway just as the car's passing the horses as well. There isn't room. I shove Leo into the verge as the van accelerates past, missing my left leg by an inch; consumed with horse rage, I'm sticking my finger up at him and shouting, but he's round the corner and gone. It's very unsettling, and worse is to come.

There's an odd pattering noise on the road behind us. Susie and I are just turning our heads to see what it is when a jack donkey straight from hell cannons full tilt into Apollo's rump, out of its field and out of control, intent on murder or sodomy, all bared teeth and deafening roars of rage. Apollo's beside himself with fear, bucking and plunging all over the road as Susie fights to control him and beat the donkey off with her bare hands, but it lunges forwards on its hind legs, bellowing over Apollo's tail, trying to bite them both. I'm carrying a whip but the donkey takes no notice of the blows raining on its bottom, and Leo's reversing in fright in case I hit him by mistake.

There's a car coming. It can't get by and I flag it down. The driver gets out to help but there are hurtling hooves everywhere. We're going to have to try to catch the thing. I'm off Leo, snatching his headcollar rope from his neck, but the donkey's caught the driver with a thumping kick and he's flying, hurled in a perfect arc over a ditch ten feet wide, turning in the air and landing spreadeagled on his back the other side. Apollo, lashing out in panic, misses my head by a whisker, but amazingly the driver's scrambled back and between us we manage to get the rope round the donkey's nose and drag it off.

Susie's white with shock, but she's still planted in her saddle and she hasn't even lost a stirrup. There are cheese and Marmite sandwiches all over the road and Apollo's trembling uncontrollably, but Leo, whose powers of observation I sometimes question, insists on making friendly overtures to this satanic beast just in case it's female and fancies him. The driver volunteers that his name is Dominic, and that he was careful to turn himself as he was propelled over the ditch so he didn't land on his face and spoil his beauty. He says the donkey comes from the estate behind us where he works, so we truss it up with Apollo's headcollar rope as well for extra safety, and drag and shove it up the road.

Dominic informs me it escaped last week and attacked a horse and carriage, resulting in a broken leg for the driver's wife who fell out when their horse careered off up the road. The problem, he says, is frustration: the donkey's fiancée is pregnant and she's not interested in sex. I don't give a toss about the donkey's excuse; we could have had a very nasty accident, and when we reach the château and find the owner outside in the garden, I lay into him in my best French with no expletives deleted. He listens politely for ten minutes until I run out of breath, when he tells me he's a builder working here on a contract. The owner's out.

Dominic fetches the donkey's headcollar and anchors the creature firmly to a tree, and by the time we get back to Susie and the horses, Apollo's calmly eating grass. We go our separate ways full of thanks and bonhomie. When a police car comes into sight half a mile down the road, Susie and I wave it down, spilling out the last hour's horror story and demanding that action be taken. No chance. There's an expressive Gallic shrug from inside the car: I am *désolé*, Mesdames, but where this ass resides is not in my *département*.

Ass, indeed.

We need coffee, with lots of sugar. We stop in the next town, ushered to the coffee shop by a friendly black-and-tan dog with big eyebrows. It's time to get back on the GR65 – it must be a lot safer than the road today. We join the Chemin on a trail through the woods, stopping to examine an elaborate black-and-white *pigeonnier* on stilts, and pausing again at the tiny chapel of St Sernin. Susie and I both go in, leaving the horses with instructions to stand still outside as there's nowhere to tie them. They'd like to follow us, but they're too fat to fit through the door. Leo elongates his neck and peers in to see what we're doing. What we're doing is looking through the travellers' book left there for the pilgrims to write in – it's inscribed with the words '*Priez Pour Nous*': pray for us.

Quite.

18. TIRED GONE CRAZY

This flappety head flopdoodles along,
Meandering after my feet;
Though I know they're all mine, I can't make them connect,
Can't walk a straight line in the street.

The words that I speak aren't at all what I think,
Misplaced, they fall out in disorder;
These pages are shuffled, outsortable-un,
My brain has slipped over the border.

At night it hooks on to a minor obsession
That picks through the pattern of sleep;
By morning my eyes are bagged up into sacks,
My skin's folded down in a heap.

Then it's over. I'm into that soft second wind
Where the cracks have all gone from the paving,
And people in blue at the edge of my sight
Are only delphiniums, waving.

And in fact I haven't felt so fit for years, even though first thing in the morning I'm a rusting robot, my joints so stiff that when I stand on one leg to put on a sock I can't crank my foot up high enough to do it. But the stiffness wears off when we get under way. By the time Susie and I have finished pottering round St Sernin we've been travelling for more than five hours, but the break gives us that second wind and it seems no great physical effort to climb back on the horses and carry on. Intellectual capacity is another matter, though – Susie's trying to teach me Spanish from a textbook as we ride along, but my mind remains geared only for the minutiae of daily life. She's throwing Spanish verbs at me but they're bouncing off Leo's spotted haunches, spattering down like pebbles on the road before they can get anywhere near my brain.

We pass a gîte sign in the hedge pointing down a valley as small as a bear pit, and the English owners are delighted to have guests. They're still restoring their old property but there's room for all of us, although some careful fencing has to be carried out round the improvised horse field. They grow flowers for the market in Moissac and, apart from the risk that Leo and Apollo will stretch their elastic necks over the fence and eat the canna, there's already a problem with a wild boar living in the woods next door that has the same idea, and with a large rodent that raids the water-lily crop in the lake full of basso profundo bullfrogs. The rodent's a *ragondin*, a branch of the coypu family unwisely introduced to this area from South America some years ago, since when it's caused havoc. Susie and I have already passed one on the way here, a bundle of greyish fur curled up in the undergrowth, probably digesting water-lilies.

By nine o'clock the heat's already stacked on the valley floor, and the swarming flies ignore the stifling stink of citronella spray and cram themselves into the horses' sweaty armpits, round their eyes and in their ears. Apollo's wearing his nose net and Leo blasts them out of his nostrils periodically, but they seem to be immune to copious cans of repellent, and I'm considering smearing Leo with garlic to see if that has more effect.

The GR65 follows a lane dotted with sun-bleached wooden tables where jugs of water are left out for the pilgrims, and cherries are for sale for one euro for a big punnet. Once out of the valley we're on a ridge again, the wide River Tarn sparkling along to Moissac below us, but the Chemin signs disappear suddenly when we reach the town, leaving us on the cobbled pedestrian precinct in front of the abbey church of St Pierre. This could be bad news if one of the horses drops a crot – we have no plastic bags with us, and Moissac's chic shoppers aren't looking too impressed by the arrival of travel-stained horses and riders with a huge fanfare of insects. We trot hastily away across the Garonne canal bridge, and here are the St Jacques scallop shell signs again, pointing us back over the canal and up the hill to a sweeping view of the tangle of canals and rivers idling across the plain below.

An Arab horse stud materialises at the side of the road, with a conveniently empty field for Leo and Apollo, but first they have to be scrubbed and deodorised in a proper horse shower. Neither of them has seen such a thing before, and they're ushered under the hose snorting with alarm; reduced for a moment to clean sleek seals, they waste no time in finding a dust bath in their field and plastering themselves in mud, before challenging a slim filly with an impeccable pedigree to a race.

In the drowsy afternoon we drive back to Moissac. I left a message for a sailing friend before we left England to say we'd be riding this way in early June, but we're nearly three weeks late and, not surprisingly, he's already passed through in his comfortable motorboat on his way to the sea. The moored yachts are rocking imperceptibly on the Canal Latéral de la Garonne and they remind me of another life, another ambition: to bring *Jorrocks* here one day from Bordeaux and follow the canal to Toulouse, where it becomes the Canal du Midi, and then on through the Languedoc and out into the Mediterranean. This is probably Plan 287.

In the church, the dramatic tympanum shows the Apocalypse

and Christ in Majesty, and to my surprise a wonderful painted patterned interior lies beyond it. St Pierre is a major pilgrimage church with layer upon layer of architecture from different ages, from a seventh-century stone sarcophagus, rough to the touch, to a series of wooden statues depicting the internment of Christ, five hundred years old, but so perfect they could have been finished yesterday.

The church was affiliated to Cluny in 1047, and about fifty years later the monks built the cloisters whose 116 columns are still throwing stripes of shade across the sunshine pouring down the long walkways. In the fifteenth century, the church was secularised and later demoted to a saltpetre factory, its cloister capitals mutilated, and it was another four hundred years before it was realised that this was a part of France's heritage worth saving. Paradoxically, it was only months later that progress, steaming through in the shape of the construction of the railway line from Bordeaux to Sète, resulted in an application to destroy part of the cloisters. Fortunately, it failed.

We have a fruitful wander round the town. The St Jacques Museum has a reproduction of a mediaeval map of all the pilgrim routes to Santiago, some winding down the eastern side of France to run off the map into Italy, and they cause me to dream up Plan 288 immediately: to ride Leo to Rome. More prosaically, we buy a book called *Miam-miam-dodo*, the pilgrims' bible of the Chemin de St Jacques from Le Puy to Saint-Jean-Pied-de-Port. This peculiar title is the French equivalent of *Yum-Yum-Zizz*, or *Board-and-Lodging*. It shows the route in chunks that are walkable in a day and all the hostelries that welcome pilgrims, including their horses if necessary, and it's the most practical book we've acquired. Susie and I spend the evening sitting out under a pink sunset poring over it and marvelling at how easy plotting the route has suddenly become.

The radiant sky correctly predicts another scorcher next day, and we're down to our skimpiest shirts when we weave our way back over the Garonne canal to the towpath to try out a variant of the main Chemin. The GR65 itself has enough zigzags over the hills to reduce Susie to wobbly silence, but its deviation via the towpath has a variant of a different kind: a traveller wearing even less than we are. Nothing, in fact, apart from a bumbag correctly positioned over his bum. Even Leo, now in a white sunhat comprising cloth ears too long for him and a tasselled fringe, is wearing more than he is.

We're on the path squeezed between the canal and the river when the hiker pops up out of nowhere on the other side, jogging in the opposite direction towards Moissac. He goes out of his way to wave and shout a greeting to us, but a mile further on we find he's really gone out of his way – he's doubled back invisibly, and is there at a canal lock waiting. We have to cross this lock. Monsieur Bumbag is full of smiles, leaning casually against the parapet and offering Susie and me all sorts of good advice about the Chemin, but it's difficult to have an ordinary conversation with someone who's stark naked, and there's something even more unusual about him, although we can't immediately pinpoint what it is because we're trying not to stare. It isn't until we've crossed over and the man has vanished suddenly as a boat approaches the lock that we realise he's completely brown all over, the even tan uninterrupted by a single pubic hair. We're relieved not to encounter him again, but three days later news of him catches up with us: he was unwise enough to engage three stout matrons in conversation as they stomped along the towpath and, unlike Susie and me, they didn't pause politely to pass the time of day with him – they called the police.

The Chemin crosses the canal again and then the wide River Garonne, leading on through picturesque Auvillar to a campsite listed in *Miam-miam-dodo* where horses can be accommodated *à l'attache*. Leo and Apollo are both clodhoppers who would get wound up in their picket ropes if they were tethered, and we haven't the heart to leave them tied to Bessie all night sleeping on their feet, but there are no objections when we produce our electric fence.

We're moving into the Gers region of soft hills and shady trees. An English couple have been camping at this site for months while they renovate the home they've bought in the next valley: a three-storey farmhouse with a barn, 25 acres and panoramic views, all for £60,000. They pull a box of local wine from the boot of their MGB and give it to us in case our resolve needs fortifying, but in fact we're all very cheerful because finally we seem to be approaching the bottom of France. It's impossible to judge exactly how far we've come, because our equestrian map is the only one we have that shows the whole country and there are no distances marked on it, but it looks as though we've travelled close to a thousand miles. Not that we dare congratulate ourselves, in case it's tempting providence.

Immediately ahead is the town of Lectoure by the River Gers, where Peter's daughter Kate is to join us for a couple of days to ride with her father in the lorry. It's a boiling hot journey there but it's like that every day now, and soon I shan't bother to record it. The GR65 is clearly marked both in the Chemin book and in *Miam-miam-dodo*, and following it is easy, but it's not only because of the scallop shells and red-and-white GR signs painted on stones and tree trunks – there's also a nasty trail of mucky crusty lavatory paper and worse. Why don't the pilgrims bury their mess? Plan 289 is needed: to market a lightweight folding trowel. Lunch-time is spent at a prudent distance from the Chemin under some umbrella pines where we turn the horses loose, safe in the knowledge that they won't stir out of the nearest patch of grass.

Lectoure's perched on a pepper-pot hill, and Leo and Apollo are streaming with sweat by the time we reach the top. Susie sits in the shade with them while I go off to ask the tourist office for a horsy address, returning to find Apollo still dozing with his chin resting comfortably on Susie's head – but Leo hears me unwrapping a Magnum ice cream, and in seconds all I have are a few dribbles on a stick. We humans book ourselves into various types of accommodation around the town for two nights:

Susie into a proper pilgrim gîte for the first time, Peter, Bessie and me into the public car park, and Kate into the upmarket Bastard Hotel. She gets the preferential treatment because she's on holiday, although the rest of us have our eyes on her hotel swimming pool.

We treat ourselves to dinner at a smart restaurant, where Kate's struggle with a steak as tough as my rawhide Spanish gaiters catches the eye of the chef – he's unimpressed by her imploring looks, and addresses her as though she's an obstinate toddler who wants to get down from the table before she's finished: it's perfectly well-cooked and she must eat it. Kate gives up, but the chef doesn't – he wraps the steak lovingly in foil, fashions it into the shape of a duck and gives it to her when we leave. We spend some time dodging round the town to find a dustbin.

By the next evening, Susie's gîte is filling up. This is our first close encounter with other pilgrims, and it's quite an eye-opener – I'm keeping quiet about my lack of religious fervour, yet find that conversation flows most easily with Heinrich, a devout and intense Roman Catholic from Germany. There's Jean who looks disconcertingly like the Mekon from the *Dan Dare* comics that our father used to buy for us as children so he could read them, and wan Gervase whose enthusiasm Susie and I suspect is greater than his fitness. And there's Alarm Clock Man, wound up tight, who's going to have everyone out of bed and marching by six o'clock tomorrow morning. In the meantime we cook our individual suppers and eat together companionably in the spartan kitchen, sharing our box of wine and gesticulating in several different languages.

Monsieur Alarm Clock still hasn't surfaced when Susie and I leave at eight o'clock next morning. Heinrich and Gervase have left together an hour ago, but the horses are sprinting along thanks to clouds of mosquitoes and horseflies, and we catch up with them on another short-cut variant of the Chemin. They're sitting in the grass with their boots off, resting outside a gîte rented by a surprised Welsh couple on a week's holiday who'd never heard of the Chemin de St Jacques before they arrived here, and whose week so far has been spent handing out carafes of water to thirsty pilgrims. They thoughtfully provide whole buckets for the thirsty Leo and Apollo.

Susie and I follow the GR and the blue-and-yellow EU signs all day. She seems to like the organisation and predictability of the marked pilgrim route, but I'm uneasily saying goodbye to the pioneering spirit of independent navigation, although I have to concede that I'm seeing a lot more of the countryside now I haven't got my nose buried in one of the seventy-odd IGN maps we've traversed so far. I suspect that, with her strong beliefs, Susie feels supported by the presence of other pilgrims on the road. As for me, I'm curious to meet them, but I don't need to know they're there.

Anyway, I'm literally distanced from them more than Susie is because apparently Peter doesn't count as a proper pilgrim, entitled to sleep in the pilgrim gîtes in France and the *refugios* in Spain, because he's driving a motor vehicle – and it's easy for me to make a choice between sleeping in a dormitory and sleeping in Bessie. I'd rather have the snores of a man whose every cadence I know than the guttural chorus of strangers, and at least I can roll Peter over if he makes too much of a racket. I might get a black eye if I tried that out on someone in a *refugio*.

In Condom, Susie and I manage to ride the wrong way along the bank of the River Baïse. We right the situation by shinning up a pedestrian path a foot wide on the top of a wall. Susie walks up leading Apollo, but I can't be bothered to get off Leo, and it isn't until I reach the top and see that one small step sideways would have sent us down a fifteen-foot drop to the river that I think, oh well, it didn't happen, and carry on. Leo's faith in me is absolute, and because I never gave it a thought, neither did he.

Our whistle-stop tour of the cathedral later is just enough to convince me that I don't find its angular Gothic architecture as appealing as the rounded Romanesque, and we can't visit the St

Jacques Church because it's locked – so most appealing of all is Kate's offer to buy us each a large pizza for supper. We go back to tonight's campsite to find a forest of tents has sprouted while we were in the town. It's a bikers' convention, and macho gorillas in leathers are sprawling in the grass, gnawing on barbecued bones, while some are freaking out because there's a lonesome toad looking for a bath in the shower block, and they're too scared to go in. Madame Campsite is summoned, but she says the toad is just a *pauvre bête* – a poor beast – and she declines to remove it.

In the night, the fine weather breaks with a rumbling thunderstorm, and multitudinous snores and farts from the tents have Susie and me out of bed at 6 a.m. to find the temperature's dropped by at least 15°. So much for taking the sunshine for granted. It's a cool cloudy day on a ribbon of road westwards, and then an abrupt turn south on to a track. With extraordinarily bad timing, we clank over a metal bridge and surprise Gervase with his trousers down right on the Chemin. He struggles to heave up his white Y-fronts, speechless with embarrassment. Susie tells him kindly that we won't wait for him as she can see this is a very bad moment, but I'm wondering darkly how many miles of the loo paper are his responsibility.

Miam-miam-dodo has come up with a proper equestrian centre on the GR at Escoubet and, while Peter's taking Kate back to the train station, Monsieur offers to replace the horses' worn-out shoes, although he isn't a qualified farrier. I decide not to risk Leo with his difficult feet, but there's no choice where Apollo's front shoes are concerned as he's lost his toe clips again. With twenty miles without a break behind him today, he behaves impeccably, even though there's no vet available to sedate him. Madame cooks an elaborate four-course dinner for us; she has the time to do it because the huge gîte is empty at the moment, quiet before the rowdy onslaught of eighty children for next week's circus school.

There are some disadvantages in relying on the GR65, as we

find out the next day when it takes us along a stretch of the main arterial road, crawling with articulated lorries welded together nose to tail. There's a mile of exhaust fumes before we're off into the Armagnac countryside again, with its neat vineyards, fields of young maize and brilliant sunflowers turning their faces to follow the sun's track across the sky. The next disadvantage is a *passerelle*: a tiny pedestrian-only footbridge over a wide ditch. It consists of two narrow planks of concrete with inexplicable hoof-sized holes in them, and there's no alternative but to slam the lid on our imaginations, get off the horses and show them where to put their feet. Leo watches attentively, snuffling at my hand and pointing finger probably because he's hoping I've got a Polo for him, but he picks his way over with extreme care, while Apollo decides he has a better idea, which is to jump over the whole ditch. Unfortunately, he miscalculates the width and jumps straight into it, scrambling out again with his dignity in tatters while Susie struggles not to fall in as well on the end of his reins.

I phone a gîte *d'étape* in Nogaro as we're riding along and once again I'm told that horses *à l'attache* are accepted, and once again no-one minds when we use our electric fence to create a little enclosure instead. Leo and Apollo have no objection to walking under the pilgrims' washing line to get to it, and the pilgrims don't mention the horse hairs that stick magnetically to their drying boxer shorts. The gîte's in a very noisy location next to the road, the local flying club and the Formula 3 circuit, and the afternoon's entertainment is all laid on, from the man taking his Ferrari for a spin round the racetrack to the tiny aeroplane practising take-off and landing. Monsieur Air Traffic Controller is very relaxed, murmuring incomprehensibly into his microphone and occasionally wandering into the middle of the airfield to check the sky for approaching gliders.

There are familiar faces in the gîte: Alarm Clock Man who's now relying on an electronic watch; Jean the Mekon; a softly spoken Asian pilgrim who photographed the horses yesterday, and the unfortunate Gervase, who's looking even more pasty and says he's going home because he's twisted a ligament in his knee. Actually, I suspect he's terminally embarrassed at meeting Susie and me again, and can't face the thought of our paths crossing for the next six hundred miles or so. Heinrich's well ahead of us now, but he's left a note in the pilgrim message book to say how much he enjoyed our conversations at Lectoure, and to our sorrow we never catch up with him again.

Tomorrow we should get as far as Aire-Sur-L'Adour where our sister Tessa is joining us for a fortnight with her backpack, and we'll have to pause for a couple of days while she's with us so Peter and I can fly home for Clara's graduation. Then we'll be crossing the border into Spain; Susie's had a spell of Chemin with no mountains, no ravines and no precipices, but even though there's not a hill in sight at the moment she's becoming pensive, brooding about the next obstacle: the huge rampart of the Pyrenees, rearing up invisibly somewhere ahead of us.

19. SIBLING RIVALRY IS ALIVE AND WELL

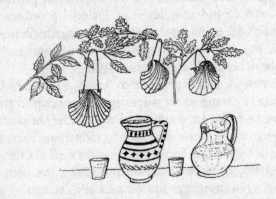

Tessa's on the telephone from Toulouse. Her backpack's caught a different flight and there isn't a hire car left in the city, so she'll have to catch a train to Aire-sur-l'Adour. Susie and I ride there along the GR, Leo and Apollo greeting all the pilgrims we overtake and collecting pats and strokes as we pass. It's just as well they're popular, because they're contributing their own trail of crots to the Chemin, and it's impossible to tell when this is going to happen in time to steer them off the path and into the undergrowth. There's a pilgrim joke doing the rounds: don't follow the scallop shells, follow the crots – but at least it's not as bad as the loo paper.

We reach some *chambres d'hôte* outside Aire with just enough time to put the horses in a field and drive back to the town to collect Tessa from the station, which takes half an hour to find and then turns out to be defunct anyway. Tessa's a mile away walking up the road, having been delivered by bus, still minus her luggage, and we all squeeze into Bessie's cab beside Peter whose expression is grim at the prospect of being stuck with not just two sisters but three. He only cheers up when Madame at the gîte, who's cooked a gourmet supper for all the pilgrim guests as well as her family, insists he has several helpings of her wonderfully sharp apricot tart. In the meantime, the horses are up to mischief in their field, playing with Madame's washing on the line, licking her car and ganging up on the sheep to evict them from their shelter. But at least they've left the vines alone.

Susie and Tessa are sharing a spacious room with a view for two nights, and Tessa gets her first taste of a typical pilgrimage day off: a quick march round the ancient town (Vicus Julii in Roman times), a trip to the supermarket, another to the *laverie* and a tour of the cathedral. When we climb into Bessie again, some instinct makes me suggest that probably we shouldn't all pile into the cab in case it's illegal, so we lock Susie in the groom's compartment. Within minutes we're flagged down by two bored police officers with nothing better to do.

They don't speak English, and they don't believe me when I try to explain that we're sisters riding horses to Santiago de Compostela for charity. So where are the horses? And why is there another sister locked in the back? What has she done wrong? Questions are fired at us without a trace of humour, and then they ask Peter for Bessie's documents. He tells them with alacrity that it's not his lorry, and points at me.

I climb in the back, letting Susie out of the groom's door to prove she's not suspended from the roof by thumbscrews, and start looking for the papers. Yes. Well. I know they're in here somewhere. The old plating certificate and the breakdown insurance turn up, but that's all. The officers are asking for the French equivalent of the MOT certificate, so Peter assures them that English lorries don't need such things. They look doubtful, but as they can't read what's written on the documents they're holding, they back off under a fearsome battery of smiles from Susie, Tessa and me, and wave us on our way. The MOT and insurance certificates turn up a week later, wilting under the mattress.

Tessa's backpack has been delivered to the gîte, full of esoteric items like seaweed soup – five hundred packets of it, to judge by the weight, but Tessa's unfazed; she says she's very fit and is used to walking. She's also been weight training, and her biceps are impressive.

When the farrier arrives next morning, he shoes Leo very slowly, carefully and expensively, laboriously adding eight tungsten studs – but as a consequence Susie and I are late leaving and Tessa's gone hours ago, thundering up the road with her sturdy thighs pumping and her backpack bouncing. We catch up with her, waiting impatiently for us at our arranged rendezvous, with a thought bubble sprouting from her head that says: I told you I'd be quicker than you. Sibling rivalry is still alive and well.

The Chemin runs along the road today, and its one diversion down a track in the woods nearly ends in disaster: there's another *passerelle* in front of us, this one made of wooden slats, and it runs for twenty yards over an evil black bog. Tessa's sent ahead to jump up and down on it, and it seems sturdy enough to bear the weight of a horse. I ought to get off just in case it isn't, but I can't be bothered, and Leo willingly walks along it until he reaches a broken plank that Tessa hasn't noticed. Leo does, and in lengthening his stride to avoid it, goes straight through the next one with a terrible crack. He's tipping forwards, his front leg plunging through into space with me about to follow it, but then he calmly shifts his weight back to his hindquarters, pulls the offending leg up again and ferries me over on tiptoe.

I recover my breath in time to warn Susie that Apollo needs to walk through the bog, and she sets off along the bridge with him plunging indignantly through the mud beside her. Why should he have to get wet? He levitates on to the boards with a crash, all four feet simultaneously, but before the whole thing can collapse she's pushed him off again. Apollo's furious, and by the time they reach the other side he's covered in slime, but apart from a superficial scrape to one hind leg the only injury is to his dignity again.

It's a long haul to Arzacq-Arraziguet, and Tessa's finally

flagging. She's walked sixteen miles on her first day, and on the last hills she's been strap-hanging off Leo's tail as though she's on a tube train, but she's not going to give up and ride him instead of walking. At Arzacq there's a pilgrim gîte that sleeps seventy in dormitories, and it's a rude shock for my sisters after the congenial *chambres d'hôte* – their dormitory contains several snorers and a strange bloke from Lausanne who sleeps like a dead saint, flat on his back with his hands piously clasped on his chest.

Peter has his own rude shock next day when a tabby tomcat jumps into bed as soon as I open Bessie's door, and grinds its hard little chin along his recumbent head to scent mark him. He's not appeased when I tell him it could have used its other end to spray him for the same purpose, and it's propelled out of the door. Unabashed, the tabby sits on the ramp, patting Apollo on the nose as he sniffs at it, his ears pinned forwards in curiosity, while Tessa sets off ahead of us again. The first part of the Chemin is in remote countryside and we've agreed to meet at the Romanesque church of Larreule – but when we get there, there's no sign of her.

What's happened? We haven't passed her. We ask other pilgrims, but no-one's seen her. She has no mobile, and Susie and I envisage her raped and pillaged in a ditch somewhere, and the headlines: ENGLISH PILGRIM VANISHES WITHOUT TRACE IN DEEPEST FRANCE. On the other hand, any would-be attacker catching sight of her biceps might think twice.

We're moving on slowly, wondering what to do, when Tessa calls from a phone box: she's taken a wrong turning, and now she's behind us. I'm aware that Peter's wake-up call from the tomcat has resulted in him getting out of bed at least two hours earlier than usual – he's probably already arrived at Pomps where we're all supposed to be stopping for lunch and, on balance, tired Tessa is less of a problem than pouting Peter, so I tell her we'll carry on and she can catch up with us there. It seems politic not to mention it's another two hours' walk.

Peter's indeed waiting for us, edgy at Tessa's absence because he's agreed to transport some homeward-bound pilgrims to the bus station in Bessie. Like many we meet, they're walking the Chemin in stages, returning each year to carry on for a fortnight from where they left off. When Tessa turns up, I register fleetingly that she's not alone: she's walking with David, an American bicyclist in the mandatory Lycra who's dismounted to keep her company. I have an impression of kind eyes, a sensuous mouth, and then he's pedalling off down the road and out of our lives again, while Tessa climbs wearily into the lorry for the rest of the journey to tonight's destination at Arthez-de-Béarn.

Scallop shells hang from the trees, and jugs of refrigerated water are left out in people's gardens. More and more pilgrims are gathering on the road to Santiago, most walking with their backpacks and some on bicycles, but there are none on horses. In the absence of donkeys and cows in this area Apollo's concentrating his phobic tendencies on bikes instead, alarmed by the hiss of tyres on the road behind him and leaping forwards at the slightest excuse, to Susie's irritation. The afternoon's punctuated by unchristian swearing, and we're all frazzled by the time we arrive in Arthez to find that Tessa's checked the pilgrim gîte, found it grubby and eschewed it. She'd rather stay in a hotel, and Susie and I tie the horses to the petrol pumps outside a café while we sit down with our cappuccinos to ponder this problem. There's another one looming as well: the need to find somewhere to leave the horses for several nights near the crowded St-Jean-Pied-de-Port, while Peter and I return to England for Clara's graduation on 10 July, less than a week away.

There's no hotel for miles, and Tessa has to compromise with a campsite, a snug tent and a comfortable airbed. And what could be better than steak and chips, eaten al fresco in an unexpected rainstorm that runs watery gravy on to our plates? The friendly Asian pilgrim we've passed and re-passed is sleeping in his microscopic tent next to Susie and Tessa, and he joins us for a glass of wine. He has a pathological dislike of snorers so he'd rather camp, even though his backpack weighs him down with its tent and bedding. Tomorrow he returns to his home in Tours, this year's stint of his pilgrimage completed. Susie breaks off her conversation with him to shout down the phone to an *agriculteur* who's driving his tractor and can't hear much, but it sounds as though he may be able to help with accommodation in St-Jean if we call him back later. My turn on the phone produces another campsite tomorrow at Navarrenx, with Tessa wondering in the background whether there are any hotels there.

When the fog finally lifts in the morning, the Pyrenees magically appear in the distance, steaming along the horizon, peak after peak. Excitement clutches at me. Dread clutches at Susie, and pain's clutching at Tessa, whose right shin is too swollen from her sudden burst of long-distance hiking for her to contemplate walking with us today. Susie and I cross the River Gave de Pau and pause at the statue of St James at La Sauvelade, where the church dedicated to him is all that remains of a mediaeval monastery, before getting lost in the hills and woods as a confusion of old and new GR signs point us in different directions. The Pyrenees tantalisingly disappear and reappear all day. We make it to the old walled town of Navarrenx, where Tessa hasn't found a hotel but has appropriated a little wooden chalet for herself and Susie at the campsite; and Leo and Apollo have an electrically fenced paddock of minute proportions, thanks to the proliferation of tents and camper vans on every pitch. The tourist season has arrived.

There's a Welcome Pilgrims party in the town where the mayor delivers a rolling-R history lesson about the Navarrrrrrre region. After two glasses of the local white wine, I can't understand a word, but there's a welcome diversion outside: a wedding party is dancing out of the sombre church, the bride in a cherry red sleeveless, backless and largely topless dress and the groom in a black jacket and a black shirt, minus his tie. They spring into a Citroën whose roof and windscreen have been untidily sawn off, the bonnet strewn with blousy hydrangeas, and the car groans on its axles as the wedding guests climb in as well. Susie's gone to the pilgrim Mass that follows on from the wedding service but it's drowned by the cacophony of blaring horns, clattering tin cans and less than holy songs as the car circles round and round the town.

Leo and Apollo are complaining that they're starving. They're fed up with watching the children on the next pitch playing table tennis, and they want to be taken for a walk so they can hoover up all the available grass. After an hour of being dragged round the campsite, Susie and I are dead on our feet, and they're put back in their enclosure, sandwiched between the ping-pong table and a late arrival in a 1960s Volkswagen camper van who's astonished at the sudden appearance of two equine neighbours. In the morning the horse department's knee-deep in crots. Starving, indeed – Leo's still nicely rounded, and Apollo's as fat as a pig.

Our departure from Navarrenx is conspicuous thanks to the *brocante* that's just being set up in the square. Plastic toy animals are piled on porcelain plates, candlesticks scratch against thin crystal glasses, and there's a squash of humanity; it's not a good idea to ride down the main street, but there doesn't seem to be any other way out through the ramparts. There's a long queue of cars stuck behind us, but fortunately when we come face to face with the town's brass band its members are still ferreting round for their music and the only sound is ours: magnified hoofbeats bouncing off the walls. We clatter away across the River Gave d'Oloron into the *domaniale* forest and a tempest of horseflies.

Leo and Apollo are going mad. In the hot humid forest we canter and swat flies at the same time, as the horses shake their heads and shiver their skins to try to dislodge them; Susie and I are in danger of being dislodged as well, but at least we're making good time. We disturb a Buddhist pilgrim from Paris sleeping under a hedge by leaving a cloud of flies behind to settle on him instead, and arrive at the Ferme Behoteguya, chosen out of *Miam-miam-dodo*, well ahead of Peter and Tessa in the lorry. This is a pig farm, and the flies are here in hordes. A bucket of water chucked over each horse sweeps them off but they're back immediately with their creepy legs and busy tongues, slurping at the sweat round the horses' ears and eyes. When Bessie arrives I raid our food supply for garlic and lemons to smear on Leo tomorrow.

We're coming into Basque country now where the houses are distinctive, painted white with ornate wooden overhangs, shutters and balconies in contrasting ox blood red. The place names are written in Basque as well as French, full of complicated consonants, and to an outsider it's an impenetrable language – apparently its nearest relation is Albanian, but nobody seems to know why. Susie, Tessa and I walk to neighbouring Aroue in the glaring sunshine, passing four men playing the equally impenetrable Basque game of pelote under the critical eyes of an umpire and most of the inhabitants of the village, as they swap small rackets with curved handles from hand to hand and fly round the court. Susie pushes us into the cool church next door to see a twelfth-century stone carving of St James Matamoros raging along on a horse: he's waving his sword energetically, but there seem to be more horses than Moors flying through the air.

Peter's stayed at the farm, reading his book in the shade of the lorry to the slobbering accompaniment of a herd of pigs eating dinner, but he's having difficulty concentrating because our host and all his sons are spending a noisy afternoon up a ladder replacing a window frame, and his thought bubble is one I know well by now: What on earth am I doing here? He and I are in for a honky night in Bessie next to the farmyard.

Tessa and Susie are booked into the farmhouse with the other pilgrims, and Jacqui the Parisian Buddhist is in a tiny room directly off theirs – fortunately he seems to have forgiven us for dumping a deluge of flies on him as we passed by this morning. I decide not to risk upsetting him again by colouring my hair in my sisters' room, and then wandering through his with purple punk spikes while I'm waiting for it to settle down to the Light Golden Brown the label assures me it will become. We're still keeping up appearances, and Susie's hair rollers haven't been packed away, but although she promised her daughters she would wear her hard hat, she's now swapped it for a straw one with a wide brim, on the basis that her health's more likely to be endangered by sunstroke than by getting knocked out falling off Apollo.

More and more pilgrims are arriving and we crowd together on the terrace for *panaché*, the French equivalent of shandy, all sweating and smelling and swapping stories. Jacqui's anxious to spread the word about Buddhism: he says everyone can choose his or her own fate and it's not down to God, but I seem to recall from some dim archive in my mind that Christianity preaches something about God giving everyone free will, which I would have said was the same thing. Jacqui's very earnest, though, and I decide against a debating duel, which will have me out of my depth in seconds. I think I'll go to bed early, in fact, because tomorrow we'll begin the long haul up the foothills of the Pyrenees and plenty of will is going to be needed, free or otherwise, to keep us all trekking over the top and down the other side into Spain.

20. PYROTECHNICS IN THE PYRENEES

Tessa's looking exhausted. She didn't go to bed early last night but got into a fearful argument with Jacqui, not about Buddhism but about communism and, as there's no sign of him this morning, I assume she won and he's sleeping off the onslaught. She's decided to walk part way with Susie and me today, although her leg still hurts enough for her to wait patiently for us while I rub Leo all over with sliced garlic cloves and lemon. He smells as though he's marinating for a casserole, but it does the trick and the flies back off in disgust. We leave under an ominously metallic sky to ride to Ostabat, close to where the three Chemins de St Jacques from Paris, Vézelay and Le Puy converge. A little stone discoid monument built by the French Société des Amis de Saint Jacques apparently marks the spot, and it looks as though the GR65 goes right past it.

The first storm hits us just after Tessa's climbed back in Bessie to carry on the journey with Peter, and Susie and I sit it out with the horses in a barn stacked with espadrille soles. When it's over, the countryside is dripping and now the terrain's changing again, rougher and wilder as we reach the foothills with another storm brewing. We're relying now only on Susie's French Chemin book which illustrates bite-sized chunks of the GR, and we have to follow it wherever it goes because there's no overall view of the roads in the area.

The horses start climbing up slippery granite steps set in the hillside, careful as goats today, altering their strides to accommodate all the different widths and heights and angles. At the top, they stop to look at the view. There's a pale track in front of us, slanting down the slope again and disappearing far away over the top of another hill. It's desolate: no trees, no bushes, no alternative routes. And the sky, empty of birds, is sinking under the weight of iron clouds. There isn't a sound.

The horses walk down into the valley, the clatter of their shoes on the rocky path echoing in the hush. Then it's uphill. Some hill. It's a bare bloody mountain, and we're going to have to keep going because there's nowhere to stop. What's that over there? It's rain, a solid curtain of it belting over from the east and here comes the wind, keening and screaming over the mountains, and now the thunder's cracking the sky open, and the lightning, it's sizzling down in bolts and Jesus, it's scary, scary as *hell*, perhaps you'd like to have a word with God, Susie, can you hear me, Susie? So will we all get out of here without being fried? We'll have to stop. I'm not going over the summit when the horses are clanking with metal.

We get off. There's a small bramble beside us, a pretend shelter, and I snatch the sheepskin off my saddle before it's soaked, and stuff it under my mac. Sorry, Leo, I'm going to let you go in case the lightning homes in on you. But the horses stay glued to us, their backs to the din and the deluge, and if I move a step, Leo moves with me. I reckon he's decided that if he's going to go, I'm going with him, so we all stand together and wait. And wait.

It's going over. The rain curtain hooks back to show the next storm churning towards us across the sky, and in the brief lull we run with the horses up through the seething mud on the track to the top. Just over the summit there's a chapel with two sodden French pilgrims and several sodden cows standing in its lee; we're about 1,000 feet up and I'm not stopping here with another storm coming, I'm slithering and sliding down the other side of the hill, but now Leo's pulling back. I can hear Apollo neighing. Where's Susie?

I can't believe this. She's stopped in the most dangerous place on this naked mountain to photograph the little Chapelle de Soyarza, so sure is she that God and St James are looking after us. And, of course, she's right – the storm kindly holds back until she's finished and we're down in the shelter of the woods again. I suppose you could call it coincidence.

In the excitement we manage to pass the St Jacques Monument without seeing it. We catch up with Peter and Tessa at Ostabat – once an important gathering point for thousands of mediaeval pilgrims spilling out of its inns, now just a small village I'm too drained to appreciate. We're starting to get tangled up with the main road, the D933, and according to Susie's book the Chemin sways to and fro across it from here to St-Jean-Pied-de-Port. We spend the night at a horse-friendly hotel in Larceveau right on this busy thoroughfare, and then it's a hot trek through the valley to St Jean, with a steady stream of pilgrims striding along in shorts and muscular sandals with thick straps. We pass a strange man who's walked all the way from Germany fully kitted out in lederhosen and leather boots. He's tapping along with a proper gnarled staff and a hairy goat-hide backpack, and I have a sudden horrible feeling that if I catch sight of his eyes under the brim of his floppy black hat, they'll be glowing like little red coals.

Every now and then the Chemin does indeed stray on to the unpleasant main road. I shall have to get used to it, though, because we'll be following it over the Pyrenees to Roncesvalles in a few days' time as it tracks the course of the river, its tarmac covering the oldest of the pilgrim routes. The alternative Route de Napoléon is much wilder, much higher, and out of the question for vertiginous Susie. We've been having a spirited discussion as to whether it's suitable for horses anyway, given that it's so rough and steep and apparently roamed by herds of native Pottock ponies with their protective stallions, but it's academic: we're not going that way, and we shall never know the answer.

St Jean is seething with pilgrims and tourists. We squeeze our way up the Rue de La Citadelle and through the narrow stone arch at the Porte de St Jacques, Leo and Apollo slipping on the cobbles down the other side to the pilgrim centre. The staff are intrigued by the appearance of two spotted horses from England, but their data sheet that has to be completed has no box to tick for equine pilgrims. We fill out all our details anyway, including the horses' names, and our pilgrim passports are stamped with the green ink image of St James with his staff and hat. It seems strange to think that this is the final stamp of our journey through France – it's 9 July, and it's taken us exactly three months and a day to get here.

We're deep in conversation with other pilgrims when there's the sound of horseshoes coming down the street. Leo, who's been in dead-donkey mode all morning, wakes up with a turbo snort as the other riders pass by on their way back to a local equestrian centre. He's skating on the spot with excitement and then he tows me down the street behind them, blurting crots all over the cobbles and scattering tourists into the craft shops for shelter. I don't have any plastic bags with me, let alone rubber gloves, so we'd better get out of here.

Susie's phone conversations at Arthez with the *agriculteur* have successfully resulted in a billet on a farm for five nights. Our host is obsessively tidy – he and his wife run immaculate *chambres d'hôte* in their house with big bedrooms opening off the polished stairs and landings, full of occasional tables with fragile legs and ornaments arranged just so. We go clumping up in our riding boots to Susie's and Tessa's room, which to Susie's dismay contains one double bed, but there's a bolster she can stuff down the middle to avoid any powerful thumps or kicks from Tessa, whose injured leg is now on the mend. When we come down again, Monsieur Obsessive's looking doubtfully at Bessie's untidy presence on his forecourt – he'd like us to hide her somewhere round the back, but his wife tells us cheerfully to ignore him. He's a maniac, she says reassuringly.

His sheep are very well trained. They're neat little *brebis* who come trooping into their miniature milking parlour every day and line up in their individual stalls, and their milk's made into a strong traditional cheese unmelodiously called *ardi gasna* in Basque. Leo and Apollo are turned out in their field with them, but the sheep have mown it as smooth as a cricket pitch and the horses set off to explore. I'm not unduly worried when they disappear over the brow of the hill, but it's as well Susie and I walk the boundaries to make sure – it turns out to be another field *sans frontières*. One side drops down a precipice on to the railway line and another melts into the verge bordering the main road, while a third leads into the neighbours' vegetable garden. The obedient *brebis* wouldn't dream of straying in there, but Apollo and Leo are striding towards it looking understandably pleased. We push them back into the lower part of the field where we can see them, and put up the electric fence.

Monsieur Obsessive's vet breezes by to give the horses the necessary health check for their export certificates into Spain. He asks me if Leo is well, and I assure him that he is. He asks Apollo the same question directly. Apollo says he's fine, thank you (by searching the vet's pockets for peppermints, which amounts to the same thing) and the paperwork is done, although it has to be sent to Pau for stamping and I feel obliged to point out that it's supposed to be signed 48 hours before departure, not five days. The vet smiles and shrugs.

In the morning Madame takes Peter and me to the station and, as we leave the farm, I observe a hundred and fifty brebis rowdily shouldering each other out of the way to get at the horses' salt lick in a rare display of insubordination. We have to catch a train to Bayonne, the TGV to Bordeaux, a plane to Gatwick and a lift by car to Royal Holloway for Clara's graduation ceremony.

A few hours later, feeling completely disorientated, I find myself sitting in the university chapel watching my luminous daughter come forward to collect her degree. The chapel organ crashes triumphantly through its bass register and pale English sunlight filters through the windows. Everyone is very polite with their canapés and Pimms in the quad and marquee afterwards, and I'm thankful I managed to disinter a pair of cleanish black trousers from the bottom of my plastic clothes box in Bessie.

Clara's fizzing and bubbling all the way home in the car. I keep on noting English registration plates with surprise, and saying '*merci*' instead of 'thank you'; Oliver's looking at his escapee mother with a faint air of disapproval, and my father when I visit him is stuck in his garden hedge, strimming nettles at 89 years old, abandoned by his daughters. Our own garden has closed in on itself, four feet high in dead poppies and sowthistles, the roses strangled.

The cat's ecstatic to see us, but Fred is less than ecstatic when I phone to admit we haven't even got to Spain yet. When I left, it was still his winter vest season: now he'll be in shirtsleeves and gold cufflinks, the office window open, the breeze shuffling the papers on his hopelessly untidy desk. From his tone I can tell he's wondering whether I'll ever come back, and I'm wondering, too – this plunge into the world of unpaid bills, grimy house and jungle outside is completely overwhelming. I'd rather be out on the Chemin with its uncomplicated pleasures and problems, although Peter would probably rather settle comfortably back into his leisurely days of retirement: not only is he missing his golf centenary year, but there's been a complete dearth of golf courses in the Basque country. It's as well we're due to fly back tomorrow, before he gets entrenched. I realise there's no time to visit my mother – I know time means nothing to her now, and that when I see her again she probably won't even realise that I've been away, but I still feel guilty.

The journey back to Gatwick in Clara's clapped-out Metro is petrifying. We leave late, and she's exhorting the car to go faster, but it's panting and juddering along on three cylinders, and when we finally get to the airport British Airways decide not to let us on the return flight to Bordeaux, even though it's still loading. Perhaps it's because I'm carrying two dressage whips. The staff raise their eyebrows and look at Peter speculatively when I say they're for beating off aggressive dogs in Spain, and it's only after a lot of argument that we're pushed on a flight to Toulouse. There still isn't a single hire car to be found in that city, and our slow train putters along, pausing to rest for half an hour somewhere in the wilderness before expiring at Bayonne – where we're met at midnight by two pairs of gimlet eyes belonging to my sisters, who've had to come and pick us up. Peter and I sit in the back of their car like naughty schoolchildren, and daren't say a word.

We have one more day to spend in St-Jean-Pied-de-Port, before leaving on Sunday to cross the Pyrenees when, in theory, there'll be no lorries on the main road, as they're forbidden by French law to travel on that day. Peter and I are still in the doghouse for missing the flight – Tessa's quietly simmering, but Susie's on the boil with frequent explosions. Eventually, I realise it's mostly because of her extreme anxiety about the mountains tomorrow, and since Apollo's keeping a low profile in his field, I'm copping it instead. But I can give as good as I get, and Peter's relieved when the other two drive off to Bayonne to return their hire car. He always knew these sisters were nothing but trouble, and it's just as well Penny's not here as well.

He and I spend a typical tourist day in St-Jean, climbing up to the citadel to admire the view over the river from the ramparts, and amassing bottles of Irouléguy wine and pairs of multicoloured espadrilles. And he buys me a tiny gold scallop shell and a curly Basque cross, which are clipped to my necklace either side of its resident black pearl. I can't quite decide if they're religious symbols or my good-luck charms, but it hardly seems to matter.

By Sunday morning peace has been restored, but Leo's looking for trouble after five days' rest and not enough grass, in his opinion. He dances up the road to the border at Arnéguy where I expect Customs and Immigration to be lying in wait for foreign horses with dubious documentation, but there's no border there at all. Tessa joins us on foot at Valcarlos to trudge with Susie and Apollo up the long ascent towards the Pas de Roncesvalles. She's slow because her leg's still hurting; Susie's slow because she's also on foot, leading Apollo and fighting the demons of vertigo; and Apollo's slow because he's weighed down by his new shoes, which are as thick as railway sleepers and far too big for him. But Leo's running out of patience, spooking deliberately at the lorries nonchalantly ignoring the no-Sundays rule. It's not easy to slow him down, and every quarter of a mile we have to stop to let the others catch up, which means five minutes of fidgeting about in the road – and if he throws his head in the air one more time I'm going to end up with a nosebleed.

But in the end, the constant climbing wears him down a little, and I have time on this day of fitful sunshine to look around at the fairy-tale mountains and the dense forest beside us, where bandits used to ambush unwary pilgrims. Ahead of us the N135 with its wide hairpin bends winds on and on. The temperature's dropping, the intense blue sky is turning grey as we reach the chapel at the Ibañeta pass, and suddenly it's as though, halfway through a trip to the theatre, the curtain's lifting on a different play.

PART TWO: SPAIN

21. FOLLOWING THE YELLOW ARROWS

This is sunny Spain, on the south side of the Pyrenees. But it isn't sunny. At 4,000 feet the wind's vicious, thrashing our hair round our heads like helicopter rotor blades. It's hard to look cheerful for Susie's camera, and when the prints come out they show triplet mops with rictus grins. The modern chapel at the pass with its cross and bell to guide pilgrims lost in fog is closed, damaged by vandals. It's been built to replace the ruins of Charlemagne's chapel, and when we sit down on a convenient monument nearby we're sitting on a chunk of history: it's dedicated to Charlemagne's nephew Roland who died here in the eighth century. His death led to the epic *Song of Roland*, passed down from troubadour to troubadour through generations, with multiple fine-tuned variations.

It's a proper tall story of treachery and heroism, and it goes something like this: Charlemagne crossed over the Pyrenees into Spain to rescue the local Christians from the Moors, who by then had radiated all over the country, but when he arrived he decided that peace with the Saracens was a more pragmatic option. His brother-in-law, Ganelon, and Roland were with him, and Charlemagne obviously liked his nephew's company. Jealous Ganelon was supposed to be making friendly overtures to the Moors, but instead he plotted Roland's death by giving away Charlemagne's return route through the narrow Pas de Roncesvalles. The rearguard was led by Roland and, as they filtered into the pass, the Moors were waiting for them.

It was a blistering battle of clashing chain mail, headless Saracens and speared horses, but then the Moors began to get the upper hand. Too late, Roland blew his horn Olifant to summon help from Charlemagne ahead of him, but with such amazing force that his head exploded and he fell, breaking his sword on a stone as he dropped so that it couldn't be snatched up by the triumphant enemy. Apparently his avenging uncle returned and wiped out the murderous culprits, but it was too late for Roland, who was lying dead where we're sitting now. The only flaw in this opus is that in fact it wasn't the Moors who killed Roland – it was the Basques, justifiably furious that they hadn't been liberated after all.

Anyway, it's icy up here, not a good moment to linger over legends, and we move on down the woodland track to the monastery at Roncesvalles with its high frowning walls, away from the road at last. There's a mass of pilgrims at the *refugio* waiting to get their passports stamped, and we queue for seats at a long table strewn with forms that have to be filled out, using pencils anchored on lengths of string to prevent them disappearing into pilgrim pockets.

Presiding Señor speaks little French and no English, but we understand him well enough when he says he doesn't like horses, and that it's absolutely impossible to accommodate them anywhere here. He gets the gimlet eyes treatment. He stares back. I'm wondering whether the smile-battery treatment might work better when suddenly he caves in and escorts us to a perfect little field on the other side of the road, complete with the Sacred Virgin's Fountain in the middle. An overexcited small boy is anxious to help with the horses, but he's chattering away in a language I can't understand: why, oh why, didn't we make the time to learn Spanish on the way through France?

Three vultures have arrived from the mountains to circle on the thermals above the field. Well, you keep your beady eyes off our horses, you lot – this isn't the sort of welcome I'd imagined. Susie and Tessa insist on taking me off to pilgrim Mass in the church. I'm more concerned we'll come out to find the horses reduced to a rack of ribs, but mass seems to be mandatory, and the church is packed with other *peregrinos* like us. At least that's one Spanish word we know. The service is conducted by priests in rustling robes who chant quietly in Latin and Spanish, and then we're all blessed in about six different languages. When I glance at my sisters to see if they're impressed, Tessa's been soothed into a deep sleep and Susie, who took an overdose of seasick pills this morning to combat the vertigo, has fainted dead away.

Tomorrow Tessa's catching a bus to Pamplona on the first leg of her journey home to America. To her relief there's a hotel here and we have a last enormous dinner together, with little conversational input from me as I have my nose in our Spanish dictionary, searching for different ways of saying piss off to a vulture and indeed to the ferocious dogs we've heard a great deal about. And I'm looking at our maps. We had eighty to guide us through France – we have two of Spain.

But we also have a book I bought in London called *A Practical Guide For Pilgrims*. This contains a series of very simple maps dividing the route into 31 stages varying in length from eight miles to about 23, so in theory the energetic pilgrim could complete the Chemin, now the Camino Francés, in a month. There's a duplicate set of loose maps so you can carry your 'Map of the Day' in a neat transparent envelope on elastic round your neck, and there's plenty of good advice for pedestrians, cyclists and motorists. There's none for horse riders, but Susie and I have already decided to follow the walking route come what may, because the only consistently practical alternative would be the main road.

And there's another reason: apparently the Camino is marked with yellow arrows for its entire length, crystal clear since its adoption as a World Heritage Site in 1993, so hopefully we shan't get lost. I'm still mourning the loss of my pioneering days of navigation, but asking the way when you speak the language is one thing – trying to make yourself understood when you don't is another. Trying to find accommodation for Leo and Apollo off the established route could be even worse: if Señor at the monastery is anything to go by, it's going to be difficult enough at the *refugios*. I have an uneasy feeling the horses won't be made as welcome as they were in France.

Our first full day on the Camino is cold, drab and bleary with fatigue, thanks to a night spent hauling heaps of clothes on top of the duvet for extra warmth while Susie rattled round in the back of Bessie, digging out all the stinking horse rugs to pile on her sleeping bag. After waving goodbye to Tessa in the early morning chill we go trotting along a neatly gravelled path through the trees beside the main road, a Camino motorway tidily signposted. Some bicyclists are here as well as the foot pilgrims, but they politely ring their bells as they approach and Apollo doesn't take fright.

My early derogatory mutterings about American-style tourist trails cease abruptly when the paths disappear and evil descents through the woods take their place, treacherous, narrow and down steep rock faces where Leo and Apollo look puzzled at our requests to follow when Susie and I can't work out where to put our own feet, let alone theirs. Leo decides the only safe way is step for step behind me with his nose buried in the small of my back – one slip and I'd be propelled down the rock, but the tungsten studs in his shoes are doing their job and he's more sure-footed than me.

The sun finally brightens the day as I'm poring over today's map, which doesn't seem to be quite accurate, or else I'm still not used to its layout. Progress is from the bottom of the page to the top, not from the top to the bottom, and it feels as though we're going backwards. The book was published in 1998 and since then a flood of EU money has started refurbishing and indeed re-routing the Camino in places, so we decide to rely only on the arrows, scallop shells and stylised blue and yellow symbols that proliferate along the Way. We pass foot pilgrims on the upward gradients, where Leo and Apollo like to accelerate, and then they pass us again on the downhill paths, sidling cautiously by as the horses pick their way slowly along. To the left is the Venta del Puerto, the Inn of the Pass, a deserted cowshed apparently unworthy of the euro coffers.

Our destination tonight is Larrasoaña on the River Arga. The arrows take us off our map again and on to a new road of bubbling tarmac that reverts suddenly to dirt, scuffling along above a hideous cement works bellowing dust down the valley. Some years ago two English horsy travellers were here, the Hanbury-Tenisons on borrowed Spanish horses, and they were allowed to camp by the river under the trees. We aren't. Dapper Señor who runs the *refugio* in the town hall proudly shows us their entry in the pilgrim book, and then looks aghast when we produce our electric fence. He directs us to a patch of weeds spanning a footpath, and Leo and Apollo have to go messing morosely around in the brambles.

The *refugio*'s heaving with pilgrims and there's no space for Susie, who's already tripping over bodies in sleeping bags on the floor as she fights her way to the loo. Where's the handy supermarket? Well, the village shop, then? We find two pieces of cheese and three of cake at the local bar, where finally someone's pleased to see us: Merou the barmaid is a radiographer in disguise, and she speaks English. Her day job's at a hospital in Pamplona, our next stop, and she phones the police to check that we may ride through the city. They say we can't, under any circumstances – horses are dirty, or in other words, they drop crots. This seems marginally hypocritical, given that the festival of San Firmin has only just finished and herds of dung-splattering bulls have been rampaging through the streets, but the police are adamant. Merou has the answer, though: ride through the city anyway and if anyone stops you, say you're stupid English and don't speak the language. Which is true.

The bread van hoots its way down Larrasoaña's narrow street early in the morning, stopping at front doors where cloth bags and notes are pinned to the knockers stating the number of loaves required. Merou's phoned the *refugio* at Cizur Menor, just beyond Pamplona, to book a piece of ground for Leo and Apollo, an act of kindness that makes up for Susie's and my unpleasant shock at finding that someone's stolen the horses' rock salt lick out of their enclosure during the night. They can't do without it, particularly in hot weather, but I'm not counting on the chances of finding a salt lick shop in Pamplona.

Following the walkers' route is an interesting experience again: there's the tiptoe through the field full of loose horses, who fortunately aren't dazzled by the array of spots before their eyes although Leo does his best to entice them over, and then the stretch on the main road where the lorries hurtle by and we have to dismount and walk the horses behind some pedestrian pilgrims, facing the traffic. Then suddenly the Camino crosses the road and scrambles up some rocks: it's a magical mystery tour, and we don't know what to expect from one moment to the next.

Peter and Bessie pass by in time to see us climbing a precipice and edging along a track the width of a pencil with a sheer drop to the left, but there's a brief concession to safety in the shape of three yards of fence pinned to the edge of the abyss. I daren't look behind me to see how Susie's getting on, and hazard after hazard presents itself: a slide down to a subway under the motorway, two flights of steps, and then the village of Villava, no village at all but a suburb of Pamplona, where suddenly we're on a dual carriageway queuing at a set of traffic lights. When we move on again I have to park Leo repeatedly between cars to let the lorries by, but he ignores them – Narcissus is neighing at himself, gazing intently at his reflection in shop windows.

The horses haven't been allowed any snacks this morning in the hope they won't produce any crots, although Susie and I have plastic bags and rubber gloves with us just in case. The yellow arrows direct us round the edge of this fortress city at the foot of its walls, over the old stone Magdalena Bridge – and straight into the pedestrian precinct. There are people everywhere, and we have to slow right down.

I can feel Leo arching his back, but there's no convenient side alley to dive down. Leo, please, please don't … he's groaning with the effort of producing a steaming pyramid, looking around with benevolent satisfaction as I scramble off him. A fascinated audience assembles as I find the gloves and bag and scrape it all up, and Susie's chortling complacently – until Apollo does the same thing. Serves her right. I have plenty of time to set up Peter's camera and photograph her grovelling on the cobbles as an even bigger crowd gathers, and an elderly señora helpfully hands out two more bags and directs us to the nearest wheelie bin. We lead the horses away with dignified smiles along the main avenues, past two police officers who are too busy directing traffic to try to redirect us, and into the city park for lunch.

The cheese and Marmite sandwiches have a certain aroma about them thanks to the rubber gloves in the same saddle bag, but they get washed down anyway with a bottle of Pulco, which we thought was lemon squash when we bought it – astringent, refreshing and guaranteed to strip the enamel off teeth in thirty seconds. I reckon it's neat lemon juice. The horses attract some strange looks among the prams and toddlers, and we make ourselves scarce before the police catch up with us, cutting across the university campus and up the long hill to Cizur Menor. The *refugio* there is very clean, very well organised and has a separate dormitory for pilgrims who snore – which is completely empty, as no-one's going to admit to such an antisocial habit.

In response to Merou's phone call Señora has arranged a field on the hill overlooking Pamplona, alongside a fortress with the red and white flag of St John of Malta waving cheerfully off the top. She directs us to an agricultural supplies shop on the outskirts of the city and, after a lot of pantomime, leaping eyebrows and dictionary consultations, we manage to buy another salt lick for the horses. Our visit to Pamplona itself is less successful; it takes an hour to find somewhere to park Bessie, with a long walk at the end of it to the Gothic cathedral with its polished hardwood floor, each panel numbered, and its organ upstairs rumbling and squeaking under the faltering fingers of a music student. Our visit's cut short as always by the constraints of time: we need to find Airtel so we can register our new Spanish SIM cards for our phones, but by the time we get there it's so late it's closed, while the restaurants are also closed because it's too early for Pamplonians to be eating. A frugal sandwich later we return to Cizur Menor to find that the horses have somehow managed to knock down their electric fence – there's nothing to stop them visiting Pamplona themselves, but such is their respect for the white tape that they haven't dared step over its snaky length lying on the ground.

Our book of maps shows relatively short hops from here to Burgos, which is about ten days away on the edge of the *mesetas*, the high plains, which we shall have no option but to cross in the searing heat of midsummer. We decide to limit ourselves to one map a day, even though the distances are less than we would normally ride. We don't know what surprises the terrain of the Camino may have in store, and if we skip the rest days then the shorter distances probably won't make any difference to the overall time we take. Susie's worried about tomorrow's ride up to the Sierra del Perdón, a ridge that looks on the map as though there's a precipice to descend the other side, but it turns out to be the day that shakes off any nostalgic yearning for the fat days of France, and ushers in enchantment of a different kind.

At seven o'clock the early sun is gilding Leo's and Apollo's silky summer coats and the rolling corn fields beyond them, and we get into a stubble field beside the Camino early on, the horses bouncing with pleasure at the open space and the chance to canter. At a gap in the far hedge there's the unusual sight of a Bedford camper van with an old X-registration English number plate. It belongs to John from South Norwood who roams the Camino from April to October, dispensing coffee to passing pilgrims for one euro and practical advice for free. We suspect he's also waiting for a lady pilgrim to walk by who'll turn out to be the love of his life.

Beyond John, the hills stretch away to the horizon, brilliant white wind turbines striding along their crests, their sails lazily churning up the sky. As we climb the Sierra del Perdón below a line of them, we can hear them humming, but silly jokes about Don Quixote tilting at windmills have to wait until we're right at the top and Susie relaxes when she sees that although there's a steepish scramble down the other side, it's nothing compared to others we've faced since leaving Roncesvalles.

Parading along the top of the ridge is a metalwork frieze, silhouettes of pilgrims on foot with their staffs, their donkeys and horses and dog, and beyond it the Camino winds away through dusty villages to Puenta la Reina and our next stop. We're right in the middle of Navarra, its capital Pamplona spread out in hazy sunshine far behind us now; there's yellow broom and scrub and evergreen oaks sprouting in the scree going down the hill, and now we're seeing montjoies, mounds of stones piling up as pilgrims add their own pebbles. Then it's an easy ride, loping again through the stubble to cross the mediaeval bridge over the River Arga, and a climb up to the *refugio* on the hill that John's recommended, austere as a boarding school, its eight long washing lines flapping with pilgrim pants and socks.

22. BREAKFAST AT THE FOUNTAIN OF RED WINE

Droves of dusty pilgrims come sweating up the hill to check into the *refugio*'s dormitory for a small handful of euros for the night. Susie appropriates one of the sixty beds, surrounded by glistening bodies splayed out reading, sleeping, writing up their journals, or simply glazed with exhaustion from the relentless sun and the hot wind that's blown them all the way from Pamplona or Cizur Menor. Susie and I don't have the blistered feet that they do, thanks to Leo and Apollo, but unlike the other pilgrims there's no crashing out for us the minute we arrive: there's a corner for the horses to be found and fenced, water to be carted, food to be prepared.

At this *refugio* the horses are welcomed, patted and fussed over, but again there's no pasture except weeds on the triangle of ground next to it. We have emergency hay rations which will be needed soon, but they're going to be difficult to replace. In this dry land there are no hay fields, and the livestock has to put up with straw. No doubt Leo and Apollo will as well, in time, but it will need to be introduced gradually or its coarser texture might give them colic. In the meantime, they're becoming experts at finding the choicest plants and eating them down to the ground, and we've doubled their rations of dried alfalfa and concentrates.

We roar down the hill again to Puente in Bessie, bypassing the graceful bridge with its six arches, and drive on to visit the funerary church at Eunate which stands all by itself in the middle of an empty field. It's intriguingly octagonal, its alabaster windows letting in pale honey-coloured light, and it's fenced in by delicate colonnades. It reminds me more of a Roman temple than a Christian church, but probably that's just the view of a heretic: in fact it was built by the Knights of St John in the twelfth century, and was a pilgrim burial ground for those who didn't make it to Santiago. A sobering thought.

George from America turns up to chat, and we share a bottle of wine as the heat drains out of the day. George is 71 years old and is walking to Santiago on a whim, but he's having trouble with his legs which are quaky with fatigue. The whim is to atone for all his sins at this stage of his life by making the pilgrimage, which he hopes will allow him to whistle through purgatory and straight into heaven when he dies. He's a Roman Catholic, and Susie's so deeply intrigued by his belief that purgatory is a kind of pre-celestial purification chamber that they get into a heavy discussion, the practical outcome of which is that Susie misses her turn to wash up the supper dishes – which she swears isn't on purpose. The *refugio* locks its doors at 10.30 sharp, and at 10.25 she and George are still so immersed in conversation they're both on the point of getting locked out. I scamper in with them to clean my teeth at a proper basin, and nearly get locked in – stern Señor doesn't want any pilgrims escaping after lights out.

We wake to the promise of a stinking hot day. Leo's wearing not only his white bonnet but also sun cream on his vulnerable pink nose. He's very particular about what kind of cream he likes and, of course, it's the most expensive unscented hyperallergenic stuff. He objects to the smell of anything else and turns into a giraffe when I'm trying to rub it in. Apollo doesn't have this problem as his head's the colour of speckled charcoal and his muzzle is dark, but his back's still causing Susie concern, sprouting hard little lumps by the end of each riding day, which she continues to anoint with Vaseline. So far the skin hasn't broken, which would make him unrideable until it healed, and it's also helpful to him, although it slows us down, that Susie gets off and walks so much in hilly country because the additional height when she's riding makes her vertigo worse.

By half-past nine it's 35°C, but it's a dry heat in this arid landscape and it doesn't bother any of us; fuelled by weed power, and still on the edge of hunger, Leo and Apollo fly up the rocky inclines. We reach a huge expanse of stubble and suddenly both horses are off like rockets in an explosion of farts, racing, pulling, muscled legs like pistons; that flying saucer whirling by is Susie's straw hat and, in seconds, we're nearly at the top of the hill, eyes streaming, no hope of stopping and no idea what's the other side.

I transfer all my pulling power to my left rein and manage to haul Leo round in a circle. Out of the corner of my eye, I can see Susie doing the same thing with Apollo, and behind her some stationary pilgrims who appear to be open-mouthed with admiration at our spotted racehorses. Little do they know the middle-aged owners have turned to jelly with fright. When Susie's retrieved her hat from half a mile away and we've pranced and bounced our way right to the top, it turns out there's nothing more daunting ahead than more miles of stubble. We could have kept going and crossed it in minutes.

The wind's blowing us along to Estella, a short hop of twelve miles from Puente la Reina, and the Camino unexpectedly passes through what appears to be somebody's house. We ride through a doorway, across a stone floor and out through another doorway, meeting no-one and fortunately leaving no trace apart from the dusty imprint of hooves to puzzle whoever the owner may be. Then we're on to a stretch of the original Roman road with a Roman bridge, defeated for the first time by such a steep downward flight of steps that I have visions of equine somersaults. It means sneaking through the middle of a vineyard to avoid it, cursing the horses' conspicuous colouring and not helped by Apollo's delaying tactic of lying down for a roll in the deliciously soft earth. Susie hauls him to his feet before he can turn right over and squash his saddle.

The *refugio*'s in the middle of the busy town and it doesn't cater for horses. The nearest alternative is a campsite pulsating with yelling children on holiday; it's not a good place but we haven't the energy to look for anywhere else. There's a tiny piece of ground with a shady tree in the middle, but Leo's still excited from the morning's gallop and starts hurling himself round it when horses from a trekking centre stop here to rest, and we have to move our two to the stubble opposite. I'd been starting to worry that Leo's looking lean but these horses are greyhounds by comparison, covered in old bumps and scars and all in ill-fitting shoes. One is wearing a *serrata*, a brutal noseband with metal teeth on the inside, which has skinned its nose to raw red – the RSPCA would have a field day here, but this is a different culture, a different attitude. Susie and I had assumed that the horses in northern Spain would be as carefully treasured as the magnificent Andalusians in the south, but so far nothing could be further from the truth.

Tomorrow's map will take us to Los Arcos but it looks as though, like Estella, it's going to be too big to be horse friendly, so we decide we'll carry on to the village of Torres del Rio beyond it. The Italian lady who runs the *refugio* there assures Susie on the phone that she can find a field for Leo and Apollo, and tonight we sweat it out in Bessie until her planks finally cool down at about 2 a.m., by which time a disco is in full head-banging reverberation in the hall next to the lorry.

Breakfast is taken at the monastery at Irache, where there's an unusual fountain – a Fuente del Vino that spouts red wine instead of water. The wine is tart, dry as sloes eaten straight from an English hedge; it makes me shiver and grimace but Leo and Apollo think it's wonderful, and Susie's giggly for the rest of the morning. Hunger and wine put Leo into super-march mode, so disinhibited that when I stop to photograph Susie with a mountains-and-monastery backdrop, he forgets I'm still on top of him and decides it's his turn to lie down and roll, flapping his ears foolishly at me when I tell him off about the new scratches gouged out of his saddle.

We're always on the lookout for the legendary ferocious dogs, but so far they've either been friendly or simply aloof. They fall into two categories: jolly-dogs and nanny-dogs. Jolly-dogs look like Tibetan spaniels, fluffy, yappy and scuttling busily about on short legs, while nanny-dogs are usually huge, silent and dignified, but they wave their tails slowly when we greet them, and sometimes they condescend to be stroked. Their job is to look after the sheep that roam the seamless fields, and today we meet several at once when we turn a corner to find a flood of two hundred sheep and goats about to engulf the horses. Leo and Apollo stop dead with surprise as the bleating tide surges round them in a cloud of dust and din of bells, and then they're all gone, galloping home with their canine guardians loping along behind, ignoring us completely.

The horse field at Torres del Rio is the worst yet, but the *refugio*, with its airy dormitory, is the best. Señora has done all she can but there's no such thing as grass here, and we have to fence off a stretch of plough that an anxiously accommodating farmer has put at our disposal. It runs alongside the main road but the verge is full of lush lucerne, and we drag up every plant by the roots and put it in a pile for the horses. When I go back to check them later, the kind farmer's pulling it up on the opposite verge to add to the heap. He gestures to me to use the farm hose to fill up the buckets, but the water's cobalt blue. I can't imagine what's in it, but it seems safer to use the village fountain. The water from some of the fountains in other villages is giving pilgrims the runs, but equine digestions seem to be impervious. Lady Aldington's bucket is in daily use but after three and a half months tied to the back of Leo's saddle it's turned into a sieve, despite Susie's best efforts with the bicycle puncture repair kit. As for the bicycle, it's got a flat tyre again and is completely useless, as Peter observes as he continues to haul it out of or into the lorry at least twice a day. He's itching to present it to the nearest villager.

Pilgrims are cooling off in the bar with their beers after the seven miles of slog along the blinding white track between Villamayor and Los Arcos, where long-discarded milestones lie upside down beside the road. We join the others for tortilla and salad, comparing journeys and exploring why we're all here. There's just one English pilgrim amongst them all, and she's from a village two miles from Faversham, and there are two Americans, who come from Tessa's home town of Portland. This is the second time one of them has walked the Camino, and I ask him why he's doing it again. He doesn't strike me as a masochist, and he isn't religious, but he says it's for the camaraderie: he made eleven good friends on his first trip and he still stays in touch with them, years later. The Camino has bound them all together.

Susie's found another octagonal church, Santo Sepulcro, which has a lantern on top of the main cupola that used to be lit to guide lost pilgrims. She's registering wonderment, but I'm registering concern at the state of the sky, which has turned black. A violent electrical storm sends the pilgrims running into the *refugio* and Peter and me down to the field where Bessie's parked for the night, slopping water out of the buckets from a refill at the fountain. The storm stops as quickly as it started, but it's a weary night in the humid lorry, disturbed by headlights on full beam and the horses clopping restlessly to and fro in the plough, moaning about the lack of grass. I creak out of bed at 6 a.m. to an inauspicious start to the day: I've forgotten Bessie's parked on a slope, and crash the ramp down on my head; the gas runs out as soon as I put the kettle on, and cold coffee with old milk isn't great. I'm still searching for the Marmite, which has inexplicably vanished, when Susie appears from the *refugio* looking as though she's just had a tranquil chat with St James. By now I'm in an unequivocal grump – my shirt's already sticking to me, and if it wasn't for a promise to the Pilgrims' Hospices back home to make it to Santiago come what may, I'd be thinking longingly of England. My office, even. Well, maybe not.

Logroño on the River Ebro is our next major town, and we've no intention of staying here tonight. It marks our passing from the first of the seven Spanish districts we have to cross, Navarra, into the second, La Rioja, and on the way here the Barranco Mataburros, otherwise known as Mulekiller Ravine, has recently been flattened to a gentle incline, courtesy of the EU – to Susie's relief. Close to Logroño some entrepreneurs have set up a stall for pilgrims with cold drinks for one euro each. A wrinkly señora smiles at the horses, giving them chunks of rock-hard bread and whole buckets of water for free while she peers underneath them to see if they're *castrato* or if they still have their balls. She shakes her head mournfully on discovering they haven't, and I'm not sure she understands my pantomime to illustrate that Leo's under the impression he still has his.

The city's full of traffic lights. When the first set turns green we cross the Ebro at a hasty trot on the Puente de Piedra, the Bridge of Stone, and then pause briefly at the cathedral to peer up at its famous statue of St James Matamoros on a horse whose balls are impressive by any standard. And now the main thoroughfare is six lanes wide, and we're passing the parliament building right in the centre, still doggedly following the yellow arrows as the traffic builds up on every side. Leo's as impatient as ever when the lights are red, nudging a motorcyclist ahead of him in the back of the neck, and Apollo holds up the traffic behind us while he snuffles conversationally at a small child on a pedestrian crossing.

Our relief when we finally escape into the suburbs is short-lived: trotting past a gateway ahead of Susie and Apollo, I catch a glimpse of a tall grey stallion with no headcollar on. I assume he's attached by a foot to something, but when I turn to look back, he's arrived in the road between Apollo and Leo with a territorial glint in his eye. Susie can see another rampant-donkey episode looming but the horse is only hobbling, his hooves so overgrown he can hardly move, and she slides Apollo rapidly past. We hammer off down the road and out of sight to the sound of desperate neighs, hoping as we follow the arrows on to a neat new cycle track that the day won't hold any more surprises.

It does.

The Camino leads off across an industrial wasteland, but there's grass on either side and we decide to stop and let the horses graze beside a convenient row of little back-rest trees. But as we dig out the squidgy cheese and Marmiteless sandwiches, I notice a flash of red Lycra in the bushes behind Leo and Apollo. There's a man in dark glasses there, who's inconsiderately stopped for a pee extremely close to us. Except that he's … what? Oh, no. Susie, that bloke's *masturbating*. Over there. *There!* Susie's peering in the right direction but she can't focus on him without her glasses. Probably just as well. But I'm damned if we're going to be driven out of our picnic spot by some, er, wanker, and now I come to think about it, we have a lethal weapon: the mobile phone. I need to speak to Peter anyway to tell him where we are, and when I put the phone to my ear the man moves out of sight, while Peter sounds as though he's trying not to laugh when I tell him indignantly what's going on.

But when I finish speaking to him the man's back, at it again, closer than ever, with his shorts round his knees. How *dare* he! All my irritation with today floods into my head at once along with a red mist of utter rage. Without thought, I'm on my feet, running at him with the phone to my ear, bellowing into it the only Spanish words I know off by heart so far, which are a rough translation of: '*I have an electric fence I'd like to put up in your field!*' Surprisingly, it does the trick – he's off like a supersonic rabbit, pulling up his shorts as he bounces through the undergrowth, and two minutes later we see him pedalling furiously back towards Logroño, fully kitted out in all his Lycra with his cycling helmet pulled down over his ears.

Perhaps he wondered what I was going to do to him with the *eléctrico*.

23. SAINTS PILED IN HEAPS

Look for the man with fur on his face. At least, I think that's what the barman in the smart restaurant says. We've strayed into a manicured park with an artificial lake when we should be at an equestrian centre, but in the hurry to leave lunch-time's uncomfortable scene we've overshot it by several miles, and it's not worth going back. It takes some time to track down a likely looking beard but it is indeed the warden, and he speaks good French. He takes the unscheduled appearance of vagrant horses, vagrant riders and a large lorry with a vagrant driver completely in his stride, and shows us to an immaculate field of lucerne and orderly trees at the far end of the park next to the security office. It's the absolute antithesis of last night's patch of bare earth, and Leo and Apollo are so frantic to get their heads down and start troughing that it's hard to get their bridles off.

There's another storm grumbling up, making the radio masts next to the office hiss and crackle with static, and Susie gets the tent up just in time for us to sit inside with our bare legs and feet poking out to clean up in the sluicing rain. In the evening two riders from the equestrian centre pass by on the first gleaming, rounded horses we've seen in Spain, and later one returns in a truck with a sack of pellets for Leo and Apollo, for which he will accept no payment. We daren't ask him what they are, since clearly we're supposed to know.

The ride to Nájera is also in complete contrast to the previous few days, the countryside warm with the scent of wet earth after the rain, the Camino passing through wildly untidy vineyards. Leo and Apollo have spent the night gorging themselves and can only amble along at a snail's pace, crawling over the bridge to the *refugio* in the monastery, where we're told there's nowhere for the horses to stay – so there's another trudge down to the river to water them, and debate what to do next. Here they attract the attention of the gypsy children jumping in the shallows, who arrive in seconds in a squabbling, jostling pack. The horses are used to being patted from head to foot, but out of the corner of my eye I notice one of the boys take a fish out of a bucket, casually kill it and offer it to Apollo, who politely opens his mouth. *No* is a universal word the child certainly understands – he shrugs, pulls the fish away and equally casually pokes its eyes out with a stick.

Susie and I take the horses back across the river to a private campsite, which has ominously large gates with locks. We're starting to feel uncomfortable about this place, and the campsite owner is obviously security conscious for a reason, but he refuses to help. Horses are dirty and no, we can't stay. He also refuses to phone the police to ask if we may camp at the municipal site, but he does give us their number, so Susie and I toss up to see who's going to be lumbered with making the call in her non-existent Spanish. I lose. I manage the words horses, camping and, of course, the electric fence, but the police say no. I think they say there's a problem with the gypsies, that the horses might disappear, and minutes later two officers turn up in their car, smile engagingly, tell us to wait where we are – and then drive straight off again.

We wait. And wait. Leo and Apollo are dreaming under the

trees, Susie's passed out on a bench and I'm buckling at the knees, falling asleep leaning against a post, while Peter's immersed in another book – which is nothing new, as he's forced to spend most of his time waiting for us anyway. The days of verdant golf courses are long gone. Two hours later, the officers return triumphantly with a captured horse owner in his truck who leads us to his stables above the town – where with great pride he shows us a filthy yard full of farm machinery and dog shit. We register unconditional delight. And it does have two great advantages: a high wire fence, and a complex arrangement of locks on the gate, so it's completely secure. He propels a pile of lucerne over the fence into the yard and the horses are in seventh heaven.

At the *refugio* we're offered showers and our passports are stamped. Peter's silent with fatigue: we've had no break for more than a week, and he looks as though he could do with a night in a hotel. It won't be tonight, though – this is an uneasy place, and even though the horses are locked in we wouldn't risk leaving them on their own overnight. He's revived by an abundance of Rioja wine instead, followed by a pageant at the monastery, a re-enactment of the history of Nájera full of grandiloquent gestures and many references to the Camino. The accompanying music is appropriately mediaeval, with sudden random interjections from *Pictures at an Exhibition* by the nineteenth-century Mussorgsky.

By the time we walk back up the hill to a restless night in Bessie it's very late. A police car comes racing up at 2 a.m. with its blue light flashing, prowls along the yard's perimeter and drives away again; the officer's probably kindly checking the horses are all right, but it leaves us jittery. And there are other noises we can't identify and have no intention of investigating, but at any rate there's no muffled clopping sound of horses being led stealthily away.

We're not sorry to leave Nájera behind and set out on the twelve easy miles to Santo Domingo de la Calzada, riding through a gentle landscape where every inch is intensely cultivated. There's no such thing as set-aside here, no fallow land, and we even see a surprising little square of hop bines. Village stores are a rarity, but there are shops bursting with new John Deere tractors instead, thanks to the EU money pouring into the agricultural economy.

Santo Domingo has a legend with a number of versions: it tells the story of a couple and their son who were walking the pilgrimage road to Santiago in the Middle Ages. They set off from France, Germany or possibly Greece – you may take your pick. On the way they stopped for the night at a Santo Domingo inn where the daughter of the house, affronted when their son refused her lusty advances, hid a bag of money in his belongings and then accused him of stealing it.

The boy was hanged for it, and his sorrowing parents carried on to Santiago. On the way back they passed the tree where he was still suspended, and to their astonishment he was alive. They rushed to tell this incredible news to the judge who had sentenced their son to death. The judge (a serious glutton, by the sound of it) was about to devour an entire roasted cock and hen, and scathingly he remarked that the boy could no more be alive than the dinner on his plate. At that, of course, the crispy chickens leaped to their blackened feet crowing, and hopped off the table: it was impossible, a miracle, and the boy was cut down, his innocence proved.

High on the west wall of the cathedral an elaborate coop with a grille has been carved, where a pair of fluffy white chickens strut and cluck to commemorate the event. If the cockerel crows when you're in there it means a spell of good luck, but they're just roosting quietly as we look round what to me is an unharmonious mixture of heavy Gothic, simple Romanesque and garish modern red and blue stained glass windows. Peter finds a piece of wood nailed to a column; apparently this is the very branch from which the youth was hanged, but needless to say I'm more concerned about the chickens, bored up there in their niche, day in, day out, although later we see the relief team waiting in a more orthodox pen in the *refugio* next door for their fortnight's stint of duty.

The Cistercian nuns at the Monasterio de la Encarnación offer Susie a bed for the night, but the dormitory has two tiers of bunks and the only one available is on the top. She eyes the drop to the floor dubiously, and then asks the beautiful young man occupying the lower bunk whether he objects to her riding boots under his bed. 'Of course not,' he tells her expansively, 'for it is not *my* bed. It is *our* bed.' Vertigo forgotten, Susie's overwhelmed by his generous pilgrim spirit, not to mention his melting brown eyes – but it is not to be.

The nuns have also offered their garden to Leo and Apollo. It's a lovely thought but there wouldn't be a flower left after two minutes, so regretfully we take them out to the edge of the town and cadge a field from a man who keeps a steel-grey Andalusian stallion with a voice like a trumpet. Señor and his family kindly incarcerate him in a dark stable where his muffled blasts of excitement can be heard all night, and here too we receive warnings about horse thieves. We haven't seen any likely candidates but it's not worth the risk, and Susie resigns herself to a noisy time in Bessie parked beside Leo and Apollo, so that Peter and I can have a night in a hotel in the town. He and I have slept in the lorry without a break for three weeks, and he's relieved to be able to sit up in bed and get out without having to crawl horizontally backwards off a large parcel shelf, slopping his toes into the washing-up bowl as he feels for the floor four feet below him.

The Camino leads out of Santo Domingo over the Rio Oja on the main road bridge towards Belorado, passing out of little Rioja and into the wide district of Burgos where, beyond the sprawling city of the same name, the high Castilian plains lie – the *mesetas* at last. Burgos is already causing us concern. We're told the city itself is substantial, with a long run in on the major road, and we can go smack through the middle, or get tangled up with the lorries on the ring road, or take a lengthy diversion with no map.

We can't decide, but in the meantime we're preoccupied with today's track running alongside the main road from Logroño to Burgos which is hardly reassuring – the lorries are nose to tail, and Peter and Bessie pass us, crawling along in the queue.

Norbert from Switzerland runs the *refugio* in Belorado, which is temporarily housed in a garage. Normally, it's next door to the Santa María Church, but there's major restoration work going on in both buildings, with saints piled horizontally in heaps and pews upended, their feet crumbling with woodworm. St James is here, both as a pilgrim and as Matamoros, and this warrior image is my favourite so far, less bloodthirsty than most, with no Saracen heads flying by – he's just looking heroic in his armour, his hair and cloak flowing behind him.

The garage *refugio* is on a tiny street leading to a ruined house that's been bought for the community, where both parish priests are busy slashing down nettles with their sickles, wearing trainers and minus their dog collars. Beyond it there's enough land tucked under a limestone cliff with a ruined castle on top to create a terraced field for Leo and Apollo, their grazing area on a level with the rear of the church tower and its untidy nests of long twigs, all overflowing with impatient baby storks clacking their beaks for food.

We can park Bessie beside the house. Well, that's if Peter can get her there. She's as wide as the village streets and there's plenty of good advice dished out by old ladies in their doorways, all conflicting, on the best way to drive a lorry past a house without amputating the roof. Bessie's heavy body tilts this way and that on the lumpy lanes, getting temporarily stuck under gables and scoring scratches along walls, but with a lot of shouted encouragement, Peter reaches the house, sheeted in sweat and in need of a large whisky. God knows how he's going to get Bessie out of here again in the morning. He and Norbert sit up far into the night, consuming a whole bottle of whisky between them from our booze store at the foot of the mattress, before Norbert reels off to his temporary bedroom in the sacristy.

Susie's up before me in the morning, owing to a keen but unpopular pilgrim turning on the *refugio* lights at 5.30 a.m. She managed to have a leather fly fringe made for Apollo yesterday afternoon and she fits it over his browband, but the tassels are a bit long and he stares through them like a mad rocker looking for a motorbike. The baby storks are awake as well, bullying their parents with a remorseless din of beak clattering, and Norbert's wearily laying the *refugio* tables outside in the street for breakfast. He looks like a man with a severe headache, but he sends us on our way with a smile and exchange of addresses.

On the vile N120 main road, Susie and I get off to lead the horses on the left, facing the monster lorries, but she and I are more daunted than Leo and Apollo by the traffic and they saunter amiably along, occasionally nudging us in the hope of a Mars Bar, until the yellow arrows point across country again towards the lonely Montes de Oca. In times past, the pilgrims had plenty of reason to be apprehensive about these mountains because they were densely forested, completely uninhabited and full of bandits and wolves. They remain wooded and uninhabited and, for all we know, full of wolves, which still exist in the mountains of northern Spain, but there are no noticeable bandits any more although walkers are advised not to risk crossing them at night.

There are plenty of pilgrims whose faces and clothes we know well by now. One beefy bare-legged lady wears a distinctive apple green dress belted at the waist, and we've passed each other several times over the last few days as her dress becomes more and more forlorn and travel-stained. Not that I can talk – my riding trousers are going to walk around on their own soon, they're so stiff with dirt, and the left calf has worn completely through where I have to push Leo over on to the right-hand side of the road. Thirteen hundred miles after leaving England, he's still insisting that English horses walk on the left.

Villafranca Montes de Oca is the last village before we climb up into the mountains. There's a St James church here but we can't be bothered to find out whether or not it's locked, as many of the Spanish churches are, and carry on up the path. At the top, the air's so clear the whole sky shines on woodland striped in emerald and indigo shade, and picks out a pilgrim fountain spilling moonstones. There are patches of clover for the horses, a seat for tired pilgrims … it's tempting to collapse spreadeagled under a tree for the afternoon, but we need to get beyond San Juan de Ortega, the next hamlet, or it'll be a long hike through or round Burgos tomorrow to somewhere horse friendly on the other side. We carry on through oak and then pine forests, and slither down the final descent on the other side of the mountain to San Juan.

There's a pilgrim church here, and a monastery, a bar, a Coca-Cola machine, a fountain pouring into a trough – and a field. Well, that's quite good enough; Peter's already arrived, having successfully extricated Bessie from Belorado, so we make a unanimous decision to stay, and Susie and I will just have to put up with a long ride tomorrow. The *refugio* with its sixty beds is in the monastery, and there are fierce notices pinned to the walls: cold showers only, and all clothes to be washed in the fountain. A small French pilgrim called Daniel staggers in, his hands dripping blood, having fallen flat at the top of the last hill and rolled to the bottom, clawing at the gravel on the way to try to stop himself. Peter raids our first-aid kit to patch him up, but there's nothing that can be done about his chest, which he says is hurting, except to offer to carry his rucksack in the lorry tomorrow.

My disgusting trousers take a trip into the horse bucket, followed by a rinse in the trough, which by now is full of soapsuds, before they join the soporific washing strung along lines and fences. Pilgrims are flaked out asleep in the dormitories at four o'clock in the afternoon, but Bessie's too hot to rest in and I wander into the cool church to find Susie's already deep in conversation about its history; apparently it was begun in the twelfth century by San Juan, who dedicated himself to helping pilgrims, but its pure Romanesque lines were finished later in the Gothic style. San Juan himself is in here, resting comfortably in his sarcophagus while extensive restoration work goes on around him using EU euros in six figures. Looking round, my eye is caught as usual by carvings of animals; there's a depiction of what looks like Androcles and the Lion with a thorn in its paw, but I can't be sure.

We're running out of energy for cooking elaborate meals, and over yet another supper of corned beef and salad, Susie and I discuss tomorrow's route. In the end we haven't the energy to try to work out a diversion round Burgos either – if we don't follow the arrows we're likely to get lost anyway, so we decide to take the horses through the middle and hope for the best. Tomorrow is 25 July, St James's Day, and our 109th day on the road. It seems fitting that we should spend part of it at perhaps the most important city on the Camino, once the capital of Castile in the heartland of Spain, and the crossroads of numerous major routes. These days the big roads still radiate from Burgos like starfish tentacles: to Logroño and Pamplona behind us in the east, León and Santiago ahead of us in the west; towards Santander, Bilbao and San Sebastian on the northern coast, and due south to Madrid. From the city it's three hundred miles to Santiago, so we're nearly halfway along the Camino.

It's a cheering thought to take to bed, but I'm awake early with a sense of trepidation. San Juan is sombre in the morning light and some of the pilgrims have already gone, whispering by before the dawn, although an American girl who arrived late last night is still outside on the ground on the air mattress we lent her, a motionless mound in her sleeping bag. As we ride away, there's an undignified squelching from my trousers, which have failed to dry out overnight. The horses are keen to get going, untroubled by any thoughts of the hazards ahead: the heat, cars, lorries, buses, crowds, inconvenient red lights and all the noise and stink of an urban thoroughfare through a big city.

24. WHERE YOU CAN SEE THE WORLD IS ROUND

Outside San Juan de Ortega there's a choice of three Caminos: the one on the right joins the N1, to the left is the N120, and ahead are layers of rock and shale through pine woods up to the top of the Sierra de Atapuerca, where ten years ago the remains of perhaps the earliest homo sapiens in Europe were found. We go straight on, as Susie's vertigo is preferable to either main road. The woods are thick with flies, blown away when we emerge on to a high plateau of heather and ragwort, purple viper's bugloss and a surprising fanfare of hollyhocks. Daniel's struggling ahead of us with his bandaged paws, his backpack left behind to travel in Bessie, and we pass Johan and Anthea, tall German pilgrims in their sixties who are often to be seen walking along hand in hand. Far below, Burgos sprawls across the cornfields, and a stop for breakfast at Orbaneja is a good delaying tactic for everyone; we linger over *cafés con leche*, the butter and marmalade dripping out of our tortillas.

And then it's down to the plain, Susie swiftly dismounting and leading Apollo because there's no avoiding a high bridge over the A1 motorway, another over the main railway line to

Madrid, and a final slog for four long miles through the suburbs on the pavement bordering the dangerous N1. As usual, Leo would rather be ridden than led, but if I rein him in to keep him to Susie's walking pace he starts crabbing sideways, showing off and taking up the whole pavement, so I have to get off, cursing him for his impatience, and put up with repeated shoves in the back for the next two hours.

It's as hot as Hades in the city: the horses are surrounded by humanity in business suits, in tight skirts and stilettos, or in ragged shorts and clutching pilgrim staffs, and we have to move into the slow lane of the main street where they're hemmed in by double-decker buses instead. At last the Telefonica building is ahead of us with a yellow arrow pointing to the right, and now the lanes wind round the old town, through an archway where Leo and Apollo stop to ask a string quartet for chocolate, and into the pedestrian precinct full of cars that shouldn't be here. We probably shouldn't be here either, at least not with a horse that's spraying crots like shrapnel, and I have to walk a considerable distance with a carrier bag of smelly shopping before finding a wheelie bin.

The extravagant Gothic spires of the cathedral come into view, the arrows pointing up the hill behind them. Calm at last, the horses trudge along like two old donkeys, the ringing of metal shoes on stone adding tympany to the distant susurration of Gregorian chant. Susie and I are shattered with heat and fatigue but in fact there's no need to go further than the park, where the *refugio* spreads through long huts round a quadrangle. Its wardens welcome us to the St James's Day celebrations, and Leo and Apollo are no problem at all. Peter has talked himself and Bessie into the park as well, but not for long – pilgrims, horses and bicycles may be acceptable, but there's a strict no horseboxes rule according to Señor Jobsworth from the council, and he's here to enforce it. The lorry's banished to the sports centre car park beside the busy road out of Burgos.

Somewhere in Bessie I've packed a dress. It seems very odd to be wearing it, and sandals instead of riding boots; Susie's unearthed a skirt, and now we're ordinary tourists, joining the elbowing mass in the cathedral. I'm trying to look earnest but it's hard to take it all seriously – it's as though every architect and builder and stonemason down the centuries has competed for first prize in exaggeration. There's fretwork and latticework and curlicues and frescoes everywhere, but it's overpowering, altogether too much; it's better to sit in the shade outside and watch the world go in and come out again, looking as glazed as me.

This is the home town of El Cid, and there's a statue of him in the square on his warhorse Babieca. If the story is to be believed that El Cid was a warrior hero rather than a mercenary on the make, then the tale of his final battle is a fair mixture of the ingenious and the macabre. Under siege by the Moors in Valencia and about to breathe his last, he ordered that his dead body should be strapped upright on his stallion so that he could lead his men to victory one last time. That night, Babieca carefully and obediently proceeded towards the enemy camp carrying his pale master, stiff as a board with rigor mortis, sword hand fixed in the air, with the rest of the troops following behind. Not surprisingly, the Moors took to their heels at this apparition of resurrection, only to be run down and slaughtered. The bodies of El Cid and his horse lie in the cathedral now, but I'm too swamped by the multitude of chapels and tombs and saints when I'm in there to do more than shuffle by without stopping.

Peter's day is made by the lady barber. He requests a short back and sides with gestures that are rather too explicit, and she scalps him with a tiny pair of scissors, standing so close that her pneumatic right breast is bouncing off his nose. His expression changes to trepidation when she attacks his eyebrows with a pair of shears, and to downright refusal when she opens a pot of hair gel. I'm quite in favour of it – sticky stubble could be an effective trap for the mosquitoes that pour nightly through the gaps between Bessie's planks, which are shrunken and bleached by the sun and the wind.

We get back to the *refugio* to find that St James's Day Mass is in progress in the quadrangle, the visiting priest vivid in his robes is crowded by pilgrims and local dignitaries. Susie's in there somewhere, but Peter and I sneak round the perimeter with dinner for Leo and Apollo in their enclosure behind the dormitory. We've had to put a warning notice on the fence after finding fearless toddlers in there clinging to the horses' knees, their mothers oblivious both to the electricity and to the half-ton of weight supported by each set of clumsy hooves. Now there's a TV crew in the enclosure with a camera trained in close-up on Apollo's loud spots, and they advance on Peter and me with inviting smiles and fluffy microphones. They seem to want a complete resumé of the trip so far in fluent Spanish, and it's an interesting experience to be interviewed at length when you don't speak their language and they don't speak yours – but we manage appropriate sounding words for spirituality, charity and religion several times.

Thanks to the generosity of the city worthies, dinner is free for those who've been given government-issue sun hats with the word Burgos and a scallop shell printed on them in lemon yellow. We clamp ours on our heads, and tuck in to tortillas and cheese and chips and pimientos and apples and pastries and red wine before collecting Daniel to waddle back to Bessie and the whisky bottle for a nightcap to help his cuts and bruises. The lorry's not in the greatest location for a good night's sleep – the orange street lamps glare in the uncurtained windows, and my efforts to shut them out with judicious arrangements of towels and drying-up cloths only deaden the colour slightly to ochre. Peter puts in a plaintive request for us to stop sleeping in public car parks when we get home again.

At six in the morning the full moon's still out, and Susie and I manage a relatively early start to avoid the rush-hour traffic, passing the mediaeval Hospital del Rey, which offered shelter to pilgrims for hundreds of years until a fire consumed most of it in the nineteenth century. The Camino leaves and rejoins the main road, weaving alongside the river, the railway line, and through orderly vegetable plots as the day heats up. In Tardajos we turn off finally towards the *meseta*, trotting down a ribbon of lane past the horrible sight of a starving cat demolishing one of its relations. Startled by the sound of hooves but determined not to let go of its trophy, it scampers ahead of us carrying a bloody spine with two tabby legs attached.

But this disgusting image passes swiftly into memory, as Leo and Apollo home in on a little nun waiting in the road beside her convent to hand out silver pendants of the Virgin Mary to all the pilgrims she sees. She's delighted with the horses who are checking her for peppermints, coming up close to stroke their necks and tell us the Virgin will protect us on our journey. Susie hangs her pendant round her neck and I tie mine to Leo's saddle – a religious symbol for my sister, a talisman for me.

And then we're out on the plain, where corn fields meet a horizon so vast you can see the world is round, and where the only shadow at midday is thrown by a lone vulture circling overhead. It's nearly 40°C again but we take the breeze with us as we trot and sometimes canter where there's stubble, dust devils whirling the residue grain and corn stalks into the sky, the shimmery haze dancing over the plateau.

We've heard that pilgrims either love or hate the *mesetas*, marvelling at their desolate grandeur or cursing the endless slog through the desiccating heat and emptiness. Today for me they're magic, the rolling wilderness of the sea I love transposed to land, glass green changed to fudge and clotted cream, and Susie and I agree that travelling by horse must be the best way to see them. We can appreciate the landscape's easy undulations at a walk, or we can lope across, eating up the miles if we find the distance daunting. The horses are enjoying the open space as well, Leo not confined by my left leg pushing him to the right, and Apollo realising that if he's quick enough he can grab whole ears of corn before he gets told off.

Mulekiller Hill, the Cuesta Matamulos, is a sharp stony scramble down to the pilgrim village of Hornillos del Camino, with its single street lined with tables and chairs. We stop for coffee and cake. There's nowhere to tie the horses, so we sit holding them, which they mistake for an invitation to dine and Apollo wastes no time in helping himself to a teaspoon which Susie rescues as it's disappearing down his throat. My drink is next. He knocks over my cup, spilling coffee all over the table, and spends blissful minutes running his tongue languorously over the surface with his eyes closed. Susie apologises to the waitress, but there's nothing for her damp cloth to wipe up – Apollo has licked the table clean. While I'm complaining to Susie about her horse's lack of manners, Leo's elongating his top lip over my cake and then it's gone; and my money's also gone as I've just spent the last of it for today, so that's it – no coffee, no cake.

At least there's water in the next valley. An oasis appears in the desert: it's Fuente Sambol, the spring of Sambol, with its mini *refugio* built from the ruins of an old hospital to treat sick pilgrims, where Javier the artist-in-residence has painted the surrounding walls with blood curdling depictions of St James Matamoros in primary colours. There are trees, thick grass, and the cold spring pouring ceaselessly into a deep stone tank. A Danish pilgrim stopped by for a lunch break two weeks ago, and she's still here: the attraction seems to be Javier, and we speculate that perhaps she'll stay here for ever in this speck of green under the wide sky.

She dives enthusiastically into the tank. Leo's drinking out of it at the time, having missed out on the coffee, but he's quite unperturbed by the shattering splash and expanse of voluptuous flesh in his water trough, and Susie photographs her bobbing head beside his muzzle. We pause for lunch among the supine bodies in the shade; like us, some are carrying on for a few more miles to Hontanas, but for an hour while the sun is at its fiercest there's an excuse to sprawl there with them, the horses grazing quietly under the pines.

The Camino leads away into nowhere, Hontanas only visible at the last minute in a fold of the land, all mellow stone houses and ladies in black dresses knitting in the street. It looks as though nothing's changed for centuries, but it has: an ancient señora tells Peter in animated Spanish that there's a tap in the village these days, thanks to the increasing number of pilgrims each year. For decades she had to fetch water from further up the hill, but now it gushes coldly at great pressure from this wonderful tap. I'd like to ask her why her husband didn't fetch it for her, but I don't have the words.

Peter's understanding of the language is increasing daily: for some reason the Spanish assume that he speaks it, and he's often treated to short history lessons. Yesterday's was that during the decades of Franco's rule the Catholic Church was in cahoots with the General, and if you weren't a Catholic you couldn't get a job. Further, according to his informant, St James is only a myth and now there's a bandwagon rolling to make the Camino just a tourist trail. We wonder if there was ever a time when it didn't have that dimension, but at least it's bringing occupation to the villages, and amenities like the Hontanas tap. There's even a bar here, but it's run by a disagreeable man who says crossly '*No vende pan*' when I try to buy a loaf of bread from him. One of our guidebooks strongly advises women travellers not to stay in his *refugio*, so perhaps business isn't good. Or else I'm just too old to catch his wandering eye.

There's only a fiery slope of bare stubble for the horses to eat, and there's no shade. Lucerne and knotgrass straggle beside a new house next to it whose owners say we may put them there to graze, although they're not the owners of the land, and Leo and Apollo spend a contented evening rummaging in the hedge for damsons, ignoring all the extra lucerne we've painstakingly picked and dumped in their enclosure with them.

Susie's booked herself a bed in the main *refugio* in the village, where the dining room has a glass floor so you can view the Roman ruins underfoot. Dinner is seven euros for each of us, and has an unusual sequence of courses: a large bowl of spaghetti followed by two fried eggs, one lettuce leaf, a tomato, and then an apple, all washed down with an agreeably cold red wine. Most of the pilgrims staying here are French, which makes conversation easier. They're curious about Peter, anxious to know what the pilgrimage means to him and, after a moment's calculation, he tells them he's walked 45 kilometres erecting and dismantling the electric fence, and has planted four thousand fencing poles in the ground. And that, he says with a smile, is his Camino.

At twilight it's so warm that he and I are still sitting outside, the combine harvesters and tractors at work in the distance with their headlights sweeping the plains. When I look at Peter, squinting at his book in the dusk, I can see he's lost weight from the heat and effort of driving seven and a half tons of unwieldy lorry on narrow roads and tracks: even his ankles have slimmed down to racehorse elegance. The only golf he's played so far in Spain was on yesterday's nine-hole course at Burgos, and now his time's spent driving to where Susie and I expect to be at the end of each day, reading the last of his books, and trying to keep himself cool. His sense of humour surprisingly is mostly still intact, and he's refused to let me contact any of our relief drivers so he can go back to England for a break – either he thinks no-one else would put up with Susie and me, or the temptation not to return might be overwhelming.

And there's a sense of unity between the three of us, even though as individuals our temperaments and interests are diverse. If all goes well, it's only another two or three weeks to Santiago and, after months of living from day to day, we can dare to look ahead: the goal is almost in sight. That goal probably means something quite different to each of us. I can hazard a guess that at one end of the spectrum Susie's pilgrimage has a great deal of spiritual significance for her, particularly now we're in Spain and the pilgrim route is so defined. I'm somewhere in the middle – not sure yet, still too occupied with organisation to think about an inner journey, my only determinable focus to raise as much money as possible for the Pilgrims' Hospices by getting to Santiago in one piece. And Peter's at the other end of the spectrum, basically honouring a contract to back us up and drive the lorry as long we don't expect him to do any cooking.

But it's a lesson in tolerance, in adaptation, and we're getting better at it as the days go by. Susie's not taking so long to get going in the morning, and whilst it's an annoying fact for me that you can only travel at the speed of the slowest, it does have advantages – not only is Apollo's back still holding up, with no open sores, but neither horse has suffered any leg strains or sprains so far. Like me, Susie also has the objective of raising funds for the Hospices and, for my part, I've been marched into so many churches by now that ecclesiastical architecture is leaving an indelible print on my mind.

As for Peter, he likes to give the impression that this is a hard labour of love for me and he certainly wouldn't be here otherwise. And no doubt that's true, but mixed in with the tedium of waiting is a burgeoning hoard of funny incidents and anecdotes, along with the scarier moments of manoeuvring Bessie down streets that are narrower than the lorry, to file into his prodigious memory and fish out later when we go home. He and I are close, companionable, and never more so than when travelling together – although I doubt he anticipated, any more than I did, that something I wrote to him years ago would prove to be so prophetic:

> *This man is unexpected.*
> *He's my humorous companion*
> *On a long, long walk.*
> *He pretends he is a dove.*
> *He is a hawk.*

This man has many layers:
Some may yet surprise him.
Some he lets me see,
And some I think will stay
His own mystery.

This man loves me with unhurried fire;
He strips me down
To nakedness of skin and thought
With gentle urgency.

He has me caught.

25. A PLACE REDOLENT OF OLD BLOOD

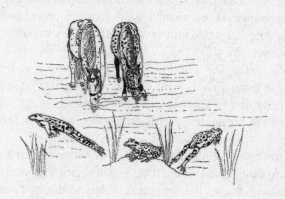

Dawn on the *meseta* is a ghostly affair, a monochrome palette of buttermilk corn, a whisper of pale rabbits that normally we would never see. When the fireball of the sun splinters the horizon I point the camera unkindly at the jet black silhouette of Susie and Apollo; between them they look like some satanic centaur emanating flames, but it needs to be recorded that on one day we actually set off before the sun got up.

It's still quite cool when we reach Castrojeriz, built by the Romans and with a ruined castle on the hill above, and we skirt round the bottom to find another hill beyond, a huge shining pimple in the plain. The Camino goes straight over the top of this one, and Leo and Apollo trot to the summit in their usual uphill travelling mode, with Susie and me smiling guilty greetings as we overtake pilgrims panting along on foot and some pushing their bikes. The whole lot pass us again on the downhill stretch which is so steep that we both have to get off and lead our horses, picking our way along a track that appears to be made of shards of glass. The hill is full of gypsum, flashing and sparking in the sun.

The evocatively named Río Pisuerga is crossed by a long Romanesque bridge with eleven arches, and now we're into Palencia, squeezed between the Burgos region and the elongated stretch across León. The Montes de León, beyond the city itself, is another range of mountains we'll have to cross, and then there's the one into Lugo and central Galicia. But we won't think about that yet. We still have a long way to go on the *mesetas* and today, like yesterday, I'm caught in a rhythm, a cadence of travelling, a conscious thought there's nowhere else I'd rather be than here with my amenable horse, swinging along with his ground-eating stride across this huge plain with the hot wind blowing.

The river at Boadilla del Camino has a shallow ford, where Leo and Apollo stand cooling their legs and gulping, surrounded by panicking frogs. It saves using Lady Aldington's bucket, which is becoming more brittle by the day – really it ought to be in a museum, but we have to use it all the time because most of the drinking fountains have no troughs, and large horse muzzles don't fit under spouts. Susie and I are both terrified that the bucket will disintegrate before we get home, and the puncture repair kit patches are becoming as numerous as Apollo's spots.

We reach Frómista in the burning afternoon, slowed by the stony surface of the towpath that runs along the Canal de Castilla, the water moving silently beside us, no frogs, no fish, nothing. Another town, another church; even I have heard of this one as it's reputed to be the most perfect Romanesque church in Spain. Running the whole way round the eaves outside is an amazing frieze of carved animals, demons, gargoyles and flowers, all of them different; inside, the rows of pillars with their carved capitals stretch from one end to the other, but the church itself is almost bare. It's been deconsecrated, and the spirit has gone out of it. Not even the storks are supposed to nest on it now.

The local horse owner provides Leo and Apollo with a locked enclosure, adding a generous bale of mixed hay and straw and an invitation to park Bessie by the dung heap. He doesn't really want payment for tonight's board and lodging, and only accepts ten euros with reluctance. We fill all our water containers from a tap in the town, suspend them by the spare headcollar ropes from the back of the lorry, and Peter transports them without spilling a drop.

On the second trip to the tap we're greeted by a young man and his uncle standing in front of what appears to be a shack with mustard walls. Not so. They insist on a conducted tour, and once inside the door the first thing to catch the eye is a beautiful old Basque stove, all blacklead and polished brass in this stunningly tidy bodega. Proudly, we're shown the entrance to the Underworld, a staircase to the caves filled with wooden barrels and rack upon rack of wine produced organically, without chemicals.

After two glasses of clear cold rosé on top of a dehydrating day with no food, I'm rapidly feeling no pain. We're still standing around grinning vacantly when Señor Horse Owner turns up to see what's happened to us. Several glasses later we've all got bendy legs, and our lack of Spanish has ceased to be a problem – slurred words sound pretty much the same in any language. Bessie's driven erratically back to the horse field clinking with bottles of rosé and home-made red wine vinegar, and in a disinhibited moment Peter takes an experimental swig out of the latter with the result that he's up surprisingly early the next morning, wearing a thoughtful expression and eyeing the dung heap.

The wind blows like fury all night, covering everything from the saddles to our clothes in pungent dust. At eight in the morning it's relatively cool, but the *mesetas* show us a different face today. A gravelled track purpose-built for the pilgrims, a *senda de peregrinos*, runs beside the main road from Frómista for the twelve miles to Carrión de los Condes, punctuated by twin sets of bollards to prevent traffic driving on to the track. Each bollard should have a decorative blue ceramic tile with a yellow scallop shell on it, but nearly all of them have been damaged or chipped off, and it's a nasty desecration on a somehow soulless route lined with pilgrim picnic sites full of stone barbecues and convenient rock-slab tables. This is a result of the commercialisation of the Camino, and there's no way of knowing whether the vandalism is the work of disenchanted locals or pilgrims greedy for souvenirs.

However, Susie and I are inspired by a dangerous sense of enthusiasm due to the speed at which we cover the distance, and after a brief coffee stop in Carrión, decide to push on, launching ourselves into the longest, hottest, slowest afternoon of our lives.

Calzadilla de la Cueza is only ten miles away, but the gravelled path gives way to the old Roman road, a nightmare of big round pebbles and angular stones that slide under the horses' hooves and make them stumble. Trotting is out of the question, and now we can understand the wearisome monotony that envelopes the foot pilgrims toiling along in the dust and glare of midsummer. The parched corn rattles; it's so thin that sometimes it's hard to tell whether it's been cut or not, but riding on the stubble is no better than the track anyway – the pebbles are even larger, the stones grown to flints. The horizon holds confusing images of water, but there is none; the guidebook says we cross three rivers, but there's only the heat quivering in dead riverbeds. A sudden dust devil whirls up in front of me, throwing stubble into the air and startling Leo, but now the wind too is dying, the horseflies catching up in squadrons to marshal whole formations of smaller flies that ricochet off our noses like gunshot. We get slower and slower.

Where the hell's that village?

There's a spike sticking up out of the plain. Or else it's another mirage. No, it isn't – it's a spire. The rest of Calzadilla church materialises as the Camino drops down the slope, and there's Peter talking to Johan and Anthea, and there's the happy sight of the other two substantial buildings in the village: a new *refugio*, a new hotel. Peter's thoughtfully booked himself and me into the latter so that we can wash off the clinging debris from last night's muck heap, and Susie heads for the *refugio*. The hotel owner's proud to have pilgrim horses staying in his yard: he says he recognises that Apollo is a Percheron, a cart horse, which Susie doesn't take as a compliment.

The village is ruled by an enormous dog wearing a collar spiked with nails. He presents himself condescendingly to be patted, but even I have to decline – his coat is unusually full of scurf, and I don't want to end up with mange as well as punctured palms. He presides gravely over our dinner, eaten outside beside the empty fountain as the breathless night drops like a curtain on the *meseta*. The rules at Calzadilla de la Cueza are strict: lights out in the *refugio* at half-past ten exactly, and the hotel door locked at the same time. Unaware of this, we're still sitting outside with Johan and Anthea, garrulously into the beer, but Señor's unamused by the loud giggling and banging on the door and we're severely reprimanded before being allowed in and sent to bed.

Another airless day, the temperature climbing to 40°C by early morning. The pilgrim path is the new version again, gritty rather than stony which makes for faster going but files down the horses' shoes with great efficiency. Their front ones are worn down to the hoof; we're brushing their feet with corn oil three times a day in an effort to keep them hydrated, but the shoes are working loose, clacking with each step. God knows where we're ever going to find a farrier. We can only hope they last until we get to the city of León – with a population of more than 130,000, there must be a blacksmith there somewhere.

By midday we've crossed the border out of Palencia to reach Sahagún, once the site of the most powerful Cluny monastery in Spain, although little is left of it apart from amorphous humps on a hill and a neoclassical arch rearing across the road out of the town. There's a connection with Charlemagne here: on the night before his army's battle against the Moors, some of his men stuck the points of their lances into the ground and by morning they'd taken root, sprouting branches and leaves. This must have caused considerable problems for Charlemagne's men, and I'd like to know who won that battle: the disadvantaged French or the fully armed Saracens. The poplars growing beside the river are descended from those lances – or so they say.

Today in the blinding sunlight Sahagún has a certain decaying grandeur, but in the restored Church of La Trinidad a positively luxurious municipal *refugio* has been created in its upper level, with bunk beds curtained off from one another and feisty showers thundering with hot water. Señora Warden assures us there's accommodation for horses down the road, and she's right. It's in the bullring. Or to be precise, it's under the bullring.

It's the strangest billet yet. A man with a van and a key arrives to let us in and, to judge by the number of old crots, there've been plenty of horses here before ours. Everything is here that's guaranteed to trip or maim a horse: broken bottles, guttering, lumps of concrete, machinery bristling with shafts and spikes, and lengths of chain. It's too heavy to move, too much to fence off even if we could force the posts into the iron ground. All we can do is to point out every hazard to Leo and Apollo, and tell them not to get tangled up in it. Not surprisingly, they haven't the faintest idea what we're on about. Señor unearths an old bale of disintegrating alfalfa mixed with husks of shrivelled corn cobs, and we shake it out in a coughing cloud of dust. The horses think it's wonderful.

When I climb on the roof over the bull pens to search for the mains tap, I'm looking down on a place that's charged with the oppressive atmosphere of an ancient, primitive sport, from the lifting metal gates with their heavy counterweights to the scored sand in the bullring and the discarded Coke cans flashing silver under a white hot sky. Susie's uneasy about leaving Leo and Apollo here – she thinks the place is redolent of old blood, and I expect she's right, but the more immediate reason could be the municipal rubbish lorry reeking inside the gate. When we come back later to check that the horses haven't cut themselves to shreds they're perfectly at ease; they've finished every last crumbling blade of alfalfa and are resting in the deep shade under the spectator stands.

As the temperature soars in the afternoon, the baking town's deserted. There's some shade thrown by Bessie, standing beside the road and the railway line. A siesta's a wonderful thing, but not easy sitting in a wooden chair in the street, every breath sucked away into the furnace. I doze off, jerk upright, write another guilty postcard apologising for the dead silence of the last six weeks, and doze off again. In the evening, we lay the supper table neatly next to the lorry, and smile *holà* at the procession of little old ladies who walk past very close so they can see what these curious foreign pilgrims are eating. Boring old corned beef and salad again, so nothing new there.

The morning's much cooler, and we risk two legs of the journey in one day again, the price paid this time in horseshoes rather than overheating. The gravelled path runs for more than twenty miles, following the route of the original Camino Francés through El Burgo Raneros to Mansilla de las Mulas. For the final four miles, Leo's front shoes are clanking so furiously that I'm sure they're going to fall off, in spite of frequent stops to oil his hooves and whack the nails in again with a hammer. Mansilla is as far as they're going to take him, and Apollo's are no better, although both horses' hind shoes are still in reasonable shape as they don't take so much weight and percussion.

Mansilla de las Mulas was a centre for buying and selling horses until comparatively recently; with such a tradition you'd think the well-equipped *refugio* would welcome ours with open arms. Not at all. The staff are emphatic that Leo and Apollo are not going in the *refugio* garden, but vague when it comes to suggestions as to where we might go instead. We cross over the broad Río Esla that skirts the town with its Romanesque walls, built with boulders taken from the riverbed, and hover on its banks. The day has warmed up nicely again, and Susie makes a unilateral decision that she will stay and look after the horses, while I go off on foot to look for the campsite. It's around here somewhere. Well, where? After an hour spent dragging my feet down hot little roads and through private allotments, I've practically melted, but at least I've found it. The owner's away, but enthusiastic young Mario's holiday job is to be in charge in his absence.

How can I help you? You need somewhere to stay? Please, stay with us. Two horses, one lorry? No problem. You need the farrier, *el herrero* (one necessary word we've had to learn)? No problem. Except that he can't come until Thursday evening, and today is Tuesday. Oh, well. We could do with a break – we've been riding for seventeen days, caught in the pilgrim continuum of get up, push on, stop, eat, fall into bed, drop into oblivion, get up, push on. The familiar and unfamiliar pilgrim faces are becoming a ceaseless river of humanity flowing towards Santiago; Johan and Anthea are here in Mansilla, and so is a Parisian who's had a nervous breakdown – her psychiatrist advised her to throw away her pills and walk the Camino instead, and we often see her striding along, the worries smoothed out of her face. There's one pilgrim we'd like to meet but never do: he's reputed to be dragging a heavy wooden cross the whole way from Roncesvalles to Santiago. He must be a very tormented soul.

What bliss, what decadence, to lie in bed beyond 5.30 a.m., with Leo and Apollo stretched out on the ground sleeping peacefully beside Bessie. We've created a field in the woods on the other side of the perimeter fence, but Mario tells us to bring the horses on to the campsite at night because there are thieves in the village. When the site owner returns, he banishes them to the wood again, on the basis that they might chew his own carefully nurtured trees, and with Apollo's record we can hardly disagree. But the horses are unhappy with the rank grass there and stand over us like big dogs, begging.

There's a little Spaniard down the lane who's scything a square of alfalfa on his allotment, and he insists on giving Leo and Apollo exactly a quarter of his entire crop, for which he resolutely refuses payment. There's enough to last the horses for two days, and they bowl us over ecstatically when we reappear lugging the rich greenery. They're honed to super-fitness now, their muscles bulging; always on the edge of hunger, the days of ambling along in dead-donkey mode are in the past.

As for Peter and Susie and me, we're all as lean as lurchers, bursting with the good health that comes of being outside in the open for sixteen hours a day. I can't begin to imagine how it will feel not to be a nomad any more, to be confined to an office, to a desk, to the claustrophobic box of an interview room at a police station. Shivery thought. Shove it away.

After supper we walk into the village for a drink or six with Johan and Anthea. By drink five, we're into philosophical discussion, teetering between righting all the world's wrongs and the usual topic of conversation between pilgrims: why are we here? Anthea's content with a long walk in the countryside with her husband, but for Johan there's another dimension that he can't explore, which is to walk alone with his thoughts. He says that one day he'll return on his own, and Anthea is understanding, but for her this journey in his company is enough.

We see many pilgrims setting off together and then walking separately within an hour, meeting up again in the evenings. Although Susie and I are companionable, it would probably be the same for us if we were on foot, given that her natural speed and pace of life are slower than mine, but the idea of trying to put it into practice with Leo and Apollo is laughable. It's out of the question – the two horses are overcome with anxiety if they're out of each other's sight for a minute. Any attempt to ride separately would result in deafening blasts of neighing, Leo trying to whirl round and gallop back the other way, and Apollo carting Susie with his bit clenched between his teeth until he caught up again. So we shall never know what it's like to ride the Camino in solitude.

To his delight, Peter's discovered a championship golf course just outside León, and Susie and I are dropped off in the city while he rattles off in Bessie, visibly relieved to have a day to please himself. I know where Susie and I are going: straight to the cathedral. I'm not sure I'm going to like it, as I have a feeling it's going to be as overpoweringly Gothic as the cathedral in Burgos, but the reality is very different. St James the pilgrim is here in greeting, sculpted next to the central door, and inside is a flood of light from the floor to the soaring height of the ceiling, all space and suffusion of colour through window after window in the sun's glow. The mediaeval stained glass is still perfect, from the detailed depictions of saints to the intricate patterns of leaves set with strange secret faces.

Outside, the airy streets and plazas are scrupulously clean and scrubbed. I have a feeling the police will have no difficulty in finding the horses if we try to bring them into the centre tomorrow, so we'll have to find a diversion and pick up the arrows again on the other side of the city. Pious hope. Today's a day for wandering, for coffee and ice creams guzzled near a group of Russians playing balalaikas as big as barn doors, for a guided tour of the Basilica of San Isidoro for Susie, and a trip to the butcher for me. It would be great to have something other than cold meat for supper, but it takes me as long to do the shopping as it does for Susie to walk round San Isidoro: the lady butcher chats endlessly to the customers in front of me, expertly chopping and slicing and mincing at the same time. When it's finally my turn to be served, I've forgotten what the Spanish word for pork is anyway, but I'm handed an anonymous lump of meat that's later simmered into something wonderfully tender, if unidentifiable.

The farrier is diminutive, full of improbable stories, and he replaces Leo's and Apollo's front shoes for a mere twenty euros each. Unfortunately, he's run out of tungsten studs, but he says the new shoes may last the distance to Santiago, and the existing hind shoes as well, though he warns us that the gravel and asphalt paths take a heavier toll on equine legs and hooves than on human feet. As soon as he's finished, Mario and the barmaid turn up for a photocall. The barmaid's never been on a horse before, but she's certainly seen the John Wayne films: when we hoist her on to Leo, she digs her heels into his sides and shakes the reins authoritatively before I can stop her. Leo's astounded at this clear aid to leap into a gallop from a standstill but is happy to oblige, clanging his new ironmongery all round the campsite while the barmaid screams with laughter, waving delightedly at the other campers as she careers through their crockery and coolboxes.

Inspector Clouseau calls by in the morning. By then Susie and I are two hours away in the general direction of León, but he confronts Peter: he has heard a rumour, he says, that there are horses in the wood. Does Señor know anything about it? Peter's standing under the trees with a pile of fencing poles and two hundred yards of electric tape, surrounded by crots we didn't have time to clear up. No, he says truthfully, there are no horses here. Satisfied, the police officer walks carefully out of the wood again and away, brushing past the lowered ramp of the horsebox with its chaos of hay bales, spare saddlebags, a shovel, yard broom and the muck bucket.

26. DOCTOR FERNANDO

I don't hear the bicycle behind us, and neither does Leo. Inspired by yesterday's romp with the barmaid, he manages nought to sixty in three seconds when it tries to thread its way past us on the track. I've been riding on a loose rein as usual and it's half a minute's hard gallop before I manage to pull him up again, by which time we've overtaken several lorries on the road alongside and it's lucky we haven't flattened any pilgrims. Apollo's a coiled spring behind us as Susie sternly holds him to a walk, shrieking his distress: My friend! My friend! He's gone without me and I'll never see him again, never!

The Camino takes to the main N120 into León. It's surprisingly narrow and there's no hard shoulder, which means another spell of leading the horses on the left, facing the traffic – full face, in fact, when we come to a thin bridge with HGVs piled one behind the other on the other side. I switch to Leo's right, hoping the lorry drivers won't take a risk with a human that they might with a horse, and flag them down: the driver in front raises his eyebrows in disbelief, but he stops to allow us over first to an explosive symphony of air brakes all down the road. Leo and Apollo are completely calm, as they always are in a serious situation, but a worse crisis lies ahead for Susie – the arrows are pointing over a thread of a pedestrian bridge arching through the air. Pea green with vertigo, she walks with her eyes fixed on the central plank – for her, the prospect of being run over by an HGV is less terrifying.

From the outskirts of the city, the yellow arrows point straight towards the centre, but it looks as though we can ride beside the river to the left and avoid it. But we can't. The road sneakily doubles back into a broad avenue packed with market stalls and bargain hunters, and there's only one escape route – a half-built road where fortunately the labourers have disappeared for a pre-prandial siesta. Leo and Apollo trip over the shuttering boards awaiting concrete, shuffle through the sand, and suddenly we're right outside the Hostal de San Marcos, once a monastery associated with the Order of St James and now one of the most luxurious paradors in Spain.

Susie! We need to get out of here quickly, before one of the horses drops a ... Susie! That spotless forecourt, don't take Apollo up to the front door! With a look of determination I know well, she leads him over to view the decorative St James Matamoros above the entrance; Apollo's ears are buttoned well forwards, his expression gracious, charming even – he's obviously expecting an invitation to lunch.

But we escape from León without any embarrassing incidents, finding the arrows again and plodding out through the suburbs on the N120, walking on foot for miles in the slow lane. Leo's impatient, and Apollo's hungry. He hits on a solution: standing behind Susie at a pedestrian crossing, it dawns on him that her sun hat is made of straw, and he grips it experimentally in his teeth. Susie pulls away. Apollo pulls back. There's the sound of ripping and the brim is unravelling, vanishing down his neck. Delicious! Susie's left with an inverted straw chamber pot on her head and a face of fury as she yanks the brim out of Apollo's capacious mouth. All the traffic's at a standstill, the drivers falling about with laughter, and Leo seems to be the only one who's noticed, accurately for once, that the light's gone green. It's the best thing that's happened all day, though Susie would disagree – she can see an evening of soggy sewing ahead of her.

On the other side of Virgen del Camino the pilgrim trail's in a mess, thanks to the new Madrid motorway still under construction. There are arrows pointing in several different directions, but we can leave the vile main road to follow a tortuous track where the dry wind rattles in skeletal hedges, and the Montes de León are vague outlines in the distance to mark the end of our days on the *mesetas*. By the time we reach the *refugio* at tiny Villar de Mazarife we've been riding for nine hours.

We grind thankfully to a halt and … oh, no! Susie! Where's Lady Aldington's bucket? The back of Leo's saddle is bare. The bucket's undone itself in the wind (well, I suppose it's just possible I didn't tie it on properly after the last water stop) and has flown away. We're speechless. It could be anywhere, but we'll have to find it. We ask other pilgrims, draw a blank with ten of them, but the eleventh saw it in the street at the last village. He couldn't work out what it was, but it looked as though it was supposed to be something (a canvas sieve, perhaps) so he picked it up out of the road and put it to one side. We drive back in Bessie, and there it is. I could kiss him.

The privately owned *refugio* has a conglomeration of mattresses in microscopic rooms, and one loo between thirty pilgrims. Susie's worried about that, but Peter points out she'll have to put up with it – she'll need a pneumatic trowel if she tries to dig around here. Her sleeping arrangements are perfect, though; her bed is on the upstairs balcony above the central courtyard, and she's soothed into slumber by the soft breathing of rows of fellow pilgrims in the open air to either side, under an inky sky and silver stars.

Peter and I have less luck, parked outside the house with its thick sound-deadening walls – for such a little hamlet, this is an incredibly noisy place. At dusk I photograph the silhouette of the church tower opposite with four storks' nests wobbling on it, and the beak-clattering orchestra carries on long after dark in harmony with the churring crickets. Leo and Apollo, enclosed next to Bessie with half a bale of English hay as the alternative is dried earth, spend the night noisily blowing their noses in the dust. They've attracted a lot of attention from the locals, particularly a family with several teenagers who at three in the morning are still calling to them over the fence, setting off every dog in the village into a paroxysm of barking. I'm uncomfortable about people around the horses in the night, shooting up in bed every half-hour to see if they're actually in the pen with them, and stabbed through the chest with indigestion from a supper that included too much sharp vinaigrette to enliven our daily ration of lettuce and tomatoes.

EU funding is in evidence again when we leave Villar de Mazarife, passing its new tractor shop and following the Camino across the plain, now striped with irrigation channels and canals dividing fields of maize as far as the eye can see. The Spanish farmers are the rich men now, and I'm glad for them that they have the opportunity to exploit the land, their natural resource, but with a tired, uncompromisingly black and white attitude this morning I'm thinking, well, why don't the Spanish fishermen leave our fishing stocks alone, our own natural resource? We don't try to grow crops on their land – why should they have a right to our fish?

Adolfo buys us breakfast in Hospital de Órbigo. We haven't met him before, but can't resist a *holà* when we notice the copious writing on his T-shirt, which he's happy to translate: I BELONG TO THE UNMARRIED MEN'S CLUB. As he's tall, dark, handsome, speaks good English and of course he's eligible, never mind the T-shirt, Susie and I debate which one of our various daughters he might suit. He looks as tired as me; the reason in his case is because he was assigned to one of the tiny rooms in the *refugio* last night and the girl on the mattress next to his snored like a train, so in the end he lugged his bed out on to the bare ground in the courtyard, and froze instead. A lawyer from Malaga, he's walking alone for a few days before he's joined by friends, and we spend an intense fifteen minutes over coffee and toast discussing the trial by jury system, recently introduced into Spain, while Leo and Apollo doze off, tied to a gutter downpipe in the street. It's the first time I've thought about the law for months, and I can hear the cogs creaking rustily in my brain.

The bridge out of town across the Río Órbigo is Roman and, at 335 yards, it's the longest in Spain. It has twenty arches, and in the fifteenth century a jousting tournament was held on it that went on for a month, resulting in the demise of one knight and several hundred lances; Leo and Apollo are slipping on the smooth stones as we cross, and I'm surprised there were no equine casualties recorded. Beyond the bridge, the traditional route of the Camino is buried under the main road, so we take the rough cross-country track to Astorga, also waymarked, through scrub and evergreen oaks buzzing with yellow horseflies. But at least there's no traffic. The Roman town of Astorga is astride a hill, blocks of its original walls still in existence, marking the junction of the Camino Francés and the Vía de la Plata, the pilgrim road from Seville in the south. It has a new municipal *refugio* but Leo and Apollo can't stay in the garden – this time it's because there are some Spanish horses expected, arriving from the north, whose back-up team in a car have already arrived to book it.

The warden's anxious to help, introducing us to octogenarian Domingo whose little house is tucked in the maze of streets at the bottom of the town. He too has a garden, and a yard and some disused stables where he dodders round enthusiastically filling buckets with water while we fence off his apple tree, bursting with fruit, and buy a bale of this season's alfalfa from a farm down the road. Reluctantly, Domingo accepts five euros for the horses' board and lodging, and then promptly spends them on drinks for us at the bar.

The Gothic cathedral is closed, and we can't get into the Bishop's Palace either which was designed by the highly eccentric Catalan architect Gaudi, but it doesn't look to me as though it's one of his best efforts. The façade reminds me of a Disney cartoon castle, and I wouldn't be surprised to see Minnie Mouse clomping out of the door in her oversized shoes. I'm too tired for sightseeing anyway, reaching saturation point with ecclesiastical buildings, but Peter and I have a better night's sleep in Bessie in the public car park than Susie does in the *refugio*: she's managed to commandeer a bottom bunk, but her neighbour overhead is an enormous bloke who clambers past her nose wearing only a small pair of black Y-fronts. He spends the night trapped in violent dreams, thrashing and grunting and bending the bed to such an extent that Susie's wide awake for hours, worrying that his bunk will collapse on top of her. I can see the tabloid headlines: ASPHYXIATED IN ASTORGA: WIPED OUT BY WHIFFY Y-FRONTS, OR PULVERISED BY PORKER PILGRIM?

Caught in the loo queue at 6 a.m., I spot first Adolfo pottering past in the corridor, bleary after Señorita Snorer chose to sleep next to him again, and then Susie looking equally owlish as the piped 'Blue Danube' waltz crashes out at a deafening volume to encourage the jolly pilgrims to get out of bed. To defeat spongers looking for cheap holidays, no-one's allowed to stay more than a single night at a *refugio*, but I'm not sure anyone would survive more than one night here anyway. Susie wanders off through the tangle of alleys and streets to give Leo and Apollo their breakfast, feeding them the rest of the alfalfa bale as well, but when we return to saddle them up we notice some of it's still untouched. I double-check they haven't touched Domingo's apple tree, and we pile the crots under his roses, hoping they'll result in an explosion of blooms next year.

As we clatter noisily out of Astorga along the paved top of the city wall, a panoramic view opens up across the sere plain behind us to the east before we drop down towards the road to Rabanal del Camino, where volunteers from the Confraternity of

St James in England run their Refugio Gaucelmo, converted from the old parish priest's house. I'm pleased to notice as we pass last night's *refugio* that although we're not under way particularly early, the Spanish horse contingent is barely stirring. The Camino is a mixture of road and gravelled path again, already grinding down the horses' new front shoes, and today both Leo and Apollo are back in dead-donkey mode from too much alfalfa and the effort of starting the slow ascent towards the Montes de León after ten days on the *mesetas*.

At Rabanal the Refugio Gaucelmo isn't open yet, but Jabir at the bar negotiates a grassy field for the horses, courtesy of one of his neighbours – or at any rate the neighbour's wife and daughter, who invite us to use their tap for the buckets although there's a water shortage in the village. When Señor the neighbour catches up with us he's most put out by the presence of a large lorry parked outside his front door, and makes it clear there are no bucket refills on offer; but fortunately the wardens at the *refugio*, now open, invite us to help ourselves to all we want. The Spanish riders don't turn up until the late afternoon. They stopped for a lengthy restaurant lunch and then had to have a siesta under the hedge, and Susie and I feel infinitely superior, seasoned old troopers used to roughing it who've ridden from Astorga without a break.

But it seems to have taken a toll on Apollo. When Susie offers him a piece of apple, he refuses it. He doesn't want his dinner, either. He stands motionless all afternoon, not grazing, not drinking, plagued by flies he doesn't even have the energy to sweep off with his tail. Prickles of worry crawl over us. We've seen this before. Perhaps he's just tired. But perhaps it's tick fever again – Jabir says there are bad ticks in Spain. He's practising his command of English on Peter, talking about his stout dog's leather antique collar. Peter doesn't think it looks that old, but Jabir's taken aback when he tells him so – a tick collar is what he said. You don't understand?

The sound of someone droning out 'Danny Boy' on bagpipes

down the valley is enough to reduce not just Apollo to a state of melancholy but everyone else within earshot. By morning he's no better, and it's clear we're not going anywhere. We scramble through the dictionary looking for the Spanish word for vet, and unexpectedly Señor Nasty Neighbour comes up trumps and arranges for one in Astorga to be telephoned. He will come out 'soon', but Susie's frantic with worry. Apollo's eaten and drunk nothing all night: his ears are drooping sadly sideways, and his normally expressive eyes are switched off, blank as television screens. When Dr Fernando turns up in the afternoon he diagnoses a blockage, and then Susie's overcome with guilt that in her tired state yesterday morning she unthinkingly gave the horses the rest of the alfalfa for breakfast, as well as their concentrates. Leo's quick digestion coped with the resulting porridge, but Apollo's didn't.

Dr Fernando administers an injection and leaves us some powders to give to Apollo. We understand the Spanish equivalent of laxative, but getting them down him is another matter and in the end it's the wooden spoon treatment, stuffing them down his throat. He hasn't the energy to protest. We wait out the day until suddenly John of the Bedford coffee van arrives in Rabanal, and we all dine together in the horse field, the two Bedfords side by side. He still hasn't found the love of his life on the Camino, but he remains hopeful. He speaks very fluent Spanish, and fortuitously he's turned up at the precise moment that we need his help.

Dr Fernando returns, summoned at midnight. Apollo's seriously ill by now, his eyes sinking in their sockets, his normally rotund bottom sloping into flat angles. The vet examines him thoroughly, pondering over the jungle of equine guts, and Susie spends a miserable night in the lorry, getting out of bed every half-hour expecting to find her horse hooves up in the grass.

But he isn't. After another batch of injections, by midday he's drinking water again. The relief felt in the village is palpable, from the kind wardens of the Refugio Gaucelmo to the pilgrims we know and many we don't, and to Señor Nasty Neighbour who is now our best friend. When Dr Fernando returns yet again in the evening, he diagnoses fermented alfalfa and a near case of toxaemia, but leaning insouciantly against Apollo and holding up a drip bottle, he reassures Susie that disaster's been averted and in a few days' time her friend will be fine, as good as new. And his bill comes to 150 euros, less than £100, a ridiculously low sum for umpteen visits at unsocial hours – all he cares about, he says, is that the horse is well again.

In the evening we walk to the *refugio* to fill up our water containers and, while I'm attending to the tap, Susie disappears with their lids. I know where she'll be: in the Romanesque church of Santa María next door – if I'm quick I'll just squeak in, retrieve the lids before Vespers and leave her to it. But once inside the church, the first person I see isn't Susie but the wife of Señor Now Nice Neighbour, who's registering delight that I've taken the trouble to turn up. She shuts the door firmly, and summons me to sit next to her. There's no escape.

It's very atmospheric in the church as the soft light illuminates its crumbly walls and the dainty gold statue of St James the pilgrim in the corner, and the service, conducted by five monks chanting unaccompanied in Latin, goes on for nearly an hour. Their voices are very clear, very true, straining with the effort of heaving the congregation up a semitone to keep them in tune, and Señora nods approvingly when I dredge up a few Kyrie eleisons from some ancient memory of singing in the school choir.

The church is packed with pilgrims, and there are lessons and prayers in Spanish and Latin, in French and English and German to accommodate everyone. I still can't see Susie, and when we pour out into the dusk at the end of the service, I miss her in the squash. Staggering back to Bessie under the weight of the slopping three-gallon containers without their lids, my new-found holiness is wearing off rapidly – but Susie was never in the church at all: she's been waiting by the lorry for ages, wondering where on earth I've got to with the water.

And now we have to decide what to do. We've lost two days because of Apollo's illness, and it could be several more before he's fit enough to ride. The sleek Spanish horses have moved on long ago, no doubt at a leisurely pace with stops for siestas, but they're far ahead of us and we too should be forty miles west of Rabanal by now. Time is running out, and so is our money. I only allowed for 100 days away, and now it's 6 August, Day 121.

There's really only one solution – Apollo and Susie will have to travel with Peter in the lorry. But Leo and I will not. We made a promise to the Pilgrims' Hospices and to our sponsors that we would ride all the way to Santiago, and if one of us can't, then the other one must. No cheating. So tomorrow I'll find out after all what it's like to travel on my own with Leo, to ride in solitude across the Montes de León and then over the Cordillera Cantábrica, the final mountain range on the last stage of our journey into Galicia.

27. HARMONY WITH LEO IN A WILD LAND

Leo, let's go. Come on, you always go in front. What do you mean, you can't hear Apollo behind you? Trot on, that's it, up the hill, let's get out of Rabanal before you start neighing. And he does, but the awful truth is slowly dawning on him: his friend isn't here. He slows to a walk and tries to look behind, but his good manners forbid a spin round on one hoof so he rolls his eyes back instead, takes a deep breath, and the resulting agonised screech is enough to blast the heather out of the hillside. I can't hear a thing for ten minutes afterwards.

And then he settles down, whinnying hopefully at intervals with occasional hiccups under his breath until his usual inquisitive interest in his surroundings takes over, and now as we climb there's only the soughing of the wind and the muffled thump of hooves on springy turf. We're not alone; there are pilgrims to squeeze past on a path so thick with tall rosebay willowherb and broom that at times we're swimming. We pop out on the road at Foncebadón, the most dreaded spot on the Camino.

This is where the hermit Gaucelmo once built a hospice and

a church for pilgrims, and the *refugio* in Rabanal is named after him, but that was centuries ago and now the village lies mostly in ruins, better known these days for the wild dogs that skulk in it ready to attack. Or so they say. As Leo and I approach the shattered buildings, I can see signs of restoration at the church, and there's a *refugio* open now beside the road, but there are no slinking furry forms until Leo lets out a tremendous neigh which summons three of the huge nanny-dogs out of nowhere. They inspect him curiously from a distance, shrug their massive shoulders, oh, it's just a horse, and disappear as suddenly as they arrived. What's the problem?

The Cruz de Ferro stands at the top of the pass. It's a plain iron cross on a long stake driven into a gigantic heap of stones, the biggest *montjoie* on the whole Camino, and each passing pilgrim adds another stone to the pile. There are queues of them waiting patiently, not at the cross but at John's Bedford camper van for coffee. I decide not to take a break; today Leo and I can indulge our mutual inclination to push on, to keep up the momentum, to get over this mountain and down the other side. The next village, Manjarín, has only one inhabitant and that's Tomás, a well-known eccentric who keeps his little *refugio* open all the year round. At an altitude of almost 5,000 feet this is the highest point of the Montes de Léon, and I can imagine that in winter or in bad weather it's a dreary horrible trek for pilgrims. But today you can see for miles in the sunshine and, as I pass the *refugio* at 9.40 a.m. precisely, Tomás shakes a tiny musical bell, a signal for the sound of sacred music to flow over the chickens and dogs on his doorstep and away across the hillside.

Time has ceased to exist here. At Acebo the balconies of the mediaeval houses hang out over the street, and I double-check there are no pieces of them actually in the street to mark Bessie's passing, before Leo and I dive off on to the thread of track again. I know I'll have to ride the long descent to Molinaseca down the hairpin bends on the tarmac road, because the route for foot pilgrims goes over the hill on slippery granite slabs, dangerous for them and impossible for a horse, but I'm not quite sure where to leave the track, and chance it through Riego de Ambros and out the other side. A mistake – the Camino out of this village has jagged steps of rock, the snarling undergrowth closing in so comprehensively we can't turn round and go back. I get off into nettles tall as triffids and Leo stops, pulling me back on the end of his reins, his head suspended by the cloth ears of his bonnet caught on a spiky blanket of brambles. He waits patiently for me to unhook his sun hat before rushing me up the bank and out on to the road again.

It feels as though it's higher up here than it was in the Auvergne, but it isn't. It's because there are no wide sloping pastures, no gentle inclines; to the left of the road there's a drop of hundreds of feet to the Río Meruelo, the far off sound of flowing water drifting back up the ravine. And I have to ride on the left, so close to the low safety barrier that Leo's hooves are swishing through the gravel on the edge, because it's better to be overtaken by cars chugging up the mountain than by those flying down, not to mention the armies of exhilarated pilgrims on bicycles with no brakes. I'm glad Susie isn't here, and no doubt she's just as thankful. In her opinion, God and St James have decided to spare her the two most vertiginous parts of the Camino.

Horseflies are zinging up from the river, and they goad Leo into acceleration until he's bouncing down the mountain on springs. Rounding a corner, we come face to face with four outsized nanny-dogs trotting four abreast up the road. They stop dead with surprise, but when Leo and I greet them cheerfully we get four tail wags and a token woof before they move politely to one side and then melt away into the riot of wild flowers above us. I can see the walkers at the top jumping down from rock to rock as they make their way back to the road, but there are no shrieks of alarm so the prudent dogs must have avoided them. We're not far from Molinaseca now, and beyond it I can see

Ponferrada, unlovely in the distance, crowned by yellow streamers of pollution hanging in the sky.

Leo rushes to nuzzle Apollo when they meet again on the rough land beyond the pretty village, where Peter and Susie are setting up camp in the shade. From the time we stopped so he could have a long drink in the swimming hole, dammed below the Romanesque bridge, he's sensed that his friend is close by. Apollo's more muted in his greeting – he's wobbly on his legs and Susie's still worried that he won't recover, but his lurch round the mountains in Bessie all day could have something to do with it. He's probably feeling sick.

I'm looking at the map. The Camino goes into the centre of Ponferrada, which is a large town, so it'll be better to get up with the dawn and ride through before the rush hour. I'm gripped by a real sense of urgency now, fuelled by the prospect of living off our emergency rations of baked beans from here to Santiago and back to England due to lack of funds, and by the thought of sweating cheese sandwiches for lunch with no Marmite. We've scraped our way down to the bottom of the pot, so it must be time to go home.

I'm sorry for Susie that we can't just sit it out until Apollo's fit to be ridden again, but we need to push on: Santiago's only about 130 miles away now, and we're not the only ones looking towards the end of the journey – the river of pilgrims has become a flood pouring from one *refugio* to the next. Bunk space is limited, and ironically it's those pilgrims who are playing the game by heaving their backpacks slowly over the mountain paths who are losing out, turning up exhausted at the *refugios* so late in the day that it's hard to find a bed. The ones who send their luggage on ahead by road, or get a swifter friend to commandeer a bed for them, are the ones who most easily find shelter for the night. The wardens struggle to be fair, but there's an increasing air of competition: must rush, must hurry, must race to Santiago.

Leo and I leave so early that the obligatory main road's a pale glimmer in the half-light, and Leo himself must look like a wraith in the headlights of the occasional car. He's upset at leaving Apollo again, and furious neighs echo round the neighbourhood from both of them today – Apollo's definitely on the mend. We cut through the village of Campo, close to the city outskirts, where an angry shepherd's shouting at his nanny-dogs who are ignoring the sheep and playing tag instead. Worried about the time, I'd like to trot, but the road's a skating rink as we pass a sordid rubbish dump and skid over the Puente Mascarón, the bridge spanning the Río Boeza, and follow the arrows through the town. We're below the walls and fairy-tale battlements of the twelfth-century Templar castle, but I'm not stopping to look – we're in a wide avenue on the bus route, and where's all the traffic? Well, there isn't any. It's only eight o'clock in the morning, and the Spanish are still in bed.

The Camino leads out through the suburbs, surrounded by sad slag heaps, and disappears into the middle of a building. I can't work out what it is as we clatter through an archway and a quadrangle, but Leo's settling into a steady trot as the land levels out, and we never pause for ten miles of road, road and more road, lined with allotments of sunflowers, corn, melons, alfalfa and finally swathes of rampant vines rollicking through the rich earth. In Cacabelos, the middle of the street's lined with brass scallop shells, reminiscent of Vézelay all those months ago, and in a final burst of enthusiasm we canter up a minuscule track beside the main road and cut through a vineyard to Villafranca del Bierzo, arriving at tonight's destination by lunch-time.

We're there ahead of the others as a result; the *refugio* is already full, and I haven't a clue where we're going to stay. A well-meaning small boy hands Leo an armful of deadly ragwort while my nose is buried in the guidebook, but sensible Leo says thanks, but no thanks – an ice cream, perhaps? It turns out that Peter's spent the last hour trying to manoeuvre Bessie round a town that's too small for her, which is why he hasn't caught up with me. He and Susie try everywhere for horse accommodation.

The nearest solution is a campsite at Vilela whose owner welcomes us with open arms, but it's a mile and a half in the wrong direction. Leo and I clop off there at a slow walk, having completely run out of steam.

Crow lives at the campsite. He croons to his owner, purrs when his back is stroked, and has forgiven Señor who some years ago failed to notice that Crow was hopping behind him in the kitchen, and stood on his head. As a result of this mishap the bird is one-eyed, and further disabled by a club foot and defective wing feathers, which mean he can't fly, but he has two party tricks: to point his beak where instructed, left, right, up or down, and to pretend to be drunk. This isn't entirely pretence – I observe him with his beak in the beer while we're struggling to do justice to the voluminous dinner Señor's Portuguese wife has cooked for us. After ten different varieties of fish and the equivalent of a melon each, we're all on the point of exploding; supper, including two bottles of wine, together with board and lodging for the horses and camping space for Bessie and us comes to just 32 euros, about £20.

There are two main routes out of Villafranca that lead over the border into Galicia and up to O Cebreiro, high in the province of Lugo. One is the authentic pilgrims' route, now submerged beneath the main NVI road, which is tangled up with a new NVI motorway, roadworks, fast-moving traffic and no hard shoulder. The second, and a third minor route, go over the mountains in conditions that can be dangerous in rain or fog.

What's the weather going to do? In the morning, Leo, finally resigned to travelling without Apollo, stands quietly on the bridge in Villafranca while I debate the problem aloud with him. It's a dull day, no sun, quite windy. Probably no fog, but we could have our first downpour since we arrived in Spain. Which way shall we go, Leo? He's brilliant in traffic, he won't turn a hair – sod it, let's go over the mountains.

The road's so steep I have to get off in case I unbalance Leo, but he launches himself up the hill towing me like a railway carriage; he doesn't want to stand for me to get on, he wants to nip straight up the cart track ahead of us. Hang *on*, will you! I'm not going to run along behind you! An ungraceful thump into the saddle, a tight rein – no, there's nothing to the left except space up there, we don't want to go flying over the edge.

There are no pilgrims either; no-one at all. As we climb higher and higher I can see them down there, ants on the road, and the huge electricity pylons pull their lines across the mountain range first beside us, then below. Oh, let's go, Leo! Let's take a risk! He hurtles into gallop, and the *speed*! We're rocketing along the ridge and there's a long drop into nothingness beside us, but I trust him, this horse of mine and fleetingly I understand: I'm no-one's sister no-one's mother no-one's wife or child no-one's employee circled in a tight enclosure legal rules and no you can't do that no-one-time cancer patient will I live or die and no responsibilities at all ...

And *that* is the Camino, to step off to one side, to travel all alone, for me the briefest opportunity to let go of practicalities, the worries, is my husband bored, will the lorry get us home, the guilt about my sister who's suffering in the heights and drops and altitude that I love so much. Today it's just my horse and me in harmony in a wild land, and when we slow down safely, as I knew we would, Leo's equally content to swing along at a walk, stop to admire the view, and put up with the sprigs of bright heather I can't resist picking and threading through his forelock in celebration of a self-indulgent day.

He's not so happy to be confronted by two old boys ploughing with their oxen. The plough squeaks and rattles; lorries he can understand, but in his opinion a mile or two between himself and the whole contraption is safest, to the disappointment of the farmers who have lined up their cows beautifully beside them for a photograph. We zip along a steep path down the other side of the mountain through chestnut woods to Trabadelo, and then we're stuck with the old NVI for miles.

What's this? It's drizzle. I haven't seen the rain in Spain at all up till now; we've been extraordinarily lucky. There are cautionary tales in books by pilgrims who've been caught on the flat *mesetas* in violent storms, or fog bound in the Montes de León, but we've had sunshine almost every day. Now the landscape's changed in a flash to lush green, and we meet a whole herd of fat cows wobbling home. Leo checks there are no ploughs attached to any of them and stands his ground, even when the penultimate cow cannons into his nose, propelled by the one behind leaping on it. Lesbian cows, huh? I seem to recall from somewhere that this practice is called bulling – also known as bovine wishful thinking.

We leave the road at Herrerías, and the last five miles up the final mountain to O Cebreiro turn out to be totally unsuitable for any horse – granite slabs skiddy in the rain, and loose stones on a path so perpendicular that Leo has to throw his weight forwards and accelerate alarmingly just to keep his balance. No question of getting off this time – I'd still be at the bottom when he's at the top. Now it's narrow dorsal fins of rock slanting into ridges, and Leo picks his way across them at speed like a ballerina on her points, sweating with the effort but never faltering, while I'm sweating in anticipation of the sudden stumble, the cracked knees, the broken leg. It doesn't happen.

At O Cebreiro a persistent rain's falling and the temperature's dropped by 15°. Fog obscures the view back down the valley, to Susie's relief, and the two horses have a patch of ground for the night fronting the road, the wind, the rain and another expanse of fog, hiding God knows what. Somewhere in the lorry the horse rugs are buried under mounds of junk accumulated since they last needed them, but they need them now; it's so cold up here that we have to light the gas stove in Bessie, and boil up tins of soup.

Tomorrow, Apollo will be fit enough to ride again, so my solitary sojourn is over; Leo and I have covered 63 miles in three days, riding for six hours at a time over sometimes impossible terrain without any need for a break. But his shoes are suffering as a result – the new front ones are paper thin after a week, although the hind ones with their tungsten studs, amalgamated long ago with the shoes themselves, are still holding out. Not far to Santiago now, so they'll just have to last.

O Cebreiro's dotted with *pallozas*, ancient thatched dwellings for sneezing occupants choked by a central fireplace with no chimney, and here in this remote place the sky's so black at night you can see the whole stretch of the Milky Way, just as the Romans did. Apparently. Not this evening – there's a suffocating shroud of fog and a steady drip-drip of rain from the holly trees on to Bessie's roof where she's shoved into the hedge out of the way, with a camper van jammed against her front number plate. There are soaked pilgrims everywhere, and in the rackety *refugio* Susie has trouble finding space among the bodies on the floor.

Since the earliest days of the road to Santiago this little place has been an important refuge for pilgrims, placed under royal protection with the result that its now restored church is known as Santa María la Real, or St Mary Royal. It's pre-Romanesque, an endearingly stumpy building, squat so it can duck below the storms that regularly scream over the mountains. Its wooden statue of the Virgin Mary is twelfth century, and like the one in the Basilica of Notre Dame at Orcival it shows Christ on the Day of Judgment, with the body of a child but the face of a man, sitting on her lap. Mary's expression is wonderfully quizzical, her eyebrows raised, as though in surprise that her tall filigree crown has remained impossibly balanced on the top of her head.

This church has its own miraculous story, concerning a determined mediaeval worshipper who struggled up here through a blizzard to receive Communion. The monk celebrating Mass couldn't imagine why he'd bothered to come, but he received the equivalent of a divine ticking off for such an unholy thought – the bread on the communion plate suddenly turned into the flesh of Christ and the wine into His blood, seething out of the chalice and soaking the consecrated linen cloth. Personally, I would have fled down the mountain in terror, but the monk took his lesson to heart, and the reliquary of the bloodstained cloth with the priceless chalice and plate are still here in the church, safely locked in a glass cabinet.

O Cebreiro's inevitable tourist shop sells Santiago sweatshirts. Peter buys one for me, and I'm going to need it as an extra layer under my dusty, unused jumper – it's absolutely freezing here. All night the wind moans dismally, and the dripping of the rain on Bessie's roof becomes a drumming torrent that keeps us both on the verge of wakefulness. The occupants of the camper van in front have inadvertently set their alarm clock for 3 a.m., which results in a lot of Spanish swearing and clattering of coffee pots. No-one goes back to sleep, and at six o'clock I slide out of the groom's door into a solid blanket of cloud. We've a long way to go today, climbing even higher to the Alto del Poio before the long downhill ride towards Sarria, much of it on the road, and at the moment I can't see further than six feet in front of my nose.

28. THE CHAOS OF THE CAMINO

Fog. Those mysterious shapes are our horses, wet through and miserable. The waterproofing on their rugs has dried out. It's also evaporated from our macs, as Susie and I discover within half an hour's riding on the main road. Passing cars peer at us through muffled headlamps, which Leo and Apollo ignore, but this morning's pilgrims are definitely dangerous – they wear drippy ponchos draped over their rucksacks, and they rustle by like hunchbacked Quasimodos in the mist. Apollo eyes them doubtfully, skipping sideways now and then. At least he seems to have recovered completely from his near fatal pig-out, and the other bonus of this dreary morning with no visibility is that Susie can't tell whether there's a long drop beside us or not.

The dedicated track of the Camino takes over; wet, it acts less like a nail file on the horses' shoes and in places we can trot, following it blindly. The Galician government opened it in the St James Holy Year of 1993, a year when St James's Day fell on a Sunday, and apparently it runs the whole way from O Cebreiro to Santiago de Compostela. It's a welcome alternative to the road, and we wind slowly up to the heights of the Alto de Poio where a huge and dramatic statue of a pilgrim materialises suddenly out of the fog.

And then it's downhill all the way through sloping fields and damp dung-filled lanes, the clouds sitting on the chimney pots of stone farms squatting in brilliant green pastures. Is this the same country we were in two days ago? The dry heat of summer has vanished and here there's almost a hint of autumn, thanks to the influence of the Atlantic weather on the west side of the mountains. We stop in Triacastela, the three castles of its name demolished long ago; it's only twelve miles beyond O Cebreiro, but it's far enough for Apollo's first day back on the road. There's a line of pilgrims in a field waiting to book into a *refugio* and there's plenty of grass here for Leo and Apollo, but we're told we can't stay – horses must be tied up in the covered livestock market in the middle of the town.

Ours take a dim view of this edict, walking restlessly to and fro in the pen we construct for them so they can be loose, and snuffling disapprovingly at the old crots and straw spread skimpily on the concrete floor. But at least the sun's come out, and suddenly it's baking hot and all our soaked macs, breeches, gaiters, socks and horse rugs can be festooned round Bessie to dry. Susie gets a welcome reception in another *refugio*, where her riding boots join the thirty pairs of wet pilgrim trainers steaming in an odorous row outside the door. As we're oiling the horses' saddles and bridles, their reins stiff as boards, John turns up with his camper van, a wide smile and Lottie, a blonde German pilgrim with twinkling blue eyes who he's sure is his soulmate. He's persuaded her to travel with him, and that's the last we see of them: I hope they bumble off together in his Bedford happily ever after, heading for Santiago and then the sunset.

There are two routes from here to Sarria. The main one winds past the Monasterio de Samos, founded by the Apostle of Galicia in the sixth century, and it's always had a strong association with the Camino and is certainly worth seeing, but a shorter path clambers over the Alto de Riocabo. The altitude at this pass isn't much more than 2,500 feet, far lower than the recent stretches of the Camino, and we decide to risk the vertigo and go that way. It's an amazing blue and green sparkling day, a beautiful day for riding, the dew so heavy that the elastic cobwebs in the hedgerows are weighted down with rhinestones, and mist rises in fat blankets from the valleys as the sun climbs towards midday. Everywhere we turn there's a half-perceived reminder of somewhere else: Dartmoor with its high tors, Ireland with its jumble of little pastures and drystone walls, and the Auvergne when we pass through village after village where the houses are roofed with thick slate tiles, curvy as the scales on a salmon.

The earth and asphalt track of the Camino winds gently under oak and chestnut trees, easy for the horses, until we reach a very narrow flight of steps with a sharp dog-leg, right in the middle of a wood. There's no way round. I get off Leo, but he's concentrating on some ivy growing on the stairway wall and it's difficult to manoeuvre him down the steps – bending a long-backed horse into a right angle while trying to yank poisonous vegetation out of its mouth takes a bit of doing, and I wouldn't like to have a horse taller than he is. The compact little Apollo hops down behind Susie, no trouble at all.

And then it's one hamlet after another all the way to Sarria, each one thick with cowshit in the main street and in the walled lanes, and now the field boundaries are delineated, Galician and Celtic style, with slabs of slate and granite; and we pass *hórreos*, granaries stuffed with corn on the cob that are raised on stilts to keep the rats out, roofed in slate to keep the rain out and decorated with finials and crosses at each end. Everywhere the signposts are written in Gallego, in which the letter X features prominently, and we decide the Galician language must come a close second to Basque in terms of unpronounceability.

Leo and I are adapting again to Susie's and Apollo's slower pace, but although coffee breaks are welcome, they put both him and me in dead-donkey mode. The minute we pause and switch off, I could happily sleep in the grass all afternoon, and Leo sighs heavily, dragging his toes along the road with the effort of carrying on after lunch. Susie and I talk, grumble sometimes at each other because one's too fast and the other's too slow, or ride in comfortable silence. I suspect there's a whole world of secret thoughts going on in her head, a different experience from mine, because I know the religious aspect of the pilgrimage and the fellowship among the pilgrims in the *refugios* mean a great deal to her. And she's battling with vertigo every day: on bridges, on hills, on embankments – it's a debilitating obstacle I don't have to face, and she's much braver than I am.

As for me, I'd hoped to have plenty of time to read and reflect, but fat chance. If I'm absorbing any spiritual sustenance then it must be by undetectable osmosis. The three days I rode alone gave me a tiny glimpse of contemplation, but now I've settled back into the routine of pondering where we're going to stay each night, and cursing that my knowledge of Spanish is still so rudimentary. Susie and I never expected that it would be far more difficult to find accommodation for the horses in Spain than it was in France, but the nearer we get to Santiago the more problematical it becomes, and today is no exception.

On the other side of Sarria lie another thirteen hamlets before we reach Ferreiros, which we've picked at random because it looks as though it's about the right riding distance for today. We're struggling through yet another herd of cows splodging up the lane, driven by yet another big señora in a wraparound pinafore, when Peter phones: his map doesn't have Ferreiros on it, nor Vilei, Barbadelo, Rente, Marcado, Mouzós, Xisto, Domiz, Leimán, Peruscallo, Cortiñas, Lavandeira, Brea or Morgade either. There isn't a road to any of them, or at least not one big enough to take Bessie. We make enquiries at another *refugio* and suggest he turns on to an invisible track off the C535, and by the time Susie and I get to Ferreiros, Peter's already there looking shaken, stirred and thoroughly overheated – and he's been told there's nowhere to put a horse here anyway.

Refugio Señora is less than obliging. She just says no. We gather that the *refugio* owns no land at all, and what's around it is *privado* – and then Señora says it's communal land, and we need to speak to the mayor of Ferreiros. But there is no mayor. Well, we must ask the people. What people? Finally, she admits that the roped-off square of ground opposite the *refugio* is owned by the bar next door. Why didn't she say so in the first place? Susie goes in, armed with her best bad Spanish sob story, and the owner of the bar beams beatifically at her. 'Campo? *Si!*' he exclaims, and thus it is all arranged. The *campo*'s tiny but at least it's full of grass, and Señora's all smiles now, offering us the use of the overcrowded *refugio*'s facilities.

It's only five miles from here to Portomarín, but it takes two hours to get there the next day because it's downhill, and Susie has to walk – Apollo's shoes are worn so smooth they're acting like ice skates on the tarmac, and water skis in the cowshit. The pretty pilgrim path keeps vanishing, and when it reappears we meet continuous herds of happy cattle rumbling along it, either on their way to their field after milking or on their way in again for a siesta.

Portomarín is on the other side of the huge Río Miño, spanned by a high main road bridge and, having crossed it with quaking Susie's eyes fixed on Leo's heels, we have to turn sharp left and cross back again over a new bridge. It seems an odd arrangement, but it's because the Miño was dammed to create a reservoir in the 1960s and the town of Portomarín was peremptorily drowned in the process. Another town was built on the hill opposite, and apparently a fortified Romanesque church in the old one was dismantled stone by stone and rebuilt on the new site, but we can't see it from the road and it seems like too much effort to go looking for it.

Now the dedicated track of the Camino runs alongside the main C535, until the path turns into seven miles of tarmac to Palas de Rei and another livestock market for the night – the *refugio* is full again and no, we can't stay at the campsite. At least this market, lurking emptily just outside the town, has a thin veneer of grass over the acres of hardcore where we can slam in the fencing spikes to create a big field. There's also a convenient water tap, a choice of ten public loos each, and nobody around at all, so perhaps it's better to be here in the quiet evening than in the town where the *refugio*'s in chaos. The Camino infrastructure is in danger of collapse – last year a total of 60,000 pilgrims reached Santiago, but 120,000 have already streamed through this season.

We have better luck next day, with a cool ride through eucalyptus woods of dappled aromatic shade where pilgrims on bicycles whistle by, and now we're into La Coruña, the final province, clattering through another 23 villages with lilting Galician names that no doubt are full of mediaeval architectural gems.

But there's no time for exploring, and we don't stop at all until we come face to face with an enthusiastic priest waiting to catch unsuspecting pilgrims. Two on horses are irresistible, and Susie and I take it in turns to hold Leo and Apollo while the other gets a compulsory tour of the priest's airy St James church, with its fetching multicoloured statue of the saint in cloak and gold-rimmed hat. But once again it's me rather than Susie who gets the holy treatment – some Catholic pilgrims have come in at the same time and suddenly I'm surrounded by prayers, and hear myself being singled out as the one who's travelled all the way from England. Heads nod approvingly, more prayers are said, and I feel I ought to duck in case a bolt of lightning heads my way. I just hope the assembled congregation attributes my scarlet face to the heat.

The *refugio* at Ribadiso on the Río Iso is a wonderfully hospitable place – certainly Leo thinks so, when an untethered mare belonging to a German hippy comes up to greet the horses, whickering through soft nostrils. Marcel is taking her to Santiago from Rabanal, and he spends much of the afternoon riding her bareback to and fro with one voluptuous lady pilgrim after another seated in front of him, clutched tenderly to his chest from behind to make sure she doesn't fall off.

The wardens welcome us, although there've been pilgrims queuing for hours and once again the *refugio* is full. There are collapsed people stretched out on mats in the sun, camping in makeshift tents on the land next to the restored fifteenth-century building, and dozing beside the Iso. The more energetic are splashing in the icy water as we join them to wash the horses down, and everywhere there's the sound of multilingual conversation, laughter and snoring. After we've fenced in Leo and Apollo, I inadvertently join the snorers. I was intending to dump some of our filthy clothes in a bucket of water, but fall asleep on the ground on the way to the wash-house instead, with my head propped up on the Persil bottle.

Susie pitches her tent in with the horses and sundry sheep, but Peter and I have to move the lorry because the man who owns the drinks machine tells him Bessie's blocking the way to it. She isn't, and Peter takes pleasure in telling the man to sod off, safe in the knowledge that he can't precisely understand the succinct words, but it seems diplomatic to remove ourselves for the night to a nearby lakeside. It's not an early start in the morning, but it hardly seems to matter now – this is probably our last full day of riding, and when we leave Ribadiso there are still some bodies prone on the ground, forced to sleep al fresco and soaked in dew. Peter offers a lift to a thin and pretty East German girl with extraordinary alacrity, when she says she has a stomach ache so bad she can't walk, but his style's cramped by the presence of another passenger: a shaven-headed bloke with a large beer belly. There's nothing wrong with him, but his dachshund's got blistered paws.

It's another day of contrasts, of main road and purpose-built track, first through noisy Arzua which is just warming up nicely with the rush-hour traffic, and then in the eucalyptus forests of blue leaves against a cerulean sky. In the hamlet of Calle there's an outdoor pilgrim coffee shop which looks as though it's a pit stop for horses, announcing its presence with the words HAY CAFÉ, so we tie them to the Santiago milestone giggling – but *hay* just means *there*, and they have to make do with biscuits.

By the time we reach Arca, the temperature's shooting up in the afternoon sun. We had thought of staying here but it's right on the major road, the N547 now, and there's the usual pile of pilgrims and backpacks blocking the *refugio* doorway. It's been built recently, and it has stables on a balcony where we shut the doors on Leo and Apollo with a bucket of water each, but it's too hot, too noisy and we decide just to sit out the heat of the day and then carry on to Monte del Gozo, the final hill above Santiago and only four miles from the city. There's an enormous pilgrim complex there, and no doubt land enough to turn the horses loose. Not once in the last four months have they been cooped up in a stable overnight, and they're completely out of the habit.

There's nowhere to sit at Arca except on the stable balcony, leaning against the scorching metal railings, or on plastic chairs outside the closed supermarket. I manage to contact Fred using the public phone beside the road, but I can't hear much because of the traffic, and the conversation's brief: sorry I haven't been in touch, I'll be back in about a week, and what's the summer like in England? His reply is indistinct, but it sounds like: wondered where the hell you were, and the weather's some adjective followed by awful.

At five o'clock Susie and I set off again, leaving the road behind to canter along a sandy track under the cool canopy of trees. When my phone rings, to my surprise it's a Spanish journalist – someone's decided two middle-aged English pilgrims on spotted horses are newsworthy, and we agree to meet tomorrow outside Santiago cathedral. We've heard negative reports about the police shooing horses out of the city, but having come this far we're not going to be deterred. Susie and I are both experts at mulish blank looks when officials are telling us what we can't do, so maybe there's an advantage after all in our continued ignorance of their language.

The Camino continues through villages with musical names. One such is Lavacolla, but the translation is malodorous rather than melodious – it means Bottom Wipe, from the days when pilgrims used to scrub up in the river before presenting themselves to St James. Now the village has a noisy airport and a television station as neighbours, but Monte del Gozo is ahead, Mount Joy, where in the old days the pilgrims stood on the silent hill and shouted in triumph at their first view of the cathedral spires below them. And the hill is still here, though flattened somewhat to make space for the thousands who attended Pope John Paul's open-air Mass on it in 1989; rustling with dried grass, the colour drained out of it by the August sun, it's now wrecked by the sprawling monstrosity of a vast complex of barracks accommodation for hundreds.

There's no sign of Peter and Bessie. Susie goes off to try to find out where we should put ourselves and our horses and, in seconds, I have my first brush with officialdom. We're in the middle of the paved plaza, surrounded by restaurants and fast-food outlets, tourist shops and a proper public laundry, and I'm told that horses aren't allowed in. Well, tough. I'm not taking them out, because I haven't a clue where Susie's gone and anyway, Leo's got his nose jammed in a letterbox waste bin, hunting for ice cream wrappers. I quite hope he drops a crot, but for once he's being discreet, although Apollo isn't – he's hanging out his willy, relaxing at the end of a hard day. Señor Official finds some other business to attend to.

But when Susie comes back, we're categorically told: No Horses Here. What's wrong with the hill? All that grass? No horses allowed. Sorry. Stables over there (vague gesticulation to the east). And luckily there are – at a riding school right next door whose owners speak English, and they lend Leo and Apollo a little stony paddock with as much hay as they want. Above them on the crest of Monte del Gozo, a tall statue of a pilgrim raises his arm in salutation to Santiago cathedral, its sharp outline fading in the twilight, and now we're almost there: it's taken 28 riding days from the time we left Roncesvalles on 15 July, and I can't think what it will be like not to saddle up and carry on. Already reality is creeping up on us, tonight in the shape of a grey beefburger and floppy chips dished out by a bored boy in a bar.

But I'm not going to think about it yet.

29. PAYING OUR RESPECTS TO ST JAMES

Horses are allowed in the city in the mornings as long as they're out again by 10 a.m. No chance of that for us and, anyway, they get longer in the afternoons: 2.30 to 4.30 p.m. precisely. It's 3.30 by the time we've got through the uninspiring San Lazaro suburbs into the old quarter, but apart from tourists and pilgrims it's relatively uncrowded: today is a fiesta, and most of the shops are closed.

Peter walks with us for the last half-mile along the cobbled streets. We're all quiet, subdued even, Leo and Apollo pacing gently with their ears horizontal in the heat: this is the end of the road, and I don't know what to expect when we get to the cathedral. I've never looked closely at pictures of Santiago, quite deliberately, because I want it all to be a surprise.

And it is.

The huge Plaza del Obradoiro opens out. On one side runs the Hostal de los Reyes Católicos, a hospital for pilgrims long ago and now the most expensive hotel in Santiago, and, at right angles to it, the huge, French-designed Raxoi Palace stretches out its parade of arches and columns. But both are dwarfed by the towering Baroque façade of the cathedral of Santiago de Compostela, so tall I have to tilt my head back open-mouthed to see St James the pilgrim perched in his turret between the spires on either side, their pinnacles and crosses puncturing the sky. It's so ornate, so complicated, it's impossible to absorb everything I'm seeing, and its front doors are firmly shut; the Spanish journalist is waiting for her interview, the police are on our trail, and today there's only time for Susie and me to climb the two-tiered stone staircase to the balcony together, look down at Peter holding the horses in the square, and turn and hug each other. We made it, after all these months, and suddenly it seems that it was no big deal: all we did was get on Leo and Apollo, and ride them for a few miles every day.

The journalist's office is only round the corner. We leave the horses tied to a shop window during a very long interview; the resulting newspaper article describes us mellifluously as *dos intrépidas amazonas* and later there's a reference to us as *heroínas*, but I reckon it's Peter who's the real hero – no-one else would have been so extraordinarily patient as he has been. When we extricate ourselves finally from the newspaper office, we find him trying to placate the police – we should have had the horses out of here an hour ago, and we haven't finished yet. There's still the visit to the Compostella office to get our certificates, our Compostellae, inscribed in Latin, stamped and signed, to show that on 15 August 2002 we completed our pilgrimage.

The police officers are beside themselves with agitation, but we're not going to be hurried. Leo and Apollo would like an ice cream each and, anyway, a rally of Lotus Super Seven kit cars is just burbling into the Plaza del Obradoiro and we want to chat to their English drivers. The officers give up, and by the time we amble out of the city it's getting on for seven o'clock – and suddenly the horses realise that we're riding them back in the direction from which they've come. Home's that way! They wake up with a jolt and fly back up the hill.

Peter treats Susie and me to a celebration dinner in the Rúa do Franco, Santiago's centre of gastronomy, crowded with bars and restaurants specialising in octopus, lobster, scallops and fish swamped in peppers and potatoes, garlic and paprika and virgin olive oil. We stuff ourselves witless, drink far too much wine, and end up dancing in the square with all the other pilgrims who've made it here in the last few days, singing loudly and triumphantly in a haze of booze and cigar smoke and thundering guitars.

Bessie roars back to Monte del Gozo long after midnight – we shouldn't really be here for a second night, and it's difficult to keep a low profile in a lorry that's throatily down to second gear with the effort of reaching the *refugio* right at the top of the complex. While we're using the thumpingly loud air compressor to try to blow up Susie's airbed, which has mysteriously deflated, Señor Jobsworth arrives – straight from Burgos, for all we know.

Bugger off! What's he want? What he wants is that we should remove ourselves to the campsite on the other side of the hill. Well, I've had a skinful and it's amazing how much Spanish I can muster to administer an earful: *Just what exactly is your problem? What has happened to your Spanish hospitality?* and a lot of other things besides, several in four letters and probably some in Greek. I don't quite remember. Anyway, it goes on for so long that Peter and Susie have time to inflate the airbed to bursting point, and Señor Jobsworth summons up a defeated grin before accelerating away in his vigilante car, the suspension groaning as it jumps off the speed humps.

In the morning, we return to Santiago for the pilgrim Mass. It takes Peter some time to find a Bessie-sized parking space so he drops Susie and me at the cathedral; I wait by the entrance that I guess he'll use, but since he doesn't, the three of us attend the service in three different places. I'm expecting it to be just something for the tourists, but it isn't. The cathedral's packed, and above the rustling and coughing a single voice rises in song: it belongs to a middle-aged nun with a broad, tranquil face, chanting in Latin, her tone as pure and clear as a young boy's treble, and, strangely, no-one has trouble joining in the slow, beautiful responses. There are pilgrims of many different nationalities and denominations here, adventurers and sportsmen and sceptics like me, yet we all just seem to know the words.

After the priest's impassioned pilgrim sermon, blue-and-white striped golf umbrellas shoot up. I'm wondering vaguely about the likelihood of holy rain in the cathedral, but they're to pinpoint the priests moving through the congregation to administer communion. It seems a good moment for me to go and find Susie who I've spotted sitting down somewhere in the nave. There she is. I weave my way over through the packed humanity, kneel down beside her to tell her I can't find Peter and oh, *no*! God's going to strike me down *immediately*! A passing priest has popped a wafer in my mouth. I can hardly take it out again, must swallow, look pleased; can't explain I'm not a Catholic, don't think Christ was divine ... that's it, it's gone and, er, where's the wine, then? There isn't any – Susie thinks the wafers are dipped in it first. Well, it just tasted waferish to me.

And then the *botafumeiro*, the cathedral's giant censer, swings in a wide arc on its long hemp rope, higher and higher, puffing out clouds of incense to counteract the pilgrim pong in a ritual that's continued down the centuries, though these days most of us have showered and found a clean pair of jeans before coming in to pay our respects to St James.

The service is over.

Now we're in the scrimmage trying to see something of the cathedral's cavernous interior, from its kernel of the quiet lines of the Romanesque nave, through layer upon layer of Gothic architecture, to the final Baroque flamboyance of its outer shell. It's hard to take in anything at all: just a glimpse of the Pórtico de la Gloria, the internal entrance to the nave and aisles sculpted in astonishing detail by Master Mateo in the twelfth century, with its three archways where St James sits with his feet on the carved pillar of Christ's family tree, the Tree of Jesse. Traditionally, pilgrims push their fingers into its intertwined stems, and so many have done it that now the stone has worn smooth. I can't get anywhere near, and gaze up instead at the 24 old men of the Apocalypse in the tympanum above the Apostle's head, chatting away to each other between songs, their musical instruments dumped in their laps.

Susie and I face the high altar. St James is seated here, too; not in the same form as the simple stone statue in the Pórtico de la Gloria, but submerged in gold and jewels in an impossibly intricate and glittery baroque alcove. His expression is serene, unmoved by it all, waiting for the next pilgrim ritual: the climbing of the steps at the back of the alcove to hug him from behind as he gazes down on the tourist scrum. After twenty minutes, we reach the front of the queue and Susie hugs, while I put my hands on the scallop shell behind his head. He's a bit hard and shiny for hugging, but this is still a serious thank you for taking care of us, a suspension of any disbelief. We join another line of tourists and pilgrims waiting to go down to the crypt, and file past the silver sarcophagus where the saint's bones are laid, according to legend or likelihood, depending on what you believe. Outside in the hot sunshine we meet Peter who managed to reach the Tree of Jesse and then sensibly went out, avoiding any further queues.

It's time to think about getting ourselves home again, but the fact is that we're going to be here for several more days. We have to find a vet to sort out the paperwork so we can take the horses out of Spain in the lorry, but today is another fiesta, another public holiday, and then it's the weekend. We also have to dispose of some of the more bulky items in Bessie, or we're not all going to fit in. Marcel and his mare Rosalie have turned up, and they get two sacks of horse feed we're not going to use, but the next item is more contentious – it's Susie's bicycle. She phones John and there's a heavy discussion, but it's no use – if the bike comes with us, none of us will be able to get into bed.

It finds a good home in Santiago with some English residents, to Peter's relief, with the proviso that maybe Susie will come back and retrieve it one day.

At Monte del Gozo the fiesta's being celebrated by a peculiar ritual to exorcise the Gozo witches. It involves a lethal hot alcoholic concoction, poured flaming from a ladle down the necks of the five hundred bikers who've throttled in on their Harley Davidsons. And down ours, of course. As a result we decide that tomorrow we must, simply must, complete the pilgrimage properly by driving Bessie to Cabo Finisterre where the world ends in the Atlantic. We're also under orders to move to the campsite, but tonight it's as much as we can do to stagger as far as the barracks and bed. The fiery cocktail's supposed to be an aphrodisiac, but Peter and I pass out in seconds.

Manuel the vet works on a Saturday, and he relieves us of all the equine documents, which have to be officially stamped by the Spanish equivalent of DEFRA, saying he'll contact us again on Monday. By the time we've dealt with that, and moved Leo and Apollo to a proper field and ourselves to the campsite, it's four o'clock – but we said we'd go to Finisterre, and we will.

Bessie has other ideas.

Thirty miles down the road from Santiago there's an appalling din under our feet. We grind to a stop – the engine must have fallen out in the road at least. Well, it hasn't, but there's no question of continuing. We can't work out what's causing the problem, but the cab doesn't tilt and only a dwarf would fit underneath the lorry beside the engine, so eventually I find the breakdown insurance details and phone the brokers. No reply, of course – it's Saturday. Phone the insurers. They give me another number in the UK and ask where we are. Er, Spain – I'll just check the map: we're on the C550 at Freixo. A Dutchman phones from Holland, and I repeat that we're in Spain. No problem – he understands we're at an Esso garage. What? No, we're not; we're on the C550. Ah. Sorry. The message says ESSO; someone's bad writing ... a truck will come out in about six days.

What? Don't worry, madam, it's a joke – about an hour. We've retired to a nearby bus shelter with our books when a lady phones from Madrid. Please describe the lorry. I give her full details: Bedford TL, blue cab, wooden body, scallop shell on front and back; I don't think there are many like ours on this road today. Oh, so you're at a Shell garage. *No!* There's a shell stuck on the front and another on the back. Ah. Sorry. A truck will be with you immediately.

A very small lorry turns up with a very large driver who peers through Bessie's grille and diagnoses the problem at once: the casing round the fan has broken, and the rotating blade is catching on the broken metal. The dwarf who fits underneath the lorry is me. I can sort of reach the metal and turn it away from the fan, but it only works temporarily and the most noticeable result is that I now resemble an oily zebra. A bigger truck is summoned and Peter persuades Bessie to rear up on to its ramp, flattening her back number plate, and then she's winched the rest of the way for a piggyback ride to Santiago at breakneck speed with Peter as pale passenger beside the truck driver, while Susie and I steam along in the little lorry, which is frantically trying to keep up. Back at the Monte del Gozo campsite, Bessie's decanted into the car park, straightening her number plate again in the process but doing some obscure damage to the gearbox, and the truck drivers give Susie and me two smacking kisses each, tell me the insurers will of course pay their bill, and roar off into the night.

Indigestible lumpy pizza in the campsite café at midnight.

It's another four days of frustration before we manage to leave. Unfortunately Señor Jobsworth turns out to be involved with the campsite as well, and his minion Señorita Jobsworth Segunda, who's six feet tall in her socks, prowls round Bessie suspiciously. You can't camp in the car park. Why not, when there's no-one else here? Well, do you have a tent? Peter points to a pitch nearby: it's over there, and it sleeps three. He doesn't say there aren't three people sleeping in it, and I'm trying to keep the woman away from the far side of Bessie where our duvet is hanging up to air. She purses her lips: you must move your table and chairs over to the tent. Peter narrows his eyes dangerously, but says nothing. At any rate they can't evict us – the lorry's immobile until someone mends it.

We have a stroke of luck: there's an English tarmacking crew staying at the site, and one member is also a lorry mechanic. In between his motorway construction duties, he manages to remove the fan casing altogether, telling us the fan will work perfectly well without it. Peter's fixed the gears, and now the only hold-up is the horse documentation: the Ministry's demanding a complete itinerary for our journey back to England including where we're going to stop each night and with whom. Susie and I are speechless – it's impossible to predict where we'll be, and we've got no further than hoping that we get home. But Manuel solves the problem, producing an itinerary that he's created entirely out of his own imagination, and the Ministry stamp our certificate without any further questions.

Peter's worries that the lorry will struggle with a heavy load of horses as well as all our belongings are completely unfounded; there's nothing Bessie likes more than to be fully laden, and she thrums up the hills to Gijón on the north coast road in fourth gear. We're all defeated by the logic. From the extra height of the lorry cab, the views of the mountains to the right and the ocean to the left are fabulous, full of bays and inlets, hamlets and fishing boats, a reminder that the sailing season isn't over, a consolation for the life that suddenly I don't want to leave behind.

The campsite on the beach beyond Gijón is as welcoming as Monte del Gozo was inhospitable. The horses have the entire grassy car park to themselves, and in the shower block there's no boarding-school drab paint and clanging metal cubicles, but marble washstands and varnished pine doors. In the still morning, we take Leo and Apollo down to the beach where the Atlantic is bubbling along the sand in small whispery breakers.

Leo's absolutely astounded at the sight of so much water, but Apollo gazes calmly out to sea, perhaps savouring some pleasing memory of Ireland, a different experience from the one that's left him with a lifelong farrier phobia.

Bessie's gear linkage seems to be disintegrating. All fingers are crossed as we pass Santander and then Bilbao, a mass of high-rise claustrophobic clutter in the valley, and we stop for the night near San Sebastian at a hilltop farm, with a long moonlit view across the gilded Bay of Biscay, swept by the restless beam from the lighthouse. We're back in Basque country now, and it seems incredible that it's taken two days to drive the same distance it took a month to ride.

But when we reach Bordeaux, Bessie's in trouble again. Peter, who's doing all the driving because by the time Susie and I familiarise ourselves with all her idiosyncrasies it'll certainly be Christmas, nurses the lorry off the motorway, coasts into an industrial estate and then crawls to a DIY superstore in first gear, which by now is the only one still working. The DIY staff are very intrigued, and rotund Patrice and the forklift driver ponder the problem, Patrice's fat little ankles poking out of the driver's door, while Peter and the works-van driver take the gear shift to pieces. It's been jamming on a plate that they manage to free and fix, but when it's reassembled Bessie refuses to engage any gear at all when the engine's running. There's more head scratching, but Monsieur Van Driver's friend Alain has the answer: the clutch cable's too loose. He disappears into Bessie's bowels with a spanner, and *voilà!* another problem's solved.

It's now getting late, but by chance Alain works at an equestrian centre, and the horses find themselves in a proper field for the night, while we're invited to use the Pony Club kitchen and to sleep in the clubhouse if we want. Obviously St James is still keeping an eye on us. Bessie behaves perfectly when we steam back up the motorway to Tours and one more night on the road at a campsite in Vouvray, where it's back to an electric fence field on the communal land and the mayor will certainly not be deranged – it is not necessary even to ask his permission, Mesdames.

Feeling increasingly disorientated, we call in at the Château de Béhen for tea with Norbert, Hubert and their mother – we were last here on 15 April, and today it's 25 August. The horses take a break in the paddock full of peacocks that in the early spring was bare earth and now is long, luxuriant grass, and it seems a lifetime ago.

Still rising to the occasion, Bessie makes it easily to Calais in time for the late-night ferry. All the equine documents in order, but neither Customs nor Immigration at Dover want to see them: they're far more concerned that we might have two-footed illegal immigrants on board. You'd think they would check the living space in the lorry, but they don't – they insist that we lower the ramp so they can confirm there's no-one in with the horses. Leo and Apollo are clattering about, thinking it's time to disembark, and any immigrant who'd tried to travel with them would have been knocked out hours ago by the combined fumes of methane and ammonia.

Then it's down the dark deserted motorway to Faversham, back to a dusty house, an accusatory cat: where the hell have you been for so long? My journal records, 'Today we came home, and very strange it feels …'

And it felt very strange for a long time.

EPILOGUE

Faded tracks in long woods,
Muddy intersections
Scrambled, nothing clear
Except a small pebble added to a pile of stones:

There was a pilgrim here.

Those were kaleidoscope days
Painted in oils,
Washed to pale watercolour,
Sun and rain in overlap,

Land and people spilling
Off the IGN map.

Time was just for plotting practicalities
As every earthy day shut down:
No slumping on the sofa,
No slow unwind;

And it's only retrospectively
A journey in the mind.

Afterwards, Peter returned to his golf with a sigh of relief.

Tessa, who'd swapped addresses with David the American bicyclist without either of her beady sisters noticing, plunged into romance and they moved in together.

Our mother took up with us again where she left off, although she'd inexplicably acquired great fluency in French while we were away, not a language she'd ever learned.

Our father merely complained that we hadn't sent enough postcards.

Apollo became a member of the Pony Club.

Leo got bored.

For Susie and me it was a mission accomplished, and we raised a substantial sum for the Pilgrims' Hospices. But it was more than that: for Susie it was a catalyst that spurred her into joining the Roman Catholic Church.

As for me, once I'd got over the novelty of being able to sit up straight in bed, cook complicated meals and bath more than once a month, I became like Leo: restless again. The Camino settled into my memory as a chaotically happy time, the tricky bits forgotten.

Anyway, the trowels are still hanging up in Bessie, ready for the next trip.